INSIDE COUNTRY MUSIC

INSIDE COUNTRY MUSIC

BILLBOARD PUBLICATIONS, INC./New York

Revised edition published 1986 by Billboard Publications, Inc.,
1515 Broadway, New York, New York 10036. First edition published
1984 by Thumbs Up Publishing, Marshall, Washington 99020.

Library of Congress Cataloging in Publication Data

Wacholtz, Larry E.
  Inside country music.

  Interviews.
  Includes index.
  1. Music trade—Vocational guidance. 2. Sound
recording industry—Vocational guidance. 3. Country
music—Vocational guidance. 4. Music, Popular
(Songs, etc.)—Writing and publishing. 5. Interviews—
United States. I. Title.
ML3790.W24 1986   784.5'2'002373   86-4234
ISBN 0-8230-7532-X (pbk. : alk. paper)

Manufactured in the United States of America

1 2 3 4 5 6 7 8 9 / 91 90 89 88 87 86

Thank you good friends, acquaintances,
mother and father for your gifts of love.
My faith in God and your invaluable help
have made this book possible.

CONTENTS

INTRODUCTION

There's something burning inside a lot of us—a dream of success, a desire for fame, money, or maybe just happiness. It's a driving force that's hard to explain or control, and sometimes it's hard to live with. It's the thing that makes us "go for it" because we know we're special. It's the magic that makes our lives sharper, more intense, really alive.

Why are Loretta Lynn, Johnny Cash, Ronnie Milsap, Anne Murray, Willie, Waylon and so many others successful? They all have their own special stories, talents, and individualism. But they also have one thing in common—they all wanted to satisfy their special, creative passion for music. They all wanted to lead special lives doing their own thing and sharing their God-given talents with the rest of the world. And they all came to the one place on earth where music is the universal language, where people behind the scenes make dreams come true—they came to Nashville, Tennessee.

Over seven million people visit Nashville every year. Many come to get close to the one thing in their lives that remains true—the country music they were raised on, and the contemporary country music they listen to today. Country music is a good friend of the family; it's a companion on a lonely night, and the common thread of so many dreams.

Country music is a place where your dreams can still come true if, like so many of music's business people and stars, you have that little extra desire, talent, and hard-earned luck. At first, these success stories were waitresses, teachers, truck drivers, nurses, etc., just like the rest of us. They knew what they wanted to do, and they found their special niche in country music.

So where do you fit in and why do you need this book? That's simple. You may want to know more about the music business, or be a fan, or maybe, just maybe, you're one of the very special people with the inner desire for a life in music that leads to Nashville. Well, if you care that much, come with your eyes open, your heart strong, your creative talents refined, and with a very good understanding of what the music business is all about.

Some of the most talented people in the world have opened up their hearts and minds to you in this book. They are the successful people in country music—artists, managers, songwriters, producers, audio engineers, record company executives, trade writers, booking agents, and the list goes on and on. You want to know how famous artists become successful? Listen to the people who *made* them successful.

Country music is a people business. Its product may be emotions sold on a plastic platter, but it's the people in the industry and their creativity that make it magical. Songwriters create the potential hit songs. Publishers filter out the bad ones, and place the good ones with recording artists. Producers marry the right song to the right artist, and lead teams comprised of musicians, the recording artist and audio engineers to create magic by recording a song "in the grooves". Technicians master the tape, press the product into phonograph records and place them into artfully designed record jackets. Artists' managers, agents, attorneys, secretaries, promotion people, radio station program and music directors, disc jockeys and radio announcers, videotape production crews, writers and thousands of other people make this business successful. Each person is an important link in the music business' chain of success. Without teamwork, nobody would be successful.

I decided to write this book because I can't sing a lick, but I do have a wonderful love affair with country music. There's nothin' better, well almost nothing! Anyway, who wants to work at something you can't stand? So many people live on the "dreams-of-someday"—and the next thing you know they are married, have kids, need a job, have a mortgage and no time leftover to follow their inner dreams.

Instead, I moved to Nashville. I met the right people, got tons of rejection, and ate cheeseburgers at McDonald's. The industry felt too big to understand, too overwhelming and confusing; I discovered it was impossible to walk in, cold turkey, and make it. It doesn't matter how much talent you have, you've got to work with and understand the structure of this industry. Instead of giving up and going home, I decided to stay. The more I learned about the music business, the more I wanted to find out. I love it, the people, the craziness, the songs, the stories of success—Nashville's great!

Why did I write this book? Because you're like me! You love success stories. You're a fan, or a singer, or a homemaker with a dream; whatever. If you're pursuing your dream, you'll need all the help you can get. The people in the music business understand us, because they're just like us. They have dreams too, and they live them every day.

The men and women behind the "stars" are really the "stars" of this book. I want you to get to know them and to understand them. Here they really level with you. Part of what they say is not easy to hear, but it's the truth and that's important. I used a tape recorder, and transcribed the interviews because I wanted to make sure that I got the facts right and that you could "feel" their personalities. The questions I asked were the question you'd have asked.

This is really a how-to-book about success in the music industry. The dreams of Patsy Cline, Loretta Lynn, Ricky Skaggs, Elvis, Roy Acuff, and hundreds of other have come true. I sincerely hope that yours will, too.

Don't forget that the most important person in the music business is you. Without you, the client, the fan, the record purchaser and concert patron, this wonderful business would be out of business. So thank you, for your love of music and participation in the pleasure, the joy, and the message of country music.

CHAPTER ONE

SONGWRITING

Have you ever thought about being a used-car salesman or flipping hamburgers for a living? Well, that's what most songwriters do for a living. Why? The answer is easy. Almost anyone can write songs, but very few people can write "hit" songs. So, songwriters work at any job that will get them by, until they score the big one—in other words, have a "hit."

The life of a songwriter often reads like a grade-B movie script, and not all grade-B movies have a happy ending.

Most of the people who want to make a living as a professional songwriter will fail. Many will try, but only a handful will succeed. Many have some talent, but not quite enough. Many will lose determination and interest when they find out how hard and competitive it is to make it. Many won't like the lifestyle of late hours, political stroking, and living on a shoestring.

But for the winners—the truely talented songwriters—there are the compensations of personal satisfaction, respect from their colleagues, financial rewards, and even the kick of hearing their songs on the radio.

Success—or failure—frequently begins in Nashville.

Nashville is the songwriters' capital of the world. It has a wonderful, creative atmosphere; it is a place where established and famous songwriters help the younger, deserving songwriters of the future. These young songwriters are real people who are living their dreams and surviving on the hope of the next lyric. They arrive in town with the dreams and desires of youth, live for a few years in a cheap apartment on music row, jam with other writers, and discover how much talent they have or lack—and how much they really don't know. They find out, over the years, that songwriting is really learning how to express the magic of life. It's a talent that is shared by only a few.

It's interesting that our complex feelings are shared and understood best in the lyrics and rhythm of a simple song. For the songwriter, maybe it takes living life to the fullest—getting in touch with what is happening in the world or with the feeling in his soul; but the magic of the message is there.

Songs communicate in two very important

ways. The first way is on an emotional level. The music and words cause us to "feel" an emotional response to the song we hear.

To make it simple, think about the emotions you feel when you hear "God Bless America," or "The Star-Spangled Banner." (Lee Greenwood makes us feel proud and patriotic when he sings "God Bless the U.S.A.") Think about the music at a romantic dinner, or the sadness of a funeral march. You'll realize there are thousands of songs or musical compositions that make us very quickly get in touch with our "feelings."

Songs can also convey a persuasive "message" to the listener. Some examples would be the pro-war song "Over There."

Think about all the radio and television commercials you've heard in the past few days. Almost every one has a music background (bed) that is supposed to help you get the message. But what are most songs about? Most song lyrics and music are about what makes the world go around, about men and women and, of course, love.

Songs are alive with the feelings and concerns of the people of the world. A great song is like a great piece of art. It communicates its creator's feelings in the same way a sculpture or painting does. Just as a painter determines the colors and texture, the songwriter determines the rhythm and words that will flow together to create the emotions and message of the song.

Like many of the professional songwriters who helped us live with wars, love, marriage, and our everyday lives, the new songwriters of Nashville are changing the world of today. Their songs are about many of the same concerns of the older generations, but they speak to the youth of today. They say important things that need to be expressed and shared through the simple lyric of a hit song. The traditional and contemporary songwriters of today are creating new songs and music that touch the world.

Songwriters make our everyday lives a little better. We hear their creative thoughts every time we listen to the radio, watch television, see a movie, buy a record, or hear a commercial. Think about our daily lives without any music. Songs give us all a common subject to talk about and share. It is a line of communication that helps us understand one another.

Without a hit song, there wouldn't be a music business! Songwriters and songwriting are only the start of the creative process and business that is today's music industry. Everyone from the record company presidents on down knows that songwriters are one of the main ingredients of this business.

As I said, a song can be written by anyone who has the talent, the experiences of life, love of music and the business, and of course, the hard-earned "luck" and determination to succeed. But what makes a hit song? Your idea is as good as mine or anyone else's in the business. Timing, talent, and a lot of luck play a part in making a hit record, but it is ultimately the public's choice—and they can only make that choice after they've heard the record!

DON SCHLITZ

Songwriter and recording artist. Songs include "The Gambler" and "I Believe."

WHEN WE SET UP THIS MEETING, WE TALKED ABOUT YOUR TWO BASIC RULES FOR SONGWRITERS. WHAT ARE THEY?
One, in order to be a professional song-writer, you have to learn to thrive on rejection. Two, assume you know nothing.

You have to start from scratch; be ready to find that the entire world does not care to hear your overindulgences in your own heartache. But if you can take those indulgences or those heartaches and make them universal—make them into something the world can understand, something that everyone can listen to and say, "That person's talking about me,"—then you become a successful songwriter.

This, of course, does not mean that you are a profitable songwriter. A business-type songwriter goes around and pitches songs to producers, to artists, and to publishing companies. That's where the ability to thrive on rejection comes in. You'll be rejected a thousand times for each time you are accepted.

This is true for virtually everyone. It might not be true for Bob Dylan or for Dolly Parton, but it's still true for Don Schlitz. It's still true, I'm sure, for many writers who have achieved some notoriety or fame. You have to learn to thrive on rejection and bounce back and say, "That person doesn't like it; that does not crush my ego."

That's a very critical point. You're writing because you have something to give, and you want to share it with the world. For someone to reject it means that what you have to share is not worth sharing. That's how you take it, anyway. That's because egomania, or that sort of egomania, and insecurity go hand-in-hand.

It's the insecurity, probably, that makes you write songs in the first place. The ego-mania leads you to go out there and think that someone else would care. The insecurity returns when someone tells you the song stinks. The egomania makes you go home and work a little bit harder; you realize that it might take years but that you still have something to offer.

It's a constant battle.

HOW WERE YOU INTRODUCED TO THE CLASSICAL FORM OF SONGWRITING IN NASHVILLE?

A great songwriter does not necessarily have to be a performer as well. Some great songwriters are not recording artists. The person who comes to mind immediately is Bob McDill, and I will always be proud to consider him one of my mentors.

I came here in 1973 thinking I knew how to write a song. The first place I went into somebody said, "Anybody listening to songs today?" A guy came out and said, "Well, that's my job today." The guy was Bob McDill—nobody had ever heard of him or anything.

So I went in real cocky; I was twenty years old. I played him thirteen songs, a couple of which he liked. They were obviously too esoteric. They weren't country, but he liked the songs. He took me aside and said, "I want to play you something, show you what I'm doing. It's a B side of a record by a friend of mine, on a small label."

I was thinking, *He's already told me that he wants to go in and demo a couple of my songs, so this is my break. I'll be a star in two months.* No problem, right?

He took me into another room to hear the recording of the song he'd written. I looked at the label—JMI. I never heard of it. I looked at the artist—a guy named Don Williams. I never heard of him. I listened to the B side. It was a song called "Amanda"—one of the greatest country songs ever written. I realized that I did not know anything about the craft this person had spent years learning. Anyway, that was my introduction to the classical form of songwriting in Nashville.

SO YOUR FIRST EXPERIENCE REALLY SHOT YOU DOWN.

It shot me down on one hand; on the other hand, it taught me a lesson. You've got to remember that every song that is on the charts is there for a reason. You may hate it. Everybody you know may hate it. But it's there because somebody, somewhere, likes it.

LET'S TALK ABOUT SONGWRITING AS COMMUNICATION.

If you want to communicate, don't be afraid of the word *compromise.* You can compromise and learn style, learn methods, learn ways to say exactly what you feel in your deepest soul. You can learn to express feelings so precisely and so clearly that a multitude of people listening to that song will be touched.

I by no means feel that I'm the equal of a Bob McDill or of someone who can sit down and sell a song a week. I have the good fortune to be able to write for myself now; I'm the artist I write for. But when I first saw people cry at something I had written, then it hit me that it was a natural thing and universal.

The suffering that you deal with, and most songs deal with some form of suffering, has universality. We're all here on earth together, but we're all individuals; and that's a very intense thing.

YOU'RE A VERY SENSITIVE, VERY INTELLIGENT PERSON. YOU SEEM TO BE AN INSTRUMENT, IF YOU WILL, THAT CAN BRING OUT FEELINGS THAT A LOT OF PEOPLE HAVE.

I really feel it is because I have those same feelings that everyone else has. What I've done is I've learned to thrive on rejection, learned to go back and rewrite, rewrite, and rewrite, then write a new song. Somewhere along the way, the magic comes in. You feel like it's magic.

When I was writing really obscure, esoteric songs, I didn't realize that they weren't communicating anything, and my songs never did communicate anything until I learned something that only comes through the repetition of the act of work.

I do not consider songwriting an art. I consider it definitely to be a craft, a learnable craft. You do not have to be brilliant or very intelligent to be a songwriter. You have to be basically normal to be a songwriter. But you have to toughen yourself because you're going to come up against a brick wall in the most competitive business in the world. You have to have your head hunched out like a bull (if a Schlitz can say that) and go against that wall. Either your head is going to break or that wall is going to break. And if the wall breaks, chances are the head's broken with it, too. And 999 out of 1,000 heads break.

IT MUST BE A GREAT BUSINESS, THOUGH, WHEN YOU HAVE A HIT LIKE "THE GAMBLER," A SONG THAT SAYS SO MUCH TO SO MANY PEOPLE.
I wrote the song, and I thought it was a throwaway. I wrote two or three songs within two hours. The fact that "The Gambler" is so well-metered, so well-rhymed and everything, is one of those things that comes from doing the craft for so long. I didn't know where the idea came from. I'm not that smart a person, but I figured it out. For me, it's a song about my father. It's something that was given to me from the other side of somewhere. But that's an intensely personal thing. Whatever the song is for somebody else is fine. I had written everything but the last verse in about twenty minutes.

I've written two other songs within two hours—both of which I thought were great. One has been cut about six, seven times, as a matter of fact, but has never been a hit.

WHAT'S THE NAME OF IT?
"Can't Imagine Laying Down with Anyone but You." It's a straight country song. I played "The Gambler" for another songwriter—someone who had been at the craft a little longer. He (Jim Rushing) fell out of his chair; he said, "You've got to finish it." And that last verse—where the man falls asleep, or whatever happens, no one knows—took me six weeks to write. I went through all different scenarios, all sorts of things, to write and rewrite those eight lines. If you had

any conception of what the other scenarios were for the ending of that song, you would just laugh at me. But that's okay, because I just rewrote until the verse was right. I worked very hard.

It was not the first song that I wrote. It was the first song I had recorded, and because of that, all the glory that's come upon that song is what I consider very blessed and wonderful. I accept it with the utmost humility because there are people in this town who are better writers, better and more consistent writers who have known their craft longer. I didn't understand, and I still don't understand, the importance of those awards. For me, all the awards sit here in the office. In my home, I have my typewriter and pictures of my family.

IN OTHER WORDS, YOU STILL KNOW WHO YOU ARE.
Hey, if you ever want to do it for money, forget it; songwriters make as much as some poets or some philosophers. You may as well go up and sit on a mountain. It can be the greatest hobby in the world, but please, please, if you want to get into it as a business, you have to approach it as a business. You have to be hardheaded; you have to thrive on rejection.

WHY ARE YOU A SONGWRITER?
I've never been asked that. I once asked my father, who is deceased, why he was a policeman all his life. I said, "What else could you have done?" He said, "I have no idea."

I've been here in Nashville for—I'm going into my tenth year. I didn't have my first cut until I had been here four and a half years. I had a record deal for six months with Capitol Records, one of the greatest companies in the world, and I was still working a night job. So you don't go out and get a limousine right away. I was working as a computer operator, which I'd done since I was seventeen.

Right now, I have no idea what else I

would do. Why am I a songwriter? I've always loved music; I've always wanted to be a singer. I was always told that I couldn't sing.

When I came to Nashville, there was no turning back. I made that commitment, and I'm not saying that anybody else ever should, because it's very hard to do. I was determined to stay here until I either made it as a songwriter or as a computer operator. Computer operating I had down already, but songwriting took a little bit longer.

Nashville is the easiest of the three "towns" to try to make it in because it's so much smaller than New York or Los Angeles. There's so much more accessibility to producers as well as to artists and publishing companies.

NASHVILLE HAS BEEN ACCESSIBLE, BUT ISN'T IT CHANGING VERY FAST?

It has to because so many people have found out that you can come here. But if you have anything happen to you within the first five years, I mean a cut that makes you $100, you are very lucky. Never, ever go to Nashville and think you're going to live off singing or songwriting. There are 10,000 to 20,000 other people here who are your competition. And you're starting at number 20,000. You've got to work your way to the top. It's a heartbreaking job.

And it's a hard job once you get it because it's very hard to keep. Even after you write one song or ten songs, you've got to keep doing it over and over and finding new ways. Everything that can be said has already been said. You've just got to learn how to say it in a new way.

A very important thing in this town, and I think in most music, is dealing with the universality, not only in the lyrics but also in the music. The simplest melody lines are the lines that people go away humming. If you have a good beat behind it and get their feet tapping, if you can make a person smile or cry, if you can make a person feel you wrote that song just for that person—then you have gotten past the point of really writing just for yourself; then you're on your way. Then you've learned a lesson. You've learned *the* lesson.

I'd like to say one other thing. On the streets of Nashville are probably a hundred songs that are just as good as "The Gambler." It's luck. And that's why it takes so long and can take forever. You've got to be willing to give forever.

SONNY THROCKMORTON

Recording artist and songwriter for Tree Publishing. Songs include "Why Not Me?," "Middle-Age Crazy," "The Last Cheater's Waltz," "I Wish I Was Eighteen Again," and "She Can't Say That Anymore."

WHAT ADVICE WOULD YOU GIVE TO SONGWRITERS?

I have standard advice for anybody getting in the music business. You should do it because you love it and for that reason alone. If there is any monetary gain to be had, you're just that much farther ahead. I loved songwriting for a long time before I ever made any money at it. If you love the attempt itself, there is a reward in that. I'm not saying it's total reward. Hopefully, you'll get a bigger reward than that, but I've known a lot of people who haven't. For a long time I never thought I would make it.

HOW DO YOU GET INSPIRED TO WRITE A SONG? DOES THE IDEA JUST POP INTO YOUR MIND?

I think some of the best songs do just pop into your head. Some people say they have written a song in five minutes or thirty minutes, but it was after they had thought about it for a year.

WHEN YOU WRITE A SONG, DO YOU HAVE TO WORK AT IT? SET ASIDE A CERTAIN TIME OF THE DAY?

I do it when I want to do it. But I would suggest to people who want to learn how to write that they discipline themselves and spend so much time a day writing. It's like anything else. There is a direct correlation between how much work you put in and what you get out of it.

WHAT MAKES YOU SUCCESSFUL?

If I knew the answer to that, I'd probably be a lot more successful than I am right now. Maybe I put a little extra twist on it. I've never tried to copy anyone. I think that has helped a lot—and the Lord's been good to me. I've come to Nashville, spent a lot of time here, and developed a lot of good relationships with people who produce records. That's important. It means the difference between having a career and not having a career.

THE MORE YOUR SONGS BECOME FAMOUS, THE MORE YOU BECOME FAMOUS. DO YOU THINK PEOPLE APPROACH YOU BECAUSE OF YOUR PAST RECORDS?

I've always heard that, and I'm sure it happens. The initial approach sometimes comes about because of that. More importantly, it opens the door. I'm sure there are times when having a name attached to a song helps. Quite frankly, when I listen to songs to record or produce, I don't want to know who wrote it. That way, I'm not influenced by anything but the song alone.

DO YOU THINK THAT SCOTTY TURNER AND THE OTHER PEOPLE YOU CO-WROTE WITH HELPED YOU OUT?
It's all relative. From my experience any contact you have with others is good because you're trying to learn something from everybody. What I learned most from Scotty was production. He was open-minded when we were recording together; he wasn't a dictator. That was a great learning process. Together we made some pretty good records.

PROMISING SONGWRITERS OFTEN COME TO TOWN WITH SONGS BUT HAVE A FRUSTRATING TIME GETTING ANYONE TO LISTEN TO THEM. COULD YOU OFFER THEM ANY ADVICE?
First of all, try to see reputable people. Second, always respect the advice given to you. Publishing company people are listening; it's their job to find hit songs. When I was starting out and was rejected, I'd think it was politics or something. The truth of the matter was that the song was not up to the level they were accustomed to publishing. In saying that, I would also say you should never take anybody's word as a final say-so on anything. I've had hit songs that a lot of people had turned down.

YOU ENJOY IT, DON'T YOU?
I do have fun. I try not to take it too seriously. I try not to set anybody up as a god. We all have our day, and that day will pass.

THEY TURNED YOUR SONG "MIDDLE-AGE CRAZY" INTO A MOVIE. HOW DID THAT HAPPEN?
It was one of those Hollywood things. Sandy Brokaw was listening to the radio in Los Angeles. He heard the song and decided it would make a great movie. He proceeded to find the literary agent and the people who could bring it into being as a movie.

THEY HAD TO APPROACH YOU AND NEGOTIATE THE RIGHTS TO USE THE IDEA IN A MOVIE. CAN PEOPLE USE AN IDEA THEY GET FROM A SONG AND NOT PAY YOU ANY MONEY?
That's a sticky situation. They can use it and change it, and then they can use whatever title they want. They can eliminate you from that. Unfortunately you can't copyright an idea or a title. Any writer who is approached for one of his songs should always keep in the back of his mind in negotiations that nothing is for sure. If you get too hard-nosed about it, you can lose the whole thing.

CASEY KELLY

Recording artist, songwriter, and publisher. Artists who have cut his songs include Kenny Rogers and Dottie West, Ed Bruce, Loretta Lynn, Jacky Ward, The Dirt Band, Johnny Rivers, The Vogues, Helen Reddy, Tanya Tucker, O. C. Smith, and Janie Fricke.

HOW DO YOU LOOK AT SONGWRITING?
Songwriting, as far as I'm concerned, is a craft. I feel that the problem with most people who want to write songs is that they don't view it as just a "plain ol' craft," like making cabinets or building houses. They think it's something magical that happens at one o'clock in the morning.

There is magic and inspiration and all that, but mostly it's a question of seeing where you want to go and what kind of product you want to turn out, a question of learning the rules and learning the craft. It's like learning how to put the doors on the cabinet right. It's something that almost everybody has to work at. Very few people can just up and write a song. The ones that do copy another form. It may be derivative enough of other songs that it allows them to build a good song by just copying somebody else. It doesn't mean they knew what they were doing. It's like cutting all the boards exactly the same length and painting them a little different color.

CAN YOU GIVE US MORE DETAILS?
There are rules to writing songs. There's a philosophical argument concerning the inspiration versus the craft. The argument seems to be whether you can be disciplined about what you're doing or whether that hurts your creativity.

WHAT ARE SOME OF THE RULES?
You want to entertain some concept that is going to be popular or going to be accepted by the audience that you're trying to reach. If you're writing a country-and-western song, you don't talk about the same things that these "hippy-dippy, super-fly" kind of songs talk about. It's just incongruous, and the people are not going to listen to that. You have to pick a concept, or a title, that means something to your audience. The hardest thing for young songwriters to do is say one thing in the song.

HOW DO YOU LEARN TO WRITE HIT SONGS?
You start by doing it. If you can work with somebody who knows what he's doing, you tend to pick up a lot of it without knowing it. If you copy somebody else's song form, you automatically get a lot of the craft in there without even knowing that you're doing it. Or

you can just do it by trial and error, which is largely what I did.

IT MUST TAKE LONG HOURS AND DEDICATION.

Songwriting is not something that strikes you with a magic wand at some odd hours or after you've taken some sort of chemical inducement. I feel that it's something you train yourself to do. You get up and work at it. If you write every day, your body somehow learns that's when you're going to be creative. It does that preparatory work without having the drugs and whatever else. You can actually come up with a more consistent product. You're in control more. I find that I have a lot of energy in the morning.

HOW LONG DOES IT TAKE YOU TO WRITE A SONG?

I've had songs that I've worked on for years and years. One day you fool with them, and you hear them a little differently. You get something going on them. You can get hung up at various places, but it's something that you work at. It's like a job; it requires a lot of self-discipline. Some jobs are all mapped out for you; they tell you what time you've got to be there, what you have to do, and when you have to go home. For me songwriting is a 24-hour-a-day job. I'm always seeing things that remind me of songs, or I have one working in my head that I've come up with some lines for. But it requires self-discipline to be able to tell yourself, "I'm going to go ahead and go to work, and I'm going to do this."

Some people get by that by having an office. They write for a publisher. Publishers sometimes will have a room, and you set hours for yourself. The really successful people, the prolific people who come up with song after song that gets recorded, work that way. They all work consistently and have the discipline that it takes. They're not the people who just turn out songs when they feel like it.

Paul McCartney is an example of somebody who works constantly at songwriting. He's always writing songs; every day he's working on his songs. I mean, who's more consistent than Paul McCartney?

It's true in other fields of writing, too. Novelists say that they have to get up every day and make themselves write. Even if they can't come up with any ideas, sort of as a punishment, they make themselves write other stuff—copy the dictionary or whatever. What happens is you start to write. It is a creative process; it happens within your head.

HOW DID YOU GET STARTED?

Years ago we were working in a mono studio, a one-track studio, in back of what they call the Fruit Exchange in Baton Rouge. It's a place where all the grocers come to get their vegetables and fruits. A guy we called Warm Daddy was essentially the engineer. There was only one knob to turn the volume up and down, and there was the tone knob. But this fellow had been in Nashville during the Chet Atkins heyday. He took me aside one day, and he said, "You know, you almost write good songs." There were many areas in this man's life I didn't respect. He drank too much, and he obviously didn't have it together; it was not much of a job working at this place. It took me back that he was telling me I "almost" wrote good songs. I was a real hot rock 'n' roller then, most popular in about a three- or four-state area that we played in. But he pointed out some things to me about songs, and it was pretty clear that he was right.

He told me you can only write about one thing at a time, and you have to pick things that mean something to your audience. I resisted, but later I came to realize that he was absolutely right. There really are rules to follow. The longer it takes you to realize that songwriting *is* a craft and that it has well-known boundaries, the longer it takes you to get successful.

CHAPTER TWO

COPYRIGHTING YOUR SONG

A copyright is a right granted by the United States and other countries to protect the creator of a dramatic, musical, or literary work from having that work published, performed, recorded, or otherwise reproduced without his permission. For the songwriter, this means that any printed reproduction, any public performance, or any mechanical reproduction of his work should result in some financial reward. The size of the reward depends on the financial arrangement the songwriter makes with the person to whom he gives permission to use his copyrighted material. Usually, the writer assigns the copyright to a music publisher, who is then responsible for exploiting the rights—publishing the song as sheet music, getting the record companies to record the song, getting performers to sing it in live performances, and so forth. The publisher and the songwriter split the proceeds 50/50.

A law that was signed in 1976 and that went into effect in 1978 says that the creator's rights begin the moment the song or creative work is committed to paper or is recorded on tape. The work does not have to be published or registered to gain these rights. The creator merely gives "notice" of copyright on his own material by placing the symbol ©, along with his name and the date, on the lead sheets or tape label. However, registering the copyright is a good precaution against any infringement of the rights. The Copyright Office will send a certification number, and this registration is necessary if any legal questions of ownership arise. For further protection, the songwriter may want to notarize the lead sheets (melody, rhythm, and lyric sheets.) (To register a copyright and for more information, write to the following address: Register of Copyrights, Library of Congress, Washington, D.C. 20559.)

The copyright grants the originator control over the following rights: print rights, mechanical rights, performance rights, synchronization rights, grand literary and grand performance rights.

Print rights apply to the graphic reproduction of the copyrighted material. This includes sheet music, folios, and books.

Mechanical rights apply to mechanical reproductions or electrical transcriptions such as phonograph records, cassette and 8-track tapes, jukeboxes, and player-piano rolls.

Performance rights apply to all public performances—live or recorded—of the copyrighted material. This covers performances on radio, on television, and in such places as nightclubs and concert halls.

Synchronization rights apply to the simultaneous use of the copyrighted music with some sort of film medium—television, movies, film strips, or slides.

Grand literary rights and grand performance rights apply to the creation of a drama based on the story line within the material. These are book rights, theatrical rights, or screen rights.

A combination of these rights is involved when copyrighted material is used to merchandise, promote, or sell a particular product—as in commercials and jingles.

PERFORMANCE RIGHTS ORGANIZATIONS

To be a songwriter back at the turn of the century, you would have had to have done it for love, because that's about the only thing you would have received from it. Radio was brand-new, tape recorders hadn't been invented, and the only music you heard was either performed in person or performed live over the radio. Songwriters submitted their songs to publishing companies and were paid for the sheet music that was sold to the performers and musicians. Song pluggers from the publishing companies pushed one or two main songs to conductors, musicians, and performers, in hopes that the performance of the songs would make them popular. Needless to say, songwriters had to have a big hit or make a living another way.

Even in 1909, the U.S. Copyright Act granted the creator of a musical composition the right to be paid for its use in a public performance. But back in the old days, it was impossible for every songwriter and publisher to keep track of who was performing their music, so it was also impossible to collect the money.

Performance rights organizations were formed to function as collection agencies. They receive money from the people and organizations that use music, and they distribute this money to the publishers and songwriters.

There are three performance rights organizations serving songwriters and publishers in the United States. ASCAP (The American Society of Composers, Authors, and Publishers) was the first performance rights organization formed. It was founded in 1914 by Victor Herbert (in association with composers Silvio Hein, Louis Hirsch, Raymond Hubbell and Gustave Kerker; librettist Glen MacDonough; and music publishers George Maxwell and Jay Witmark) with a charter membership of 190. Today it includes approximately 10,000 publishers, 26,000 songwriters, and 2,200 associate members.

BMI (Broadcast Music, Inc.) was started in 1939 when radio stations refused to pay another performance rights organizations' increased license fee. (In 1939, the song "Jeanie with the Light Brown Hair" was played over and over until new songs were created and placed into BMI's publishing houses.) BMI has approximately 46,000 songwriters and 28,000 publishers as members. On the average, about 2,500 songwriters and 1,000 publishers become affiliate members each year.

SESAC (Society of European Stage, Authors and Composers), formed in 1931 by Paul Heinecke, is by far the smallest performance rights organization. It currently has approximately 700 writers and 500 publishers as members.

The performance rights oganizations issue licenses to and collect license fees from any business, company, or organization that uses musical or song performances in public. Radio and television stations, disco's and nightclubs, football and baseball stadiums, hotels, colleges, airlines, and even jukebox owners are just a few examples of businesses that pay fees to use copyrighted music. (Radio stations pay for the use of the songs they play over the air. Television stations pay for the music they use in productions. Nightclubs pay for the music their live bands play, and airlines pay for music their traveling customers listen to through headsets.)

Music played at nonprofit state fairs is an exception. Also, the right to perform musical plays must be obtained directly from the producers of the show and the publishers.

The organizations differ slightly in several ways. BMI is owned by the 481 radio stations that formed it. ASCAP is owned by its members. SESAC is still owned by the founder's family.

The monitoring policies are also different. ASCAP monitors and tape-records radio stations. Point values are determined by how many times the song or composition is performed in public. When it has been established how much money has been collected, then an amount of money is given for each point of value. BMI has the stations send their logs (legal documents showing what records are played on the air). SESAC pays the publisher and songwriter by the placement of the record on the three main trade magazines' charts. It samples *Billboard, Cash Box,* and *Radio & Records.* From these three magazines, it estimates where the record is charted and pays accordingly. All monies collected, except operating expenses, are paid to the members. Once ASCAP and BMI receive the money from the licensees, they pay it directly to the publisher and songwriter. In other words, they take all the money and split it 50/50, sending 50 percent to the publisher and 50 percent to the songwriter. SESAC pays the publisher, who in turn pays the songwriter.

Performance rights organizations do a lot more for their members than just collect and distribute money. Some of the most knowledgeable people in the industry work for them. These people can really help a young songwriter by listening to the songs and giving advice and encouragement. They know the right people, have connections, and can sometimes give direction to a career. After all, they are in business to serve their members, and they do!

HAROLD C. STREIBICH

Attorney and college professor. Member of the Board of Governors, National Academy of Recording Arts and Sciences. Former President of NARAS Institute.

HOW DOES THE NEW COPYRIGHT LAW DIFFER FROM THE OLD COPYRIGHT LAW?

Probably the most important single feature of the Copyright Act of 1976 is that the new copyright term is for the life of the author plus fifty years. Under the 1909 Copyright Act, the term of copyright was twenty-eight years with a renewal period of twenty-eight years, or a total of fifty-six years. Now the copyright will not terminate during the life of the author. A good example of this benefit is Irving Berlin's copyright. Without the copyright extensions that were added annually by Congress, some of his work would have gone out of copyright during his lifetime.

EVERYBODY HAS A NATURAL RIGHT TO BE CREATIVE. WHAT OTHER NATURAL RIGHTS ARE THERE?

Well, as I stated in my article ["The Moral Rights of Ownership to Intellectual Property: Part Two—From the Age of Printing to the Future." Vol. 7–1, Fall, 1976, *Memphis State Law Review*], the basic natural or moral rights are as follows:

The Right of Creation, which includes (a) the right to create a work; (b) the right to print or publish or not to publish; and (c) the right to prevent excess criticism of a work and to reply to unjust criticism.

The Right of Paternity, which includes (a) the right of recognition that a certain person wrote a certain work; (b) the right of the author to prevent others from being credited with the creation of a work; and (c) the right to prevent others from attributing to a certain person the creation of a work which he did not write.

The Right of Integrity, which includes (a) the right of the author to prevent others from altering the work so as to distort, deform or mutilate it; (b) the right of an author to modify, change or correct a published work or to withdraw it from distribution if it no longer represents the views or scholarship of the author; and (c) the right of the author to prevent others from using the work or the author's name in such a manner as to reflect on his personal or professional standing or reputation.

I ASSUME THAT PLAGIARISM REFERS TO STEALING AN IDEA?

No, it refers to stealing the actual words. Plagiarism is now an integral part of our copyright law. Yet the term "infringement" is sometimes used interchangeably with plagiarism so as to cloud the moral stigma of the harsh indictment and connotation of theft. Leonard Feist, President of the National Music Publishers Association, observed in a lecture at Memphis State University, "In our contemporary society, plagiarism is a crime upon which society frowns. Copyright infringement, however, is something like speeding. It's considered by many to be quite all right as long as you don't get caught."

THE COPYRIGHT LAW ALLOWS PEOPLE TO CREATE AND GIVES THEM LEGAL PROTECTION.

The new Act gives us a different method of copyrighting. Under the old Act, statutory copyrights were issued when the material was registered, and you had a common law copyright to protect you prior to registration. Under the new Act, the common law copyright has been abolished and the copyright holds from the instant of creation. When you finish a work, you put a copyright symbol, the date, and your name on it, and it is copyrighted. To protect that copyright, you register it like you did before, but it is copyrighted *upon creation*. You have an interim period when you can apply for the registration on it and protect yourself.

SOME PEOPLE SAY NOT TO SEND IN FOR THE REGISTRATION OF A COPYRIGHT UNTIL AFTER YOU HAVE PLACED THE SONG WITH A PUBLISHER. WOULD YOU DISAGREE OR AGREE?

We disagree because it is copyrighted from the time it is created, not from the point it is registered. First of all, you are not extending the time of protection as you did under the old Act. Under the new Act, the copyright term is for the life of the author plus fifty years. It would have made a difference under the old Act by extending protection. Also you only have a certain time period to file for protection after creation. The only thing that would limit your registration of your work is the cost factor.

WHAT ADVICE WOULD YOU GIVE TO SONGWRITERS WHO ARE TRYING TO BECOME SUCCESSFUL?

First, see what is commercial, what is selling, what people like. However, being commercial is not being a good songwriter. It means that your material will be accepted by the public and readily sold. To be a good songwriter, you must structure your pieces correctly and then play them in some type of showcase, whether it is in a nightclub, on a recording, or whatever, so that it reflects the ideas, melodies, and harmonies within it. You write for a particular artist or artists and in a certain style so it will be accepted.

CHAPTER THREE

MUSIC PUBLISHING

There are approximately 40,000 music publishing companies sanctioned by the three performance rights organizations. Of the 40,000, only a few do most of the business. Music publishers select songs from songwriters and attempt to place songs with recording artists. The publishers only receive money from songs that have been recorded and sold to the public or songs that are used by the public.

As Wesley Rose stated in the December 9, 1979, issues of *The Tennessean:* "Music publishing is a personal business and success boils down to one's track record. If songwriters and performers know they can trust a publisher to work for them and develop their careers, then they are much more willing to sign with the publisher. You've got to have a team (the publisher and songwriter) working for the same thing, and each one has to be positive about what they are doing or it just won't work. By working together, the impossible can be done. It all starts with the writers. Without great songwriters you can't have great publishing companies."

Obviously the only way to stay in the music publishing business is to select songs that have hit potential. That's easy to say but very hard to do. There are lots of stories about how one publishing company executive turned down a song while another one picked it up. Remember "You Light Up My Life"?

One of the main factors in the music publishing business is personal opinion. You as a songwriter should only submit songs you believe in. If you find a publishing company that believes in your songs and your talent, then you are part way home. Selection of a publishing company is like selecting a member of your baseball team. Find how successful they have been in the past and what their plans for you are in the future. Be careful! There are a lot of horror stories about people who were so eager to place a song with a company that they got ripped off. Some songwriters have signed writers' deals that have tied them up for years, and they never received a penny for all their work. Investigate the company. Make sure it works very hard placing your songs with recording artists. They may promise you the world, but all you really want is what is owed you. A percentage of nothing is still nothing.

Thankfully, most publishing companies are honest and sincere about their work. They screen all of the songs submitted to them and decide which have hit potential. Thousands of songs are sent by mail, or delivered by hand; thousands more are created by company writers. Out of the thousands of songs that are submitted, only a handful are selected to be placed with the company. The vast majority of the songs selected are from the professional song-writers working for the company or from writers already in the music business. The chances that a company will select a song submitted by a newcomer are slim to none. From past experience, publishers realize that the vast majority of songs sent to them by nonprofessional songwriters are simply of poor quality. They hate to waste their time listening to them; it's like looking for a needle in a haystack.

The first function of the publishing companies is to listen to and select the songs. The second function is to place songs with a recording artist. Demos of the songs are made and given to the company song-plugger. He or she will take the song to a record company A&R (artist and repertoire) person; a record producer; the artist's manager; or the recording artists them-selves. The marriage of the song and right artist is very important.

Publishing companies are paid their portion of the performance royalties from the performance rights organizations. They receive mechanical royalties from the Harry Fox Agency in New York City, which collects those royalties from the record companies. The Harry Fox Agency charges a fee of 3.25 percent of the money collected for the publishers whose mechanical receipts are over $25,000 a year. It charges 4.25 percent to new publishers. Mechanical royalties are royalties paid by record companies for the use of songs. Even an individual who de-cides to record a demo record and press copies must pay for the right of recording that song.

Publishing companies are in business because of and to serve songwriters. They filter out the poor songs and work feverishly to deliver good songs to the right record-ing artists. In addition publishing companies have people employed that are extremely knowledgeable about the music business and the personalities that make the music business operate. Their knowledge about the business and their contacts are the main ingredients that make them successful.

MIKE KOSSER

Songwriter and freelance journalist. Author and publisher of *How to Become a Successful Nashville Songwriter*, co-author of the authorized biography of Conway Twitty, and co-writer of the radio series "The History of Country Music." Former staff songwriter for Tree Publishing.

***WE'RE IN YOUR OFFICE AT TREE PUB-
LISHING, AND THERE ARE TAPES
STACKED ALL OVER THE PLACE. THEY
MUST BE FROM EVERY CORNER OF THE
COUNTRY.***
Tremendous backlog, by the way, because
the song pluggers got so bogged down with
it. They so seldom hear good material that
they just lost interest and let it accumulate.

***OUT OF ALL THESE TAPES THAT ARE
STACKED IN THIS ROOM, HOW MANY DO
YOU THINK WILL BE HIT SONGS, ON AN
AVERAGE?***
I can't give you a fair answer. I will tell you
that there should be a couple. I will also tell
you that because I have 1,000 tapes to get
rid of—these aren't all of them by any
means—my main job is to get them out of
this building. I know people aren't going to
want to hear this, but I don't have time to
listen to more than the first song on these
tapes. Very often I will listen to the first
couple of lines. If something turns *me* off,
which tells me that the writer is not aware,
I'm going to turn *it* off right then and there. I

don't think I'm doing the writer a very good
service, but on the other hand, my feeling is
that if you want to be a songwriter, you'd
better go to the music center and live there
and meet the people, because this is a
personal business.

***SO YOU DON'T THINK IT REALLY HELPS
TO SEND TAPES TO A PUBLISHER.***
I wouldn't say that, because there have
been many writers who have established
their first good contacts, or have even had
hits, by sending songs through the mail. But
I think you're really cutting down on your
percentages by not being here, by not
meeting the people.

DO ALL THE TAPES GET LISTENED TO?
Virtually every tape that I see here, I'm
listening to now. But I've got instructions not
to mail any tapes back that don't have
stamps. The company is not going to spend
any more money on those.
    A lot of publishing companies are very
reluctant to listen to unsolicited material
because of the risk. Suppose you have a

song and it says, "Love Me Tomorrow." And I hear the tape, or maybe I don't even hear the tape, but the tape is in the building. Maybe I write a song called "Love Me Tomorrow" because it just occurred to me. Or maybe I did hear it, and it did lie in my subconscious. In either case, you say, "I sent in a song to them called 'Love Me Tomorrow,' and I'll bet you he heard it, and he copied it. I'm going to sue them."

Now, your suit is based on such nebulous stuff that you don't have a chance to win, but you have a high-powered lawyer who doesn't know that. Many lawyers don't know a thing about music copyright law and the precedents and so forth, not to mention that many precedents are still being established. This guy presses the suit, and I've got a $25,000 royalty being held up. They've got an injunction holding up those royalties because this person felt I'd stolen his song even if I hadn't. This hasn't happened to me, by the way, but as a result, just because this company was open to listening to tapes, we've got a lawsuit. We might even wind up settling out of court for several thousand dollars, just so it won't hold up the royalties.

NOW, WHAT ARE SOME OF THE BAD THINGS YOU HEAR?
First of all, don't send me a tape with ten songs on it. Secondly, five years ago I would have said to send reel to reel because we're not equipped to handle cassettes. Right now I would say to send cassettes. They're much easier for us to handle. And, they're easier for you to mail. You can make quite an acceptable demo on a cassette machine. Just make sure that the voice is far enough out in front of the guitar to be heard.

Now, when you ask me, "Does the demo count," the answer is *yes*. If you're going to spend money for a good demo, it better be right. Because you're better off with a well-made guitar/voice demo than you are with a studio demo that doesn't have the feel that you wanted it to have. At least if you're working with your guitar and your voice, you

have a chance to put it down the way you want it.

HOW IMPORTANT IS THE FEEL?
I would say feel is the most important element of the hit. Feel is a combination of song and production. The song gives rise to the feel, but very often the producer can go several ways as far as the feel is concerned. "Feel" is difficult to describe, but it is a combination of the lyric and phrasing thereof, the melody, the rhythm, and the production.

WHAT ELSE WOULD YOU SUGGEST?
Send in an envelope, 5″ × 7″, with a cassette inside. I don't think you need any buffering material in it, generally, although I did see one tape that was broken apart. No more than three songs a tape. I think two is a good idea. Make sure your best song is your first song. Without a doubt, there are a few iron-clad rules, and that's one right there—because the publisher might not listen to your second song.

HOW ABOUT LEAD SHEETS?
No lead sheets, usually. Lyric sheets, yes. Lead sheets are hard to read for a lot of people. But make those lyrics clear enough in the recording so that they don't need the lyric sheets. A short letter would be fine, but most people don't read the letters. They just pull the cassette out, put it on the machine and listen.

Hopefully, you want that first song to hit them very early. They might not wait long enough for two verses and a chorus. The song that's your strongest-starting song should be your first song.

Make sure you have a self-addressed, stamped envelope. Don't write little notes saying, "Hey, I think this song would be a smash for Merle Haggard," or something like that. Most important of all, I believe it's very, very difficult to deal by mail if they don't know you. Now, people may say, "Yeah, but I went to Nashville, and I couldn't get into the publishers." It is hard, so you've got to make a war out of it, practically. I did, and I didn't know anybody when I came here. Today, it's a bit easier; you're bound to meet somebody somewhere along the line. You just keep going around, you keep writing songs, and eventually you meet somebody.

If your attitude is professional and the person likes you, he may say, "If you come to my company next week, or give me a call, I will hear you." You try to get into situations where you'll be able to meet people.

HOW ABOUT PROFESSIONAL SONGWRITING ORGANIZATIONS? DO THEY HELP OUT?

Yes, I think Nashville Songwriters Association International is for the songwriters. They have a great deal of feeling for new songwriters. For example, they have workshops every Wednesday night. Go to these things, and they'll teach you something. More importantly, you'll get a chance to meet people.

IN REGARD TO ATTITUDE AND PROFESSIONALSIM, HOW STRONG SHOULD A PERSON COME ON?

You come in so confident that you don't have to sell yourself. The songs are going to do the selling for you. You come in, meet the person, be interested in what that person has to say. There are no rules. If the person seems to be in a great hurry to get rid of you, you don't press it. If you think he's in a great hurry, you might be the one to say, "Well, thank you for your time. I know you probably have a lot of work to do, so I'll go." If the person seems to want to talk with you, then talk. Then if he wants to talk awhile, you converse with him the way you'd converse with a friend, without being a wide-eyed, eager-beaver. Try and be yourself. Anxieties show through, and they scare people off. It's something you have to work on. If you believe in yourself, you don't hype yourself.

RICHARD PERNA

Director of research and consultation for Copyright
Management, Inc., Nashville.

**WHAT DOES A PUBLISHER LOOK FOR
WHEN HE IS GOING TO SELECT A SONG?
CAN HE PREDICT A HIT?**
Considering the diverse genres that are out
there in the music world today, how can you
really say what is going to be a hit and what
isn't? There are some melodic structures
that endear themselves to the public. Look
at Kenny Rogers. He has the "Coward of the
County," which is definitely a hit song, but it
is a story song. It's a country song all the
way through. It scored real high. Then he
turns around and has "Lady," an R&B
[rhythm and blues] song and a Number One
hit. How can you tell?

A good song has something evident in
itself. Basically, the lyric is there. I think that
Nashville prides itself on lyrics. We are a
strong copyright town. Los Angeles and
New York are more into the feel type of
music where you get "in the groove."

When you come down to what really
makes a good song, there are many formats. You have the verse-chorus-verse
format, for example, or the verse-chorus-
verse-chorus-bridge-chorus format. That is

just structure. But what a good song does is
leave the public either laughing or crying. If
you can't do either of those, make them
think.

A publisher might choose a song for the
way the subject matter is put together.
Subject matter should be tied together and
compressed, instead of being scattered.
The writer has to concentrate on one particular thought. In a story song, he develops it
all the way through.

Another trick that people have gotten
away from is conversational music. I think
that some of the greater writers of our era
include Paul Simon, Paul McCartney, and
John Lennon. What makes their music so
great is the conversational lyrics they use.

If you look at the standard songs, a lot of
them are very conversational. The hook is a
big part of the music, but at the same time,
you can do without it if you structure a song
in such a way.

**WHAT A PUBLISHER IS SUPPOSED TO DO
IS CUT A DEMO, GET IT OUT TO THE
MANAGERS AND ARTISTS, AND TRY TO**

GET THAT SONG PLACED. BUT A LOT OF TIMES, PUBLISHERS ARE A LITTLE LAZY, AND IT'S THE SONGWRITER WHO EVENTUALLY GETS IT PLACED.

Talk to people who make their living from writing songs and you'll find that seven times out of ten those guys got their own songs cut. That's a high percentage.

WHAT YOU'RE SAYING IS THAT THE PUBLISHER SHOULD EXPLOIT THE SONGS FOR THE WRITERS. IF THEY DON'T DO IT, THEN THE REVERSION CLAUSE SAYS THAT THE SONGS GO BACK TO THE WRITER.

Right, after a limited time period.

WHAT WOULD BE A GOOD TIME PERIOD?

If I were a writer, I would say six months. If I were a publisher, I would say six years.

SONGWRITERS NEED TO MAKE SURE THAT THE CONTRACT STATES THE PROVISIONS FOR COMMERCIAL EXPLOITATION.

Yes. A lot of people don't realize that it's not written in the contract at all. Publishers don't ever have a firm commitment in any of their contracts; they don't ever have to do demos or pitch your songs. They just have to pay you if and when your song earns money.

THERE IS NO GUARANTEE OF HOW MUCH MONEY OR TIME THE PUBLISHER IS GOING TO SPEND ON PROMOTING THE SONG?

Right. And in a lot of areas, publishers charge the songwriter; they'll say, "We are going to charge you 50 percent of the demo expenses," and so on. It's written into the contract. Exclusive songwriter contracts are notorious for that. In some instances, I've seen it at 100 percent. It is a great game. A publisher, or maybe a producer, will go out and do a spec session and spend $2,500 to $5,000 on the session. Then when that song is cut and it's a hit, but it's not by the artist who did the demo, he says that he spent all that money doing a demo on your song, so he has to recoup that first.

AND FOR $5,000 YOU HAVE TO SELL A LOT OF RECORDS.

Right. On a record that sells a million copies, the mechanical royalties amount to $50,000. The publisher is supposed to get half, or $25,000, and the songwriter is supposed to get half.

WHAT ARE THE PUBLISHER'S RESPONSIBILITIES IN EXPLOITING THE COPYRIGHT?

A publisher must protect the songs once he has acquired them. He has a responsibility to make sure that the songs are contracted properly between the company and the songwriter. He has to make sure that the assignments are filed properly and so forth. This paperwork is very important.

Another area that a publisher has to know before I even consider calling him a publisher is the actual exploitation of that copyright. When a song is cut and is a big song, there are several areas where you can generate money. Performance rights, mechanical rights, synchronization rights, print rights, grand literary rights, grand performance rights, commercial uses and jingles, and foreign market rights. As a publisher, you have to be versed in all of these areas, know exactly what is going on, know the applicable rates and the procedures, know the people you are dealing with, and know how to get the most out of that copyright.

WHAT IS A PUBLISHER'S CATALOG?

All the copyrights that a publisher owns are his catalog. Tree Publishing has a catalog with 38,000 copyrights. But how many are active and how many do they actually know exist? I think that a catalog should be judged not only on its size but on the quality of its cuts.

I WAS ONCE TOLD THAT IF YOU GET A LARGE CATALOG AND PUT A FEW GOOD SONGS IN IT, YOU CAN SELL IT FOR A LOT OF MONEY.

Right. People are always impressed by size as compared to quality. If you look at trends in the future, I can emphatically state that people who are going to be earning money in the publishing field are going to be publishing producers or publishing artists.

DO PUBLISHERS LIKE TO LISTEN TO NEW SONGWRITERS?

Most publishers will tell you that they listen to everything. What that usually means is that their song pluggers or other people sift through the material. The problem is that so many good songwriters are walking the streets that the guy who is new and sends something through the mail, unless he has made personal contact with that particular publisher, can't depend on his song being listened to. So much of the material that comes in the mail is junk, prepared improperly. People don't always know how to pitch their work. That isn't saying that there isn't some good stuff there, too. Look at it this way. Do you want to listen to boxes of tapes or to a guy who has won a Grammy award?

BILL
DENNY

President of Nashville Gas Company, former President
and owner of Cedarwood Publishing, Hatch Show Print,
and National Tape Corporation. Past President, National
Academy of Recording Arts and Sciences.

**HOW MANY SONGS ARE SUBMITTED TO
YOU ON A WEEKLY BASIS?**
We get as much as, or more than, a lot of
people because we're right here on the
street. We have a sign out front, and we're
easy to locate. Also the name of our firm is
known. We may get a couple of bushel
baskets full of tapes a week from people
who will bring them by or send them through
the mail. We don't feel that is a major priority
for us in our daily operation. We don't try to
work on the basis of a 24-hour turnaround in
listening to songs. It's impossible because
we get so much product. We have about
four people here that listen to the material,
and they all listen to them according to their
own patterns—some at home, some at the
office.

**WHAT DO YOU LISTEN FOR IN THE
SONGS SUBMITTED TO YOU?**
Some things automatically exclude a song.
For example, some songs contain words
that are dated—we refer to them as "The
moon is blue and so are you" type lyrics.
There are songs that people write as an

expression or outflowing of their feelings
about some experience they've endured.
They feel that the song says what they want
it to say. We have to look at it from a commercial standpoint, from a competitive
standpoint. We don't want to put anything
out to producers that we don't feel would be
the best for a particular artist. We want to go
back to those producers again. We refuse
songs by the ton because we have to feel
the song has real potential.

WHAT MAKES A HIT SONG?
I don't know that there is any one thing that
can make a hit song. You can have a great
song, a sensational song, and have it
recorded by the wrong artist, or get the
wrong arrangement, and it just dies. Or you
can have a mediocre song that gets a
magnificent musical treatment, the artist
literally sings his lungs out, and it wins. In
general you've got to have a meaningful set
of lyrics—lyrics that are current in their
appeal, that are easily understood, and that
have no hidden meanings. A hit song needs
a flow to it. It has to be cloaked with a

34

musical treatment that allows the best of the lyrics to be displayed. The music, in fact, displays the lyrics, becomes a base for the lyrics, and fills in the spaces between the lines. Think of lyrics as the gravel in a bucket and the music as water. If you poured water into the bucket, the water would fill in all around that gravel and come up to the top. You'd have a full bucket, full of lyrics and full of music. The water would fill in all the empty spots.

ONCE YOU'VE SELECTED A SONG, WHAT DO YOU DO WITH IT?

We go through a process. We build a data base on our catalog. We go through a clerical procedure which involves our contracts for the songs and then a certain number of card cross indexes by song title, songwriter(s) and so on. Each card contains a certain amount of information that we have to have to market the song—copyright date, serial numbers, etc. Then we feed all that into our data base. It's an involved process.

PUBLISHERS MUST NEED A LOT OF KNOWLEDGE ABOUT WHAT IS HAPPENING IN THE INDUSTRY—WHO IS PRODUCING OR RECORDING—TO BE ABLE TO MATCH A CERTAIN SONG WITH AN ARTIST.

That's one of the biggest tricks in the business—finding the song that matches the artist. A lot of songs will match several artists, but some songs can only be recorded by one person. I don't know anybody else who could have done "Teddy Bear" as well as Red Sovine did it. It's a classic in the business.

WHAT IS A SONG PLUGGER'S JOB?

The song pluggers keep up with who is recording, and they keep in constant communication with producers and artists. The song plugger is your first contact with the industry. In addition to bringing back information that he gathers out there, he is also matching up songs with the producers and artists he sees. If he's not good at that, you suffer. He needs to maintain friendships with people in the industry so that when he has a product that someone needs to hear, he can get that person to listen to it. Our industry is crowded, and there is a lot of competition. It's important that he be able to do that.

SAY YOU HAVE A SONG THAT SELLS 100,000 COPIES. HOW MUCH MONEY WILL YOU RECEIVE FROM THE MECHANICAL RIGHT?

The copyright royalty is 5 cents per song sold; so that would be about $5,000. The songwriter and publisher share that equally—that is, if you get paid. Payment is a real problem. Record companies feel it is necessary for them to hold back a percentage of sales. They don't report the sales until a certain period of time passes. Sometimes they miscount. You may get your money or you may not. You may get it this quarter or the next quarter. The license says they're supposed to pay every quarter on records sold during that quarter. Some record companies consider records *sold* when they've shipped them. Some companies do not consider the records sold until they've gotten paid for them. Other companies say the record's not sold until the consumer buys it at the retail store. The copyright law says records are distributed when they are out of the control of the record manufacturer. Some manufacturers maintain that they have that control all the way down to the retailer. Who knows? We have misunderstandings about it all the time.

DO YOU RECEIVE MOST OF YOUR MONEY FROM THE PERFORMANCE RIGHTS, RATHER THAN FROM THE MECHANICAL RIGHTS?

No, not necessarily. A lot of records will sell well but not play very well, or vice versa. I don't know that there is any clear demarcation where you get more money from performance or more from mechanicals.

For instance, you may have a song that gets recorded by several artists, but you only have one single out on it. The single is getting the performances. Let's say the song was recorded by ten different artists, but only one artist put it out as a single. The single sold 100,000 units. But each album sold 100,000 units. You only get *performance* earnings off the single, because the albums aren't getting played, but you are selling a million records.

On the other hand, you might have a record that plays like everything. A lot of times this happens on novelty songs. They get played and played for a flash campaign for about a month. Everybody loves to hear it, but nobody buys it. It can work both ways.

HAVE YOU EVER HAD A PROBLEM GETTING MONEY THAT WAS OWED YOU?

We've had occasions when a song has sold very well and has played well but we didn't get paid. We deal with the Harry Fox Agency, which issues our licenses and collects money for us, as it does for most of the other publishers in the country. The agency went to a particular record company, did an audit, and found that we were owed some money, but the record company wasn't going to pay us. They just went out of business; they didn't owe just us but a lot of other people. It was a big hit song, but neither the songwriter nor our company got paid.

You have a lot of people in the record business who take the attitude that the money is theirs, and they don't consider the royalties involved.

IT REALLY IS A RIP-OFF WHEN THE WRITER AND THE PUBLISHER DON'T GET ANYTHING FOR THEIR EFFORTS.

The worst part is that it affects the writer. The writer's on the very end of the royalty trail. The song started with him and the royalties end up with him. It's tough for a writer to have a song do something; he sees it and his friends see it. They assume he's earning something, and he assumes he's going to get paid. Royalty time comes and there is no money. It's terrible. I don't know what else we can do about it besides constantly policing it.

WHAT ADVICE WOULD YOU GIVE TO PEOPLE WHO WANT TO GET INTO PUBLISHING?

The publishing business is a good business. It requires a very broad knowledge of the industry in general. You can't just operate as a music publisher, because music publishing affects so many parts of the business—the record companies, the artists, other contacts. To start off fresh in the business, the most important thing is to have a good product—good songs—and to have the ability to get the song heard by the people who do the recording. That means cultivating and developing one or two producers, hanging with them until you get something done with them, then adding another producer and another. It will be a long term, step-by-step process, but it's done every day.

The publishing business is for independents; it's for entrepreneurs. True, there are some publishing companies that are owned by record companies, but the big independent houses have always been built by entrepreneurs in the business. There is plenty of room for everybody.

ANY OTHER ADVICE?

Stay aware of the public taste. Public taste is a very fickle thing. It changes almost overnight. For instance, a few years ago no one would have ever thought of disco music. Then something happened. Disco records came out and people went to various establishments and danced. It was a movement all over the country. Then, all of a sudden, it was over.

There is a very big movement in country music right now. People have said that the American public is getting back to basics in its music. That is where country music is, has been, and will be. The country song deals with basic emotions in people—love, hate, loneliness. These are things that country songs speak to. Everybody understands that. Country music cuts across a lot of economic and social barriers. I don't know if it's going to be a fad and end. I don't think so. It's been around a long time, and I think it's going to stay. It reaches so many people—the banker, the truck driver, the homemaker, the working girl, the single people, and the married people. It touches all those sociological areas.

WHAT ADVICE WOULD YOU GIVE TO SONGWRITERS?

I guess the important thing would be to be professional and don't take things for granted. This is a business, and we look at it as a business.

Just because one publisher turns your song down doesn't mean it's bad. It just means that he didn't like it. There are over four hundred active publishers in the city of Nashville alone. The Southeast is loaded with publishers, and there are other centers such as New York, Dallas, Los Angeles, and Austin. Don't be discouraged. But also consider the fact that if three or four publishers have said they don't like your song, maybe you ought to take another look at it. They're in the business on a daily basis. They're going to look at it strictly on what they think they can make on that song. The dollar is the bottom line. The bottom line is whether they make a profit.

CASEY KELLY

Recording artist, songwriter, and publisher. Artists who have recorded his songs include Kenny Rogers and Dottie West, Ed Bruce, Loretta Lynn, Jacky Ward, The Dirt Band, Johnny Rivers, The Vogues, Helen Reddy, Tanya Tucker, O. C. Smith, and Janie Fricke.

WHAT DOES PUBLISHING MEAN?

To publish means to place on sale. To publish a magazine means to place the magazine on sale. When a person publishes a song, he places that song on sale. With songs it is in the form of sheet music, which is a mechanical copy of your work, or records, or whatever. What usually happens is that somebody else is interested in manufacturing the records. The publisher places the song on sale through a manufacturer. So all the publisher does is place your song on sale. When a writer sells the publishing to somebody, what he's selling is the right to publish the work, the right to place it on sale, the right to control the copyright and say who can record it, and—coincidentally—how much the publisher has to pay you.

All you're doing is creating a work; and as soon as you do, the copyright springs into effect. A publisher is just somebody that controls that right that you have. You give him the control of that right.

WHEN YOU PLACE A SONG WITH A PUBLISHER, YOU GIVE HIM THE RIGHT TO

EXPLOIT YOUR COPYRIGHT. WHAT KIND OF MONEY CAN YOU MAKE FROM THAT?

Usually, you get half of whatever income the publisher can generate from your song. The bottom line is how much the publisher can sell.

IS THERE ANY EXCEPTION TO THAT RULE?

Except in bizarre cases, publishers essentially give you half of whatever they collect. They will subtract some money for doing business in some cases. Some other, less scrupulous publishers will charge other items against your royalties and give you less than half of the money collected. Really and truly you ought to get half of everything. They can't do anything without the song. Where else do you get the kind of deal where somebody agrees to give you half of money collected for acting as an agent?

ONCE YOU GIVE THIS RIGHT TO THE PUBLISHER, IS IT HIS FOREVER, OR IS IT NEGOTIABLE?

That depends on your agreement. Sometimes it's totally negotiable. Most often you give it to the publisher forever, and that's it. But part of the new copyright law is that at some point, the rights come back to the writer, if the publisher doesn't fulfill his obligations.

IN OTHER WORDS, THE PUBLISHER IS USUALLY GOING TO BE HONEST IF HE'S HONEST AND CROOKED IF HE'S CROOKED.

Most of them will just do what's supposed to be done. They know that they're not going to get away with it in the end.

WHAT DO YOU LOOK FOR IN A PUBLISHER?

You look for somebody who is respected by the other people in the music community, generally somebody who has been around for a while; and you want somebody who believes in the material.

If you're going to shop for a publisher, you should talk to some of the other writers, especially some of the old-timers who have been around for a while. Everybody who's been around has had some bad experiences with somebody. A publisher, like a manager or anyone else, may be great for one artist and terrible for another. By and large, you'll get a feel for what the people are like.

It also depends on what you want in a publisher. I was tempted to go with Jim Ed Norman as a publisher because he had done so much production. I felt that, maybe, this would be a way of having some guaranteed cuts. I was informed that he sometimes will not even listen to the songs he has in his own company. He is completely aboveboard. He listens to the songs, and whichever ones he likes are the ones he does. He doesn't care who published them.

On the other hand, you have some publishers who are looking for an in-house situation. They want people who can write a copy of the last Ronnie Milsap thing, and

they'll produce it themselves. They'll fill their albums up with that kind of stuff.

Some writers want to be with a national company because they feel that they are hindered by a Nashville-based company. That's another thing you've got to look at when you're trying to find out if somebody can do the job for you. How is a publisher going to place tunes with people in Los Angeles if he hasn't got any connections there? If he's only had success as a country publisher and if he has no office on the West Coast or doesn't have a man out there who knows the territory, it's hard to get those cuts. You can't do it by mail.

SO IF THE PUBLISHER DOESN'T HAVE THE RIGHT CONNECTIONS WITH THE RIGHT PEOPLE, HE'S NOT YOUR PUBLISHER. IS THERE ANYTHING ELSE YOU WANT TO ADD?

Some people want a publisher who's just going to get them cuts. Some people need to have somebody who's going to supplement their income. There are small publishers who do the job of getting records cut but who cannot supplement your income.

WHEN YOU SAY SUPPLEMENT YOUR INCOME, DOES THAT MEAN THAT THE PUBLISHER GIVES YOU A SALARY?

No, it's not a salary; it's an advanced payment of a sum of money that is charged against your royalties. The company is saying that it will advance you some money based on the royalties it expects to pay you. When the royalties come in, the advance the writer has received is deducted from his share of the money. I guess some people somewhere have gotten deals where they have actually been paid a bonus; but an advance is not a bonus. It's a gamble that the company is taking. The company says, "We feel we're going to earn this much and more on you. We can go ahead and advance you this much because we know the money is going to come in."

JACK ROSS

Songwriter. Songs include the Canadian hit,
"If I Had One Wish."

WHY DO YOU WRITE SONGS?

I don't really know that I can say. I love good songs, and I admire people who can write them.

I've had a taste of having a few of my songs produced really well, and that is terrific! One of them was "If I Had One Wish." Randy Goodrum heard it when all I had was one verse, nothing else. I guess he heard something there, because he really encouraged me to finish it. Later on, when it didn't get a great response around town, he did a demo on it and tried for a year to get it cut. He didn't have any luck; but he did make me feel that I have talent as a writer, and I'm grateful for that. When the song was recorded, it became a hit.

I guess songwriting is really just another way of expressing myself—like singing, acting, photography, or doodling. It's a way of communicating feelings, ideas, and experiences. It's a way of capturing and sharing these things so other people can see their own reflections in them. There can be a real sense of fellowship between a writer and an audience. And it can be very spiritual and profound.

AS A SONGWRITER YOU ARE ALSO A SONG PLUGGER. DO YOU FIND THAT HARD?

Oh, yes. Rejection hurts, but then that's part of it. Besides, it's rarely personal. As my mother would probably say, you have to look at it as just another "learning experience." Still, I imagine it's hard for most writers to think of their songs as just so many cans of beans. Know what I mean?

HOW DO YOU PRESENT YOUR SONGS?

Ideally, I like to have an appointment rather than just drop a tape off. I want to know what the publisher thinks, and I like to get to know him a little better, too. But sometimes getting an opinion in person can be nerve-wracking for everyone—especially if the song stinks. I try to be pleasant and to always be on time. Once, I was kept waiting for four hours only to have the receptionist tell me that the guy I had the appointment with had to catch a plane and had split out the back door. Now I usually wait fifteen to thirty minutes or so; then I politely excuse myself and try again later.

WHAT DO YOU DO WHEN A PUBLISHER SAYS THAT HE REALLY LIKES THE SONG BUT THAT HE CAN'T USE IT?

He may be stating exactly what he thinks. The song may not be there. He may not hear it as a hit, and that can be due to any number of reasons. I figure that one rejection isn't any reason to put a song away. However, if the same criticisms keep popping up over and over again, I probably have something to think about. Fix it or forget it.

"If I Had One Wish" was turned down a bunch of times before Randy Goodrum finally got involved. And after our deal ran out, I kept polishing it. I've got a notebook in which I keep track of everyone I pitch my songs to. Once, just for the fun of it, I counted how many times I pitched "If I Had One Wish" before it was recorded. It totaled over 120 times. I got a call from a new artist up in Canada, Mary Lu Zahalan, and she wanted to do it on her first album. I said, "Sure." A few months later, the album came out. Radio stations started pulling it off the album and playing it. The next thing I knew, the label decided to put it out as the second single. On Christmas Day, 1982, it was Number Nineteen across Canada. In some markets, it went to Number One.

CHAPTER FOUR

RECORD COMPANIES

When you think about record companies, dollar signs seem to come to mind. The high life style of limos, women, and parties run a close second. But if you look behind the public image, or what you think record companies are all about, you may be surprised. Record companies are in the people business. They take your songs, personality, and vocal talents and gamble millions of dollars on your abilities and their abilities to make a profit. After all, this is the music *Business* and just like any other business, the bottom line is money.

According to a five-year trend report, *The Consumer Purchasing of Records and Pre-Records Tapes,* released by The Recording Industry Association of America (RIAA), record companies in 1984 shipped 679,800,000 units. Shipment in dollars (net after returns and at suggested retail list price) amounted to $4,370,040,000 in revenue. Country music's share of total dollars spent in the United States on all units (records, tapes, and compact discs) was ten percent of the market or $437,040,000.

That is approximately 68 million units shipped.

Because of the glamour and money involved, record companies hire people that can get the job done. Having "hit" records is the apparent goal, but the real bottom line is often the profit and loss statements at the quarterly meeting.

There are approximately 2200 signatory record labels according to the American Federation of Musicians. Many of the record companies are one-man operations, others are vanity labels owned by performers for ego trips and tax purposes. An article in *Changing Times* magazine stated that there are over 1000 record companies in the United States that are able to produce a first-rate recording. The real number of record companies changes daily because of the high risk factors involved in this business. Changing attitudes of the public, the economic situation of the country, the mood of the people, and hundreds of other humanistic and economic factors affect the business.

So how many major, world-wide record

companies are there? Would you believe five? They are Capitol-EMI records, CBS (Columbia Broadcasting System), Polygram, MCA (Music Corporation of America), and Warner Communications-Elektra, Asylum, (Warner Bros.) They are conglomerates, with the record business being only a part of the overall business activities. For example, CBS is also a major television network and book publisher in the United States. MCA and Capital-EMI are television and motion picture production companies.

Major independent labels are record and video companies that may have started as total independent labels, but are not part of a major label or use the distribution, and promotion department of a major label. The cost of personnel for distribution and promotion is often shared by independents or through an agreement with a major label. Examples include Artista, A & M records, Compleat Entertainment, Motown Records, and many more.

Major record companies have different branch offices that specialize in individual types (formats) of music. As an example, most of the majors and some of the independent labels have offices in Nashville for country music, and Atlanta, Detroit, and Memphis for rhythm and blues, black, or soul music.

According to the RIAA 1984 figures on expenditures by music type, the following is an example of how the public purchased different types (formats) of music for that year.

ROCK	33%
COUNTRY	10%
POP/AND EASY LISTENING	20%
BLACK/DANCE	9%
GOSPEL	4%
CLASSICAL	4%
SHOWS/SOUNDTRACKS	4%
JAZZ	3%
CHILDREN'S	3%
OTHER	10%

Many of the independent record labels specialize in only one type of music. Motown Records started in Detroit and was incredibly successful in creating the Motown Sound. Sam Phillips started Sun Records in Memphis and discovered Elvis, Johnny Cash, Carl Perkins, Jerry Lee Lewis, and many others. Some of the most successful independent labels in the past were responsible for the creation of new musical trends and for the discovery and development of today's stars.

The RIAA certifies gold and platinum records for the recording industry. A gold record is presented in honor of one million singles (45 rpm records) sold, and one half million albums (long play records) sold. Platinum records are presented for sales of two million singles and one million albums. In 1984, the RIAA started awarding Multi-Platinum records in honor of two or more million albums sold. From the 679,000,000 records, compact discs, cassettes and eight tracks that were released in 1984, the following number received a Gold, Platinum, or Multi-Platinum award.

Multi-Platinum:	109	albums
Platinum:	59	albums
	2	singles
Gold:	131	albums
	26	singles

Because of the millions of units released, you might have expected thousands of Gold or Platinum records. It's a real shock to find out that only 15% of all records released make any profit (according to the RIAA). As you can see, the few records that sell well make up for the 85% that lose money.

Today's country music is competitive, political and very, very big business. There are the traditional markets, contemporary markets, progressive country music, and very high production, labor, talent, touring and additional business expenses. The cost of breaking a new artist or promoting an established artist is very high. Digital recording and the new technologies are driving up studio production cost.

Record companies provide the money and personnel to produce the product (artist recorded on records, tapes, or cd's) and the marketing and sales staff to promote, advertise, and sell the product to the public. Everyone works together to make it successful. But who is the leader that sets the label's direction and makes the decisions?

Record label executives are very special people. They must be successful in business and in dealing with creative people. It's very rare when the two mix, and it takes a person who understands both "worlds" to bring the two sucessfully together. The bottom line may be stockholders and profits, but the product is creative. The duties and functions of a record company personnel include:

PRESIDENT: Supervises national operation of record company including national vice presidents and branch operations. Gives direction to the label and may make major decisions concerning signing of artists, producers, budgets, and major advertising campaigns.

VICE PRESIDENTS: Supervise, on a national or world-wide level, one main operation of the company. Examples include Vice President of Marketing, Promotion, Artist Development, or Operations.

VICE PRESIDENT/BRANCH GENERAL MANAGER: Supervises operation of all departments in a branch office. Reports directly to the company President. Gives direction to all department heads and makes major decisions on branch artist signings, producers, budget, and operations.

RECORD PRODUCER (STUDIO PRODUCTION): In charge of record production for the label, including supervision of additional record producers, production budgets, matching producers with the right artist, selection of songs to match the artist or the artist's image, selection of studio, musicians, and audio engineers. Supervision of mastering process and pressings.

ARTIST AND REPERTOIRE (A AND R): Finds new recording artists and songs for the label. The A and R person is the "ears" of the company. He or she screens prospective talent by listening to tapes that have been mailed in or delivered in person and tapes of songs delivered by songpluggers from publishing companies and amateur songwriters. The A and R person must know what the record company is looking for in new artists, and have a "feel" for songs that can be recorded by the current labels' recording artists.

PROMOTION: Responsibile for getting records charted in the trade magazines through establishing radio station air play on reporting stations and to help create sales momentum in stores. Trade magazines include *Billboard, Radio and Records,* and *Cashbox.*

SALES: Supervision of record sales to record distributors, retail stores, record clubs, through direct per-inquirer television and advertisement, and other outlets. Maintains daily reports of product sold and placed into distribution.

PUBLICIST (PUBLIC RELATIONS): Provides the media information, stories, press kits, and other materials that will enhance the artist's image and career, and inform the public about new record releases and tour information.

MARKETING (PRODUCT MANAGEMENT): Supervises certain artist projects, including album concepts and video scripts.

ARTIST DEVELOPMENT: Helps the maturing image and success of the artist. Long term goals are established and markets may be studied to match the artist's appearance, style, and personality to the audience perceptions.

LEGAL AND OPERATIONS: Handles contracts for the label with artist, managers, and their attorneys. Supervision of accountants and budgets, payrolls, personnel expenses, and revenue generated.

CREATIVE: Development of concepts for albums, jackets, posters, television advertisements, and videos to increase record sales.

ART: Art work, layout, photos for album covers, posters, and displays.

OTHER: Personal assistants, secretaries, and internships.

How much does it cost to put out an album? What are the individual elements of an album project and what do they cost? Who pays all the expenses? The following explains one of the hardest things to understand about the music business: the cost of doing business.

Record companies advance the artist enough money to pay for an album project. All of the expenses paid by record companies are recouped from the artist's future royalties. That means that all expenses paid by the record company are "charged back" to the artist. So it's the artist who is really paying for all reasonable expenses of the album.

Record companies gamble their money on an artist's talent, name, personality, and abilities to deliver a "sellable" product. If the record doesn't sell well, then both the artist and company lose. On the other hand, if the artist and producer spend tons of money on the production, the artist could have a million seller and not receive any royalties because of excessive expenses. The only thing the artist receives at that point is exposure. Unless you're a superstar, don't expect to get rich from record sales.

The recording artist is ultimately responsi-ble for the final product. Success or failure may also have to do with selection of songs, artist performance, production techniques, promotion, advertisement, marketing, luck, the grace of God, and which way the wind is blowing.

Record album, and cassette album expenses that are charged back to the recording artist include the following:

RECORDING STUDIO RENTAL COST

Studios have different rental fees, but a good average in Nashville is:

In a 24-track studio $100 an hour for master recording of basic tracks, overdubbing, sweetening, and mix-down. Nationwide recording costs vary from $60 to $250 an hour depending on the region of the country. Sixteen track studios rent for approximately $35 to $75 per hour. Digital recording sessions average from $200 to $300 per hour. Prices are determined by the equipment available, personnel, studio track record, and what the market will bear.

Fortunately, some studios have a cash price instead of the 50% down and 30-to-90 day payment plans. Cash up front, before the session, often gives you at least a 20% reduction from the standard rate card.

Sometimes "deals" are made to pay for the studio time. Just about anything goes when it comes to renting a studio! The only thing studios really have to rent is time, and record company executives, producers and artists know it. Therefore if a studio isn't busy, they can strike a deal for block time, additional equipment, or special rates. Just like our phone and electricity bills, studios have to pay the bills whether the place is rented or not. By shopping around, good deals for quality studios can be found.

Recording sessions are booked for three-hour blocks, with a one-hour break between sessions. Typical sessions run from 10:00 A.M. to 1:00 P.M., 2:00 P.M. to 5:00 P.M., 6:00 P.M. to 9:00 P.M., 10:00 P.M. to 1:00 A.M., and 2:00 A.M. to 5:00 A.M.. It's not uncommon for the 10:00 P.M. to 1:00 A.M. to last all night.

STUDIO MUSICIANS

The American Federation of Musicians (AF of M) rates for studio master sessions are approximately $221.00 per musician per three hour set.

Recording Rate	$196.41
Cartage	$5.00
Pension (10%)	$19.64
Total	$221.05

This fee covers the three-hour call and includes pension, health, welfare, and cartage. The leader is always paid double. Some of the better known musicians may charge double or triple rates. Union musicians are allowed to cut the basic (rhythm) tracks on three songs during a three-hour call.

It's not uncommon for the musicians to do only one song, if it's for a major record producer, artist, and label. They take a little extra time to record the song in the groove. Now add the overdubbing (the recording of additional musical instruments) like the lead guitar, strings, and horns and it's very easy to run up musician and studio costs when trying to get something perfect. Good producers realize it's in the best interest of the artists' future royalties not to run into overtime. On the other hand, it's sometimes required to make sure the final product is as good as it can be. A general rule of thumb is the more rock 'n roll and high tech the album, the longer it'll take to complete. It's a judgement call between creativity and business and it's worth a lot of money in the long run to the artist and record companies.

VOCALIST, LEAD SINGERS, AND BACKGROUND SINGERS

The American Federation of Television and Radio Artists (AFTRA) charges the following rates for recording session singers.

$ 50 per song (side) or hour, whichever is completed first. This includes the 9% gross for health, welfare, and cartage.

$ 75 for leader or 1 and ½ the base rate.

$120 per side or hour for a lead vocalist or duet.

A lead vocalist (recording artist) may take a couple of hours to complete a song. One of the biggest studio expenses is the time singers take to make their performance perfect. Background vocalists often nail their parts within the first couple of tries.

PRODUCER COST

Producers are paid anything from a few dollars to approximately $2000 per side (one song), plus points (one percent of 90% of retail price equals one point). With major artists and record labels, 12% of 90% of the retail price may be shared by the recording artist and session producer. This share can be split in any combination. A new recording artist may receive only 3 to 5% of 90% of retail price. The more popular the artist and successful the producer, the more "points" they receive.

Points are paid after the total number of records (units) sold is established. Many producers receive payment on a quarterly basis, while others wait for over a year or more until the labels receive payments from independent record distributors on records sold at retail outlets. Remember producers get production fees as they complete the sessions and turn in their master tapes. But the artist won't receive any money (unless they get front money) until all of the expenses are recouped by the record company. Some examples of producers' expenses include the following: $2000 per side, or $20,000 on a ten song album plus 6% of 90% of $7.98 retail or an additional .43 per album.

ARTIST ROYALTIES

Major recording artists are paid according to their fame, talent, and "worth" (selling power). Only the most popular superstars and new artists who are quickly increasing in fame, are offered front money. Most record companies won't pay front money to new artists and some won't pay it to anyone! Sometimes front money is used for living expenses, payment on a tour bus, tour support, and other promotional things that'll help both the artist's career and increase record company profits.

Very few recording artists could afford the cost of the album, producer, promotion, marketing, and exposure the record companies provide. To the experts and record company executives their overall investment in a "sound" act or artist is good business—but you better have a hit!

You can see how much faith and mutual cooperation the artist and record label must have in each other. They need each other to be successful and they'll only get it by working together. If an artist tries to take advantage of a label, or the label takes advantage of an artist, it's only a matter of time before everyone knows about it.

The overall quality of the production, and the selection of the songs are the responsibility of the producer, artist, and his/her manager. How well the record is promoted, advertised, and marketed are some of the labels' responsibilities.

There is always teamwork in any successful venture and loneliness in failure. If an album fails (and 85% of them lose money), the blame often falls on the artist. Few artists can make hit records by themselves, and record companies need decent product. When it works, it's music and money; when it fails, it's emotions, rejection, re-evaluation, and try again.

Recording artists and producers split a royalty (points) of 12% of 90% of retail price. The split can be a 6% and 6% to any other combination. Fame has a lot to do with who gets the most points. A major superstar and somewhat new producer may be a 10 and 2 split. A well established producer and new artist may be an 8 and 4 split. Because most artists aren't paid front money, and all album expenses are taken from their future royalties, they've got to sell a hell of a lot of

records before they get paid. Most artist know that about 80% of their income is from concert dates and special appearances. If records don't make the artist rich, at least they'll get tons of exposure, if they get radio station airplay.

Some examples of artist royalties of 6% of 90% of retail are:

$5.98 (90% = 5.38) $5.38 × 6% = 32 cents per album

$6.98 (90% = 6.28) $6.28 × 6% = 38 cents per album

$7.98 (90% = 7.18) $7.18 × 6% = 43 cents per album

$8.98 (90% = 8.08) $8.08 × 6% = 48 cents per album

$9.98 (90% = 8.98) $8.98 × 6% = 54 cents per album

MECHANICAL RIGHTS (COPYRIGHTS)

Mechanical royalties are paid by record companies (to be recouped from artist royalties) to the songwriter and publisher for the use of their songs. The current mechanical rate for use of songs on records, compact discs, and tapes is 5 cents per song or 95 cents per minute, whichever is greater, per unit pressed or manufactured. Record labels pay mechanical royalties on the number of records pressed and released for distribution and sale. They are paying for the use of the songs imprinted in the grooves of the record or magnetically recorded onto the cassette tape. Some examples of mechanicals are as follow: One song recorded on tape under $5\frac{1}{2}$ minutes in length equals the following: 5 cents x the number of cassettes recorded. One song (5 cents) × 1000 tapes = $50. Ten songs (5 cents each = 50 cents) × 1000 tapes = $500. An example of an eight minute song would be: .95 × 8 = 7.6 cents per song × the number of records or tapes pressed for sale.

JACKETS AND RECORD PRESSING COST

Record jackets can cost almost as much as the record pressings. Prices include the one-time mastering process (three steps), the records, labels, paper sleeves, four color front and back, artwork and shrink-wrap on album jackets. Some average record pressing and jacket prices are as follows:

45 RPM JACKET AND PRESSING COST
× 1000 units (60 cents each)	= $	600
× 10,000 units (29 cents each)	= $	2,900
× 100,000 units (25 cents each)	= $	25,000
× 1,000,000 units (21 cents each)	= $	210,000

ALBUM JACKET AND PRESSING COST
× 1000 units ($2.00 each)	= $	2,000
× 10,000 units ($1.17 each)	= $	11,700
× 100,000 units ($.94 cents each)	= $	94,000
× 1,000,000 units ($.71 cents each)	= $	710,000

Cassettes are high-speed duplicates made from a master tape copy. Things that effect the price include the type of tape (ferric or Chrome oxide), and length of the tape (C-30, C-60, C-90, or C-120's). There is also a one-time set-up charge of about $100 for picture and label insert preparation. Average prices for a good quality duplication of your master tape on a C-30 cassette tape with inserts, labels, and shrink-wrap are:

Cassette prices (under 30 minutes)
× 1000 units (93 cents each)	= $	930
× 10,000 units (80 cents each)	= $	8,000
× 100,000 units (55 cents each)	= $	55,000
× 1,000,000 units (45 cents each)	= $	450,000

High performance output tapes average 10 to 20 % higher.

ADVERTISEMENT, PROMOTIONAL AND MARKETING EXPENSES
Now the company has the product to sell, and it's got to let the public know it. There are several ways to inform the public, such as radio station airplay, music television, hype through the print media and trade magazines, or just word of mouth. It all costs money! Promotion and advertisement personnel are employed by the company, and additional costs include payola and other not-talked-about expenses.

Record companies produce albums and release three or four singles from the album for promotion. The singles promote the album and artist's image, while concert appearances and newspaper articles promote unit sales (albums, cassettes, and cds). The cross-promotion helps increase record sales, concert attendance, and the overall image of the artist and record company.

For a new release, it costs just as much to market and promote a bad product as a good one. When a record catches on, additional promotion money and payola are added to increase sales even more. Lots of money is lost because some records just don't make it. If you don't know anything about the record and never hear it on the radio, you sure won't buy it! So record companies must really believe in their product (records) and spend enough advertising and promotional money to make sure that the public hears it and has a chance to decide if they want to buy it. The following are some of the typical expenses for promotion, and advertisement.

Advertisement:
Trade magazines
Billboard magazine
Full-page color advertisement:	$5,170
Half-page color advertisement:	$3,425
Black-and-white full-page:	$3,810

Cashbox magazine
Full-page color advertisement:	$3,700
Black-and-white full page:	$3,300

Radio and Records
Full-page color advertisement:	$4,050
Black-and-white full page:	$2,950

National, regional, and local promotional costs are hard to figure, because several records may be promoted at the same time. Radio station and print media advertisement costs increase with the size of the market and popularity of the station or newspaper.

Independent promotion people are sometimes hired by the record companies to help push the new releases through telephone conversations with trade-magazine-reporting radio stations. Most record companies have their own in-house and regional promotion people. The average cost for a national independent record promotion campaign is about $250 per week or $2,000 to $3,000 for the life of the record.

Regional promotion men are employed to get air play on local stations. Hype, personality, money, free trips, money, lunch, women, and money are used to help persuade the radio station music and program directors. Some of it's legal and some of it is questionable. With almost 200 individual markets in the United States, "legal" and "non legal" payola can add up to big bucks.

One of the newest and most exciting forms of promotion is MTV (Music Television). Video clips cost between $20,000 and $50,000 for country music and up to $150,000 for rock music. Music videos are creating new excitement in the music business. It's questionable if MTV increases the sales of a certain song, but there is little doubt that it does improve awareness of current artist and new releases. Production costs depend on the following: Cost of the artist, staging, lighting, props, additional personnel, dubbing, editing, scriptwriting, and equipment.

Record distributors purchase records (product) from record companies and place them in record stores, one stops and rack jobbers. The rule of thumb is 40 % of suggested retail price. Rack jobbers and one stop are major, full-line discount stores like K-Mart and Wal Mart. There's less profit in record stores because they own the racks and sales volume is reduced.

Suggested retail prices are determined by sales potential (how famous the artist is and the quality of the songs and performance) and total production expenses. Record companies make approximately the following amount of money per record sold: $5.98 less 40% = $2.40; $6.98 less 40% = $2.80; $7.98 less 40% = $3.20; $8.98 less 40% = $3.60; $9.98 less 40% = $4.00.

Now, let's look at some of the total sample costs. Please remember that most of the bills are paid originally by the record company and later by the recording artist through royalties.

Each recording session is divided into the following stages of production:

First stage   Basic or rhythm tracks: The recording of the rhythm instruments and scratch vocal.

Second stage: Overdubbing or sweetening: The recording of additional instruments or musical "parts" to fill out or enrich the overall production.

Third stage: Overdubbing a vocal master: Recording lead singer track.

Fourth stage: Overdubbing background singers: Recording harmonies and additional vocal stacking.

Fifth stage: Mix: Mixing 24-tape tracks to 2 track stereo. Use of special effects and production techniques.

STUDIO RENTAL FEE

The average album takes 180 to 200 hours to complete. For our project we'll take the twenty hours per song, which would be $100 an hour × 20 hours per song × 10 songs = $20,000

MUSICIANS FEE

For our example, we'll say we used five musicians for the rhythm tracks and five musicians for the overdubbing of additional instruments for each song. Instrumentation would change on each song. An example is:

Rhythm tracks: 1 bass guitar picker
1 drummer
1 piano player
1 electric guitar picker
1 acoustic guitar picker

Overdubbing: 1 electric guitar lead
1 rhythm guitar
1 sax
1 steel guitar
1 fiddle

The cost for 5 musicians, with the leader getting double for a total of 6 musicians, would be 6 × 221 (each per three hour set) = $1326 per three hour set. For an album, the cost would be $1326 × 2 sets per song × 10 songs = $26,520

VOCALIST

We decide to hire four background singers and have them sing on three songs. At $50 per singer, with the leader getting an extra $25 (½ base) our cost would be 4 × $50 plus $25 = $225 per song × 3 songs = $675. The lead vocalist gets $120 per song × 10 songs = $1,200. Our total cost for vocalists is $1,875.

PRODUCER

We want the best producer we can find for our project. Good producers charge $2,000 per side, so our cost will be $2000 × 10 songs = $20,000

Now let's take a look at the total cost of our album project. The production costs are:

Studio rental fee	$20,000
AF of M musicians	$26,520
AFTRA singers	$ 1,875
Producer	$20,000
PRODUCTION COST TOTAL	$68,395

Now let's look at our promotion, marketing and advertisement cost. We decide that our "star" needs a lot of regional promotion and radio station airplay. In addition we want to inform the industry about our new company and artist. We decide to release two singles from the album to promote the album, artist, and company. If they take off like we expect, we'll release an additional single if necessary.

Trade magazine advertisement budget

Billboard magazine, full page four color ad:	$ 5,000
Cashbox magazine, full page advertisement:	$ 3,000
Radio and Records:	$ 3,000
Amusement Business:	$ 2,000
Total trade magazine budget per single	$13,000

Promotional budget
Regional promotion: $3,000

per single × 2	= $ 6,000
In-house promotion, give aways, radio station promotion, store displays: $5,000 per single × 2	= $10,000
Total promotion budget	$16,000

We decide to do a music video for the second single release. We shoot the works and go with a decent music video for release to MTV, VH-1, Turner Broadcasting, independent television production companies, cable television outlets and local television stations. Total music video cost: $30,000.

Total budget for advertising, marketing and promotion:

Advertisement, trade magazines ($13,000 × 2 singles)	= $26,000
Radio station promotion and store displays	= $16,000
Music video (MTV)	= $30,000
Total budget for advertisement, marketing and promotion	= $72,000

Now let's see what we're at. So far we've produced our album and budgeted for advertisement, marketing, and promotion.

Production = $ 68,395
Advertising, marketing, promotion = $ 72,000
Total cost of the master tape and advertisement, marketing and promotion is = $140,395

We've spent $140,395 on our project and still haven't pressed any records, paid the mechanicals, or artist royalties. The above figures are somewhat "fixed" while all the additional figures depend on the number of records pressed, sold, and the suggested retail price.

So now let's really have some fun and figure out what the "real" cost of our little experiment is. We'll figure the cost and possible profits on 1,000, 10,000, 100,000, and 1,000,000 albums, pressed, delivered, and sold. Our suggested retail price is $7.98 per record. In our contract with the artist, we decided to split the 12% of 90% of retail price equally between producer and artist (they each get 6% of 90%).

Remember that we're pulling two singles from the album for promotion to radio stations, juke boxes and stores. So we'll press 10,000 singles of each release. To make it easier, we'll name our production, promotion, advertisement and marketing budget, PPAM. It will remain a fixed figure of $140,395. The cost of our two singles will also remain the same at $7,800 for the following reasons:

Pressing cost 10,000 $2,900 × 2 = $5,800
Mechanicals (10 cents per record) × 20,000 = $2,000
Artist and producer royalties (none), record company uses records for promotional purposes.

MECHANICAL ROYALTIES
(5 cents per song)
(10 cents per single)
(50 cents per album)

Singles
1,000 units × 10 cents = $100
10,000 units × 10 cents = $1,000
100,000 units × 10 cents = $10,000
1,000,000 units × 10 cents = $100,000

Album
1,000 units × 50 cents = $500
10,000 units × 50 cents = $5,000
100,000 units × 50 cents = $50,000
1,000,000 units × 50 cents = $500,000

RECORDING PRESSING AND JACKETS
Singles
1,000 units × 60 cents each = $600
10,000 units × 29 cents each = $2,900
100,000 units × 25 cents each = $25,000
1,000,000 units × 21 cents each = $210,000

Albums
1000 units × $2.00 each = $2,000
10,000 units × $1.17 each = $11,700
100,000 units × .94 cents each$h = $94,000
1,000,000 units × .71 cents each = $710,000

Cassettes (C-30)
1000 units × 93 cents each = $930
10,000 units × 80 cents each = $8,000
100,000 units × 55 cents each = $55,000
1,000,000 units × 45 cents each = $450,000

ARTIST ROYALTIES "POINTS"
(6% of 90% of retail)
Suggested retail price
$5.98 (90% = $5.38) $5.38 × 6% = 32 cents per album
$6.98 (90% = $6.28) $6.28 × 6% = 38 cents per album
$7.98 (90% = $7.18) $7.18 × 6% = 43 cents per album
$8.98 (90% = $8.08) $8.08 × 6% = 48 cents per album
$9.98 (90% = $9.98) $8.98 × 6% = 54 cents per album

PRODUCERS "POINTS"

Because we also paid our producer 6% of 90% of retail his/her share will be the same as our artist.

$5.98 retail price = 32 cents per album

$6.98 retail price = 38 cents per album
$7.98 retail price = 43 cents per album
$8.98 retail price = 48 cents per album
$9.98 retail price = 54 cents per album

TOTAL COST OF ALBUM PROJECT WITH A SUGGESTED RETAIL LIST PRICE OR $7.98.

1000 albums

PPAM COST	$ 140,395	
SINGLES:	7,800	
MECHANICALS:	500	
JACKET/PRESSINGS:	2,000	
ARTIST ROYALTIES:		(no royalties until profit)
PRODUCERS POINTS:	430	
TOTAL COST:	$ 151,125	

10,000 ALBUMS

PPAM COST:	$ 140,395	
SINGLES:	7,800	
MECHANICALS:	5,000	
JACKETS/PRESSINGS:	11,700	
ARTIST ROYALTIES:		(no royalties until profit)
PRODUCERS POINTS:	4,300	
TOTAL COST:	$ 169,195	

100,000 ALBUMS

PPAM COST:	$ 140,395	
SINGLES:	7,800	
MECHANICALS:	50,000	
JACKETS/PRESSINGS:	94,000	
ARTIST ROYALTIES:		(no royalties until profit)
PRODUCERS POINTS:	43,000	
TOTAL COST:	$ 335,195	

1,000,000 ALBUMS

PPAM COST:	$ 140,395	
SINGLES:	7,800	
MECHANICALS:	500,000	
JACKETS/PRESSINGS:	710,000	
ARTIST ROYALTIES:	384,958	(Break even point is approximate on 104,748
PRODUCERS POINTS:	430,000	albums sold. Artist royalties: 895,252 units × 43
		cents each.)
TOTAL COST:	$2,173,152	

Now let's figure out the bottom line, our P & L or profit and loss. For this experiment we'll forget about any tax write off possibilities. Record companies receive about 40% of suggested retail price from the distributions for each record sold. Our suggested retail price was $7.98. Our company will receive about $3.20 per record sold. How many records did we have to sell to break even? (Remember the artists don't receive any royalties until all the expenses have been paid.)

```
1,000 ALBUMS
                TOTAL COST   $   151,125
INCOME $3.20 × 1000              − 3,200
                TOTAL COST   $   147,925

10,000 ALBUMS   TOTAL COST   $   169,195
INCOME $3.20 × 10,000            − 32,000
                TOTAL COST   $   137,195

100,000 ALBUMS   TOTAL COST$   335,195
INCOME $320 × 100,000           − 320,000
                TOTAL COST   $    15,195

1,000,000 ALBUMS
                TOTAL COST   $2,173,152
INCOME $320 × 1,000,000        3,200,000
                OUR PROFIT   ×$1,026,848
```

The break-even point for our project is about 104,748 units sold. All of the examples are abstract and figures quickly change with different levels of production, advertisement, and promotion. In addition, break-even points where the money spent has been regained by record sales also vary. It's easy to see why it costs about $300,000 over a two-year period just to break an artist. That's two albums with a budget of $150,000 each.

A lot of people don't understand why record companies won't sign them to a recording contract. Now you should understand. The cost of releasing a good product is high and very risky. Remember only 15%

of all records released make money. Who do you know that'll give you $300,000 on a 15% chance of making a profit and an 85% chance of losing money!

Hit records are memorable; flops are not. Yet sometimes the reasons for the success or failure of any given record is mysterious. In the article "In Search of Plastic Gold: The Making of a Hit Record" (*Nashville* magazine, 1979) Jerry Seabolt said,

Take *Lucille,* for instance. Everything was there. We listened to it, and every one of us knew it was an out-and-out country smash, although we had no idea it would be as big as it was. Still, it was just obviously going to be a great record, and we all knew it.

We felt exactly the same way about a record called *Neon Lady* by Bobby Wright. It was just a great song, a great production, and it was one of Bobby's best vocal efforts. It was a super record, and we all loved it. We got glowing reviews from the trades, got loads and loads of airplay. Everybody who knew what they were talking about—all the supposed "experts"—said it's a number one. But (he added with a rueful laugh) the people disagreed. They didn't buy it. *Neon Lady* peaked out in the '80 of the top 100 and was never heard from again. Who knows why? It had the same producer as 'Lucille' (Larry Butler, a man with a superb track record), got the same expenses and effort in promotion and was in all the stores.

Still want to get into the music business? It's hard to believe the emotions, creativity, money, and craziness of the industry until you've been there. It's people living life on the edge, risking money, career, time, happiness, and dreams to satisfy their inner passions. Record company personnel help make recording artists successful. Without their love of music, personalities, and desire to beat the odds, a lot of artists would never be heard.

BRUCE HINTON

Senior Vice-President and General Manager
of MCA Records, Nashville.

DO SOME PEOPLE HAVE A NATURAL FEEL OR "EARS" FOR WHAT RECORDS THE PUBLIC WILL LIKE?
Yes, absolutely. There are really two levels. There are "ears" and there are "gut feelings." I think "ears" can be acquired, to a great extent, by working in the industry day in and day out. After years of seeing which records win and lose with radio, you acquire a feeling about which records may be successful.

That is not to say that someone who has "ears" will discover the next Elvis or Beatles. That kind of phenomenon, one that can change the course of musical history, is much more than "ears." In many cases, it's someone who dares enough to try something radically different and to ride it all the way. Ninety-nine out of one hundred of these situations fail because the artist is so different that no one can hook into them. We don't hear about the many failures; we just hear about the rarefied successes such as the Beatles or Elvis.

HOW DO YOU SIGN AN ARTIST TO MCA?
The way we sign an artist is to get a consensus from everyone involved. It's a consensus, but not necessarily 100 percent unanimous. To give you an example, there was an act that some of our people in the A&R department thought the world of. They were ready to go to the bank and walk on water for this act. I heard potential in the act, but I could also say that about some other acts. Jimmy Bowen [Division President of MCA Records] agreed with me, that we were not quite hearing what the other people in A&R were hearing. However, they were so charged with the artist that Bowen said, "All right, I believe in you [the A&R group] and we're investing in you. If you feel that strong about this act, then we've got a deal." This is a case where decisions are tempered by the intensity of the advocate for the artist.

SO WHEN SOMEONE SUBMITS AN ARTIST FOR CONSIDERATION TO MCA, ALL OF YOU LISTEN TO THE TAPE?

Yes. The philosophy of the A&R department is that of a very open society. We individually and collectively hear the artist, and we all get involved in the decision before an artist is signed. The bottom line is that when an artist is signed and brought to the label, he is going to know that we really want him here. That may sound commonplace, but I don't think it is. In the pop world, you may have one person who is responsible for signing an act. I'm not saying that is wrong; we just do it differently.

DO YOU CONSIDER THE ATTRACTIVE-NESS AND SEX APPEAL OF THE POTEN-TIAL ARTIST?

More than ever. What we are looking for is someone who carries it off on-stage—the whole package of performance, sex appeal, and musical integrity. If the artist can't deliver on-stage, you may sell thousands of albums, but the chances of hitting gold are much more limited.

We are also in the process of signing some people who are very unique. Whether they turn out to be stars or not, only time will tell. But if they are unique enough, they have a good chance of cashing in.

We're not really looking for a safe singer. There are a lot of safe singers with good names and with talent that I happen to like. But I don't see them as tomorrow's artists— the ones who are going to sell gold albums.

The artist has to have a unique vision of himself. If an artist at an A&R meeting said, "Well, what do you want me to do," I think, in almost every case, Jimmy Bowen would say, "What is it that you do, and what do you want to do?" We are not just a publishing house masking as a record company. We are a label and the artist has a vital role in what his music will say and how it will sound.

HOW SHOULD ARTISTS APPROACH A RECORD COMPANY? SHOULD THEY BRING AN ATTORNEY, TAPES?

Not the attorney, because that is just costing them and I'd like to save them the money.

The best way is still the voice and the song on a cassette tape. That doesn't get you a deal, even if it is a very exciting tape. But what it does at MCA Records is create a situation where several of us can focus in on what the person sounds like.

The next step can be one of two things. If we really liked the tape, then we will either see the artist perform or we'll invite him to have a sit-down meeting with one of the A&R people. We'll get into it one-to-one and find out where the artist's head is at.

SHOULD THE ARTIST ALSO INCLUDE A PORTFOLIO WITH A PICTURE AND A SHORT HISTORY?

Yes. Someone who has not had success with this procedure, may think "What's the use, it doesn't work?" Well, it does work. It's just that we don't sign everyone who simply submits a tape and portfolio.

WHAT DO YOU LOOK FOR?

I want to know that the artist has sex appeal, and that's a very hard thing to define. It doesn't mean that you're the best-looking person. Sex appeal is something else; you either have it or you don't. Put sex appeal and good music together and you've got a home run. A case in point is George Strait. He has unquestionable sex appeal. If you go to see one of his shows, down in the front seats will be a hundred young ladies, in their twenties, with glassy-eyed stares. Those are all album buyers and probably not one album, but the entire catalog. When you've got that, it's almost as good as printing money.

HOW DO YOU INVESTIGATE A POSSIBLE ARTIST?

Artists come in from so many different situations that I don't know a quick answer to that. In many cases there will be someone involved that we know. It seems that when an artist lands at this door, he has already hooked up with someone we know, someone who serves as a reference.

It's not always that way; we've just signed

an artist who simply came through the door. We didn't know of anyone who was associated with her, but we got very excited about her tape. It was the richness of her voice, and the material was extremely good. You may hear a thousand tapes and find nothing there, and then you hear one that just stops you in your tracks. We flew her in, talked to her, checked her out, cut demo recordings, and signed her to the label.

SO THERE IS STILL THE OPPORTUNITY FOR PEOPLE TO COME IN OFF THE STREET?

Yes—absolutely every tape gets listened to. To the extent that they can, artists should make their presentations look professional and together—the cassette label should not be torn or dog-eared from having traveled through 50 offices before it got here. Whoever picks up a tape like that is not going to be disposed to say, "This is the next Hank Williams, Jr.,"because that person is going to figure that everyone else turned it down. A negative vibe is put out even before the music is heard. Also, don't cut a $10,000 demo; just make sure the tape presents the voice clearly with a high regard for material.

HOW SHOULD THE DEMO BE PRODUCED? ARE YOU LISTENING FOR PRODUCTION TECHNIQUES OR MORE FOR THE MATERIAL?

We are just listening for the voice and song. If it's a band, we'd be trying to sell whatever that band is in total, so we need to hear a tape that is a good overall representation. That can be accomplished by going into a modest studio and laying down a decent performance tape. That wouldn't cost a lot of money.

I ASSUME THAT YOU ARE SPENDING AROUND $150,000 FOR A NEW ACT TO GET INTO THIS BUSINESS?

That is just the beginning. We have to be very selective about the people we sign, because with that much money involved, we just can't record everyone who wants to be an artist.

Another school of thought, one that we don't subscribe to involves the artist who feels that he should put half of that money into his pocket. In some cases, labels may go along with that. To us, that is totally the wrong concept. We feel that if it takes $150,000 to make the record right, then that should be the artist's priority. Hopefully, that is what the artist wants, because we're not really trying to become his father or his bank. We just want his music to be successful, and then we're both successful.

A dollar and a hit are the same to us. In other words, we spend the entire $150,000 on an artist's album. Across the street, another record company may offer the artist $75,000 front money, and spend $75,000 on the album. If the artist can accept and be satisfied with a $75,000 album, then that is where he should go. We'll spend every dollar required to make the album right. It's a great weeding-out process because the artists that we sign to our label really believe in their art. They believe in putting their money into the product first.

We will cut a totally unknown artist with the same budget as our biggest star. Just because an artist is unknown, we're not going to hedge our bet by just cutting an inferior album and hoping that we get lucky. The new artist gets the "A" treatment, just like our best-selling act.

HOW DO YOU SELECT A MARKETING PLAN FOR AN ARTIST?

With an established artist, things have already been tried in the marketplace, so we've got a good idea of what works and what doesn't. We just innovate and expand on what has been successful in the past.

For a new act, we get to know the artist very well before the master recordings are final. We fine-tune our knowledge about who the artist is and what he or she is musically. As cuts are being recorded in the studio, we get feedback from the producer, and we start to get a sense of direction. This helps us formulate an approach on how we can market the record and artist. In addition, if the artist has some pop background or some pop success, that will influence our marketing strategies. There's not the same marketing plan for everyone who has come from a pop music background. It's really just a judgment call for the individual situation.

If the artist has a more traditional sound, then we may zero in on the South, because that is where the initial base needs to be built. Things almost fall into place about what the marketing should be. In Nicolette Larson's case, she moved to Nashville and let go of everything from her pop world. She just cut the cord and started fresh. She was part of the community and she was vivacious; her sparkle started working in the marketplace, and we started seeing a way to go with her.

With the marketing of the album, it was important that she sign with the right booking agency—an agency that would understand her and know what to do with her. Joe Sullivan of Sound Seventy really know what to do for her, and she in turn had a lot to offer. Because of her past pop music successes, she could help a headline country act sell additional seats at concerts, and the headline country act could introduce her to their audience.

From a marketing standpoint, we would be following behind her concert appearances in each market, to maximize her exposure. Before the concert, she would have already gotten exposure from radio-station air play. On her first trip into a market as an MCA act, we would give a reception with all of the press, wholesalers, retailers, and radio personalities, for that one-to-one exposure. Immediately after she has left that market, we would return and plug in with key displays, newspaper ads, time buys, and flyers. This approach is usually better than shotgun advertisement and marketing.

Before the concert, we concentrate on getting all the publicity we can into the local papers. As far as advertising is concerned, it will follow the concert. It's a tried-and-true concept that works.

HOW WOULD YOU GET A NEW ARTIST'S RECORD ON THE RADIO?

We are continually finding out what works and what doesn't work with radio. It's a stark piece of reality that radio stations add very few records to their air-play list each week. So having a "nice" record isn't good enough; it's got to knock you down. Radio station personnel know that we are not going to release a record just to see how it flies. In other words, radio knows we work to get the music right before we consider asking for a slot.

WHEN SHOULD A PERSPECTIVE OR ESTABLISHED ARTIST SEEK MANAGEMENT?

Whether an artist has a manager before or after getting a record contract is not a prime issue. The issue is finding a manager who will do the job and do it honestly. Of course that's somewhat easier said than done, but I'd rather artists take their time and get it right. The price is high for those who don't.

JIM FOGLESONG

Division President, Capitol/EMI Nashville; former President of MCA Records, Nashville. Record producer (of the Thrasher Brothers) and recording artist.

WHAT ADVICE WOULD YOU GIVE TO PEOPLE WHO WANT TO BE IN THE MUSIC BUSINESS?

People who want to be in the business must get a foot in the door somehow. This could be selling or stocking records, working in a radio station, filling orders in a distributorship, or even sweeping floors in any of the above. The most humble beginning can put the individual in contact with the industry and introduce him or her to people who are already in the business.

I believe that anyone who has the ability and the desire, and who is willing to make the necessary sacrifices, can have a successful career in the music industry. You must get totally involved; ask questions, be *really* curious, and let it be known that you want to be a bigger part of the industry. A job well done is almost always noticed and appreciated.

WHAT ARE SOME OF THE SACRIFICES, BESIDES TIME, THAT PEOPLE WHO WANT TO GET INTO THE INDUSTRY CAN EXPECT?

Probably the most obvious would be the sacrifice of a larger salary in order to get a start in this business. Other sacrifices could include the forgoing of a good portion of one's social life while trying to absorb as much knowledge as possible and gain experience. Intimate personal relationships *have* to be affected. Are you and/or your mate willing to "hang in there" for a lengthy period of time while opportunities slowly develop? I don't know very many industry leaders or star performers who didn't "pay their dues" over an extended period of time.

Our industry seems to offer many opportunities to "play." Playtime is necessary and important, but the music business is a business, and it must be treated as such. When it's time to work, then one must work.

WHAT ARE SOME OF THE PROBLEMS RECORDING ARTISTS HAVE ABOUT HANDLING THE FAME AND PRESSURES OF CONCERT TOURS?

It is very important that an artist have good professional management. As success

58

grows, more pressures develop. Some primary pressures would be these:

  a. Keeping a band together; handling the payroll, maintaining discipline, finding replacements, controlling morale, running rehearsals.

  b. Putting together an entertaining show with great sound, lighting, staging; keeping the show tight.

  c. Communicating with the record company, the media and the music industry, in general.

  d. Communicating with the booking agency; deciding which dates are the career builders, which offers should be refused.

  e. Finding time to relax and develop a personal life. (I think that this is extremely important. Without being able to periodically "leave the business behind," I do not believe that it is possible to keep things in their proper perspective.)

  f. Staying healthy.

PLEASE EXPAND THIS STATEMENT: "IF YOU DON'T BELIEVE IN YOURSELF, YOU'LL NEVER MAKE IT AS AN ARTIST!"

Many times in most artists' careers, they are the only ones who truly believe in their talent. Although these moments occur mostly in the early, struggling days, they can occur when an artist is on the top of the heap. One must believe in oneself. This belief, however, has to be realistic.

Even though the artist believes that his talent is unique, he must realize that the talent has to be continually developed, that more success breeds more competition and more responsibility.

WHAT KIND OF EDUCATION WOULD YOU ADVISE FOR PEOPLE SEEKING A CAREER IN THE MUSIC BUSINESS?

I believe that there are many good courses being offered in colleges and in recording workshops that could be very helpful. I am told that there are some rip-offs. Formal education provides excellent background for any career. I believe that we should never stop trying to develop our talents. I think that all musicians should study theory, if possible. Singers will have a much easier time if they learn to read music. Drummers should also be percussionists. Publicists should study journalism, and so forth.

I look for potential professionalism in a new person—someone who has a good mature approach, someone who will take suggestions and criticism, and at the same time will communicate. Professionalism to me is the acceptance of one's responsibilities and "getting on with it" in the most thorough and expeditious manner. A "pro" seldom gets hung up on insignificant details. He is able to push his ego aside and make "team" decisions.

WHY DO YOU SIGN AN ARTIST TO YOUR LABEL?

An act should only be signed when you are convinced that it is truly unique. I must feel that the act can grow over a long period of time as well as immediately compete with the best product being released.

WHAT MAKES A HIT RECORD?

It's a combination of ingredients. It's a marriage of a piece of material (song) that relates to people, an artist who can convey that message, and a solid production. If I could take only one thing, give me a great song. I'll find somebody to sing it, and we'll have a good record.

WHAT DO YOU THINK MUSIC'S EFFECT IS ON PEOPLE IN GENERAL?

"Music is a universal idiom. It is a 'bridge over troubled water.' " I subscribe to both of those statements, which I heard during a speech several years ago. Music brings people together. It transcends barriers of language and culture. It relaxes tension. It makes people happy.

LARRY RAY

Former record company executive in charge of A&R and promotion for RCA, DOT, ATCO/Atlantic, Nonesuch, Kapp, Bang, and A&M Records.

ONE OF THE COMPLAINTS THAT I HEAR TODAY IS THAT LAWYERS RUN THE IN-DUSTRY, SO CREATIVE PEOPLE HAVE BEEN STIFLED.

Lawyers and accountants. But that is true in the film business, also. That's a truism in almost any creative business today.

WHAT HAPPENS IS THAT THEY DON'T TAKE THE TIME TO DEVELOP AN ARTIST THE WAY A PRODUCER DOES.

I don't know if they don't want to take the time or that they really don't know how. I can't see how an attorney or accountant, someone who hasn't spent a number of years in the recording business, can know one iota about how to record and present an artist, much less how to establish this creative person.

I think the main thing a producer does is to pull out the talent from the artist, the deep-seeded talent. I suppose just pushing a few levers and knobs can make you a producer, but I'm not that kind of producer. If I'm working with an engineer or director or singer, I try to get to know that person and

find out what his talent is. Then I go for it. I don't see much of that today. In fact, I don't see it at all with the exception of George Lucas and Steven Spielberg (in film) and perhaps Bill Szymczyk and Benny Anderson (in records).

The only attorney that became a record man that I have a lot of respect for today is Clive Davis. And the only accountant is Mo Ostin at Warners.

WHEN YOU WERE AN A&R PERSON AT A RECORD COMPANY, WHAT DID YOU LOOK FOR?

I would look for style, creativity, something in a song or person that might be a little bit ahead of its time. I looked for that innovative, creative person. I'd also look for character and attitude. I believe the artist, no matter how talented, must have the attitude to carry it forward. If it is strictly an ego trip and not based on any substance, it won't be long before the artist falls. When he falls, every-body is a loser.

Then I had to consider whether or not to sign the artist and if I did, for how many albums. A label never makes money until about the third album, except in a case like the Doors. The average artists take a long time to establish.

WHAT ADVICE WOULD YOU GIVE TO PEOPLE WHO WANT TO BECOME RE-CORDING ARTISTS?

First, make sure your head is on straight. When you're in the business and you look around and see people that you have known well end up overdosing because they cannot handle what is going on in their lives, it can be very traumatic. Joplin is only one example. Second, don't let up. Persevere!

THERE SEEMS TO BE A LOT OF DIVORCE, DRUGS, MENTAL PROBLEMS.

Your life is like a glass window. To keep it from being shattered, you have to put up barriers, and the barriers have become part of the problem. People keep hearing, "Hey, man, you're great." Well, you're not great; none of us is great. We all have to work for that next thing. We have to strive for perfection, always.

With the type of lifestyle a performer experiences, an artist can get wasted. It happens any time there is exploitation of the flesh, like in the film business. One reads about movie stars and how messed up their lives are. Well, it's the same in the recording business. An artist has to stop every so often, find out where he or she is at the moment, make any necessary changes or adjustments, and then continue on. Our physical bodies and minds are no different from most other physical matter. If we don't change the oil and tune our car's engine, in a matter of time, it will cease working.

ANY MORE ADVICE TO PEOPLE WHO WANT TO GET INTO THE INDUSTRY?

Don't be swayed by somebody with the checkbook. If you sell out early, or start compromising early, soon it becomes capitulation, and you might as well forget it.

Writing music or books or producing records or film—each is a career that takes a lifetime. I look at Hemingway and other writers in this respect, and it can carry over into anything else we do. Hemingway held on and went through those pain thresholds to where he achieved success. In any career that deals with intangibles, such as singing, writing, recording, the artist never knows if anyone is going to accept his talent or not. There are all those pain thresholds. So-called friends say you won't make it; your family doesn't believe in it. You put all your savings in your talent; your wife or husband leaves you and takes the kids. A talented person must have the perseverance to hold on through these thresholds and to continue without setting any time limits. Time limits will destroy a creative person. One should never say, "I'll hold on for two years and make it or get out of the business." It is very unrealistic and, besides, I doubt if a person's sold on his talent, if he feels this way.

Your talent may not be accepted by the public now, but it may be accepted a few years down the road. And if you can survive, while seeking your true potential, then go for it. You will be in that small minority of creative people—secure in your talent, happy and yet sometimes pained, but for the most part knowing where you are going and, hopefully, leaving something of value behind where you have been!

GENE FERGUSON

Artist manager of John Anderson and Charly McClain.
Formerly with Columbia Records (CBS)
in promotion and management.

YOU'VE WORKED WITH MANY ARTISTS IN YOUR TWENTY-THREE YEARS AT CBS. WHAT WERE YOUR RESPONSIBILITIES IN ARTIST DEVELOPMENT FOR A MAJOR RECORD COMPANY?

All artists need help. I don't care who they are. When you deal with the public, the public will, for whatever reason, get off artists. Artists only last so long.

With major artists, the prime thing is to keep them as big as you can. In my opinion, out of Nashville the only living legend is Johnny Cash, because of his strength with radio through those years. You could say Roy Acuff, but he hasn't had the air play or the worldwide recognition that John Cash or Elvis Presley had.

THERE ARE VERY FEW ARTISTS WHO CAN REALLY SUSTAIN THAT FAME OVER MANY, MANY YEARS.

Really. We have a feeling, we don't know why, that television kills a lot of artists. The people get tired of seeing you in their living room all the time.

DO YOU THINK THAT ARTISTS SHOULD HAVE A CERTAIN MYSTIQUE?

The thing that the public should understand is that an artist is a unique commodity. They're people doing jobs exactly as we're doing jobs.

WHAT MAKES AN ARTIST TICK?

I've tried to figure that out because a very large percent have killed their own careers. They get taken up with their own ego. Their career rises faster in their heads than it does with the public.

That almost sounds like sour grapes, saying this type of thing, but I don't have to worry about that because I never wanted to be an artist. I would say that at least 70 percent of every act I've ever met, and I've worked with over 400 of them, has at one time or another begged, "Just help me to get started. Whatever it takes." Of course after they hit, they don't remember those days; they lose it so fast, it's unbelievable.

THEY FORGET WHERE THEY CAME FROM.

Exactly, they get caught up in their own importance. While I'm blasting them a little bit, I'd like to uphold them, too. What they do is very different from a normal job, and I'll explain that.

Their life on the road is torture. I traveled for twenty years. But I went by jet; I stayed in first-class hotels. It was all paid for by CBS. If a room cost me $50 a day when rooms were going for $18, it didn't make any difference because I wasn't paying for it. Artists don't have that luxury.

You have to really feel for artists because the public pounds them terribly. They never have time on their own. They have to change their names. They go to a hotel, and they sign under a band member's name so people can't locate them. The type of person that's generally attracted to them, I hate to say it, is not the better type.

An awful lot of people will want to get on their side. They'll say, "Well, let me bring you a drink. I got a bottle of whiskey. Do you want to smoke some of this? I've got a girl for you." These are the facts. It's not occasional. It's an unusual thing when it doesn't happen; that's how far it's turned around. But this *is* the life the artist has chosen.

To let the artist himself grow up and learn to be a businessman is unbelievably difficult. To let that man grow up, go out there and do his show like he's supposed to do, and walk away is not going to happen. The fans standing around the stage are thinking, "God it's the only time I'll ever see him. Whatever it takes, I've got to get to him." Tear his clothes off, scratch him, whatever.

The fans act like "goons" a lot of the time. It's amazing; I watch them. It's really sad, just sitting back, and making observations about these things.

I've seen artists who've started out and people would say, "Well, he's not very attractive. I can't imagine who would ever want to go with him." Or, "How are you going to do anything with him?" Later he will come along with two or three really fine records, and he is no longer ugly. He now has character in his face.

The public sees what it wants to see. It's the same people that hang around the politicians, film stars, and so on. The people build an image, and the artist has to be on his toes all the time. The slightest little thing can kill a career, and bad news travels fast.

I've seen two or three careers go straight down the drain because of certain things that artists did that they should never have done.

I really wish that artists would get to the point where they would see this as a business, and not as something that's going to last forever. You can't say, "Hey, I'm the New Dynasty," because the public will decide that for you. It's difficult on both sides.

SO, THE ARTIST, WHO'S A CREATIVE PERSON, IN MANY CASES MAY BE SOMEWHAT HARD TO HANDLE. THE PUBLIC MAY LIKE THE ARTIST ONE DAY AND NOT LIKE HIM ANOTHER DAY. THAT COULD CAUSE AN EXPLOSIVE SITUATION.

It comes down to each individual and how he feels about his career. Two of the very best I've ever seen in handling their careers are Sonny James and Barbara Mandrell. They may not be exactly in private life as they appear in public, but they're as close as I've ever seen. Some are complete turnabouts. They're one way in the public's eye and totally different in private. I really don't think they should be admired that much for being who they are. I think they should be admired for what they do and how well they do it. A person is a person, and a good person's a good person whether he digs a ditch or sings a song.

I HAVE A THEORY THAT PEOPLE LIKE TO WORK WITH ARTISTS WHO ARE GOOD PEOPLE INSTEAD OF ARTISTS WHO ARE GOING TO CAUSE THEM PAIN AND GRIEF ALL THE TIME.

That's true. At the record company, we would have meetings. If an artist was giving us trouble, we'd no longer want to work with him. We would shy away from him. We wouldn't push for releases, or album covers, publicity or publicity pictures. We just plain hoped the person would disappear and generally he did within two years. CBS was so big that we could just turn to the next act.

YOU WERE CONSTANTLY CONCERNED ABOUT THE DEVELOPMENT OF AN ARTIST.

I think it all stems from my love for music. Everything bends around that. You finally see the man who wrote the song, the man who recorded the song, and the man who produced the song. It's like a baby. You watch it all come together in a little piece of vinyl. Then you try to expose it to millions of people and see what will come out of it.

WHAT MAKES A HIT SONG?

The public definitely makes the hit. What makes the majority of the public like that one song, I think, has a lot to do with the current times and the differences in the song.

WHAT DO YOU THINK THE PROBLEMS ARE WITH RECORD COMPANIES TODAY?

Nashville, without question, has always been a stepchild to the labels. There's not a label in town that was born, grew, and became a monster right here in this town. CBS is out of New York; Capitol Records, MCA, are all from some place else, and we're a division of those people.

Pop music is the biggest selling thing of all and has been for quite some time. When an artist from this area has a record that sells a million copies, which is what we call a spill-over record, it goes from the country charts to the pop radio stations. It captures more radio audience than it normally would. Those records suddenly belong to New York. And when that same artist cuts his next record and it no longer spills over, he's back to Nashville again.

The ad money has never come to this town. The contract money for artists has never come to this town. I've known many cases where rock groups were given tremendous salaries and before the company could put them on record, the group broke up. Not one of the major acts here would draw that kind of money from the company when his contract was up.

HOW ABOUT POLITICAL PROBLEMS IN THE RECORD COMPANIES?

It starts right with the songs. One of the prime reasons I believe major artists fade away is that once they get into the business, the next thing is publishing and wanting to A&R their own recording sessions.

There's good money in publishing songs. So now they want to write them, to publish them, and to sing them. They want to get it all. There's no harm in that, but they finally begin to cheat themselves because they start picking inferior material.

WHAT ABOUT INTERPERSONAL CONFLICTS?

I've seen heads of labels, if they didn't get along well with an artist, never really do anything to hurt him, but they wouldn't do anything to help him, either.

For political reasons, I've seen certain talent come to a label and just spend money hand over fist. In reality, they weren't going anywhere to start with. Nobody in this business is going anywhere without a song. Those days are gone.

I've heard some of the old-timers at CBS, the people that brought the Bessie Smiths and put them on a label, talk about the days they'd see a talented person. Everybody would come in and sit at a conference table and they'd say, "This person has talent. The budget is going to be $100,000 for the next year." The talent went along and did everything they said. There was control in everything that was done.

Those days are gone. Now the labels take a vast number of recording talent. They find it cheaper to go in and cut it (vinyl is inexpensive), put it out on the street, and find out what the public likes. A lot of the music business is run by lawyers who don't know one note from the other. And still we've got to satisfy the guy in the pickup truck.

ESTELLE AXTON

Co-founder and former President of Stax Records and Freetone Records. Member of the Board of Governors, NARAS (Memphis Chapter) and the Memphis Songwriters Organization. Artists include: Isaac Hayes, Otis Redding, Albert King, Carla and Rufus Thomas, Booker T. and the MG's.

CAN YOU TELL ME A LITTLE ABOUT HOW YOU AND YOUR BROTHER STARTED STAX RECORDS?
It started in a garage. At first, Satellite was the name of the label. We then went to an old store that had just been left there. We sold ice cream in one part of the store, and we sold some records, other people's records, of course. I would try to make a few bucks, and we found that this wasn't possible in the area we were. We moved back into Memphis, to the Capitol Theater Building, right in the middle of talent. That is how we really got started.

DID YOU SEE SOME KIND OF TALENT THERE THAT THE RECORD COMPANIES WERE JUST NOT EXPLOITING?
A lot of it was luck and a lot of it was hard work. We did it all ourselves, and just took what we could spare from our salary. We were both into banking. He was at one bank and I was at another, so we would have a few dollars left over from that. I mortgaged my house and got some extra cash there. Just a typical operating hassle.

SO YOU TOOK A REAL GAMBLE?
Oh, definitely, and especially in those days. That was in the early 1960's and there just wasn't too much money around. Not too many people had enough faith in the music business to invest any money into it.

I feel that Memphis has more talent than almost any place on earth. You can see it everywhere you go, in the schools, colleges, and on the street corners. All it needs is direction. So I guess you would say experience has been my greatest teacher in being involved in the music business, from sweeping floors, putting down rugs in studios to having a record shop where I could see what people would buy. That is the bottom line on any business. Will they buy your products? You find that out in the record shop firsthand; how and why people buy certain types of records.

WHAT IS THE BIGGEST PROBLEM THAT THE RECORD COMPANIES HAVE TODAY?
Poor promotion, and the product is a little weak in some cases. They don't take enough time to listen to the songs and really

put them together with the artist to make a hit. I think that they are in such a hurry to make a buck that they don't take the time to analyze the artist and the material they are using.

HOW ABOUT ISAAC HAYES?

Isaac Hayes was a great talent. It was three or four years after he began to come into Stax and work with our people before he wrote some of his good songs and became a great artist. I can remember when he was picking out his melodies with two fingers on the piano, when he and David Porter were writing together.

HOW ABOUT SOME OF THE OTHER ART-ISTS THAT YOU HAVE MET AND KNOWN? WHAT ARE THEY REALLY LIKE?

Most of them were very humble to begin with, of course, to get their foot in the door, but we could recognize talent after we heard them audition. I think Otis Redding was one that fooled everybody. He came in as a bus driver, with a band from up in the Carolinas. We didn't hear anything unusual in the instrumentation of the band, but one of the guys said he wanted me to hear the bus driver over the mike. So we brought him in and we heard him. We thought, oh, boy, here is another Little Richard. Because he came from Macon, Georgia, where Little Richard was born and raised, and he performed a lot like Little Richard. After we had done one or two records on him he changed a lot. Otis began to phrase his words a little differently. He became quite a unique artist.

We had Albert King from St. Louis. I had been selling his records on another label, a small label out of St. Louis, but they had dropped him and weren't going to do any more. It just so happened that I had a terrific

song from Indiana. It was good; I put them together, and we ended with a pretty good artist. He got worldwide recognition. That was our first real blues, I guess. Then we went on with Little Milton and several others. We found out from the record shop that blues would sell.

SO THE ARTISTS BELIEVED IN YOU AND YOUR BROTHER?

Yes, from the very beginning, from Rufus and Carla. Rufus and Carla Thomas were our first artists to sell. Rufus was a disc jockey and was always looking for a studio to cut a record in. And that is how Rufus came to us. When he came over, he brought his daughter Carla, who was only about sixteen at that time. She had this little song called "Gee Whiz" that she had written herself.

AND IT ALSO TAKES THE RIGHT PEOPLE BEHIND THE GROUPS.

Yes, you are right. You have to direct these people because none of your artists knows anything about business. I guess there are a few exceptions. But by the time they write and perform and do their recording, there isn't much time for business. So you have to have someone who is head of the company take over and sort of direct and get managers that can help the artist. So it takes a lot of patience and money and hope and faith. I don't know. There are just so many things that it takes to be successful in the record business.

TIMING?

Yes, timing. It is a fascinating business. I can't think of anything that changes from day to day as much as the music business does. If you can keep up with it, you are a good man, Charlie Brown.

SCOTTY TURNER

A&R for Liberty Records. Producer of Willie Nelson, Waylon Jennings, Del Reeves. Co-songwriter with Slim Whitman, John Marascalco, Mac Davis, and Buddy Holly.

WHAT ROLE DO YOU THINK LUCK PLAYS IN BEING SUCCESSFUL?

A great song doesn't care who sings it. There are millions of talents throughout the world who just have not happened to be at the right place at the right time.

WHAT DO YOU FEEL THE LUCK FACTOR IS IN THE RECORDING INDUSTRY?

Many people want to get into the industry as a performer or writer or whatever. During their struggle up the ladder, it takes thoughtfully placed funding to do it. Luck plays, I would say, about 80 percent of getting the right forces together. But, sustaining talent plays 100 percent in proving it. These people can't work a full day job and then concentrate on their music for three hours a night. They are competing with people who spend fifteen hours a day on their music alone.

I was head of A&R with Liberty Records, and I had just finished a session one night. A guy wanted a song I had written for a girl who had an audition with Billy Sherrill. The song was at Central Songs because I was under contract as a writer there. The girl learned my song, "She Didn't Color Her Daddy," and she landed a CBS contract. Tammy Wynette was the artist. I got a letter from her thanking me for the song, and in her book she remembered me. I had never met her. It had to be luck.

I was at the Ramada Inn and a friend, Joe Allison, was in the room below me. He called me one Saturday morning and asked me if I would come down and rap with him because he had a meeting at one o'clock. I had taken this song with me on tape. At one o'clock in comes Roy Clark. I said, "Roy, there's no tape recorder here, but I've got your career in my pocket, and I'm going to put it in your coat pocket."

I gave him the song. And five weeks later, at five o'clock in the morning, there was the most God-awful rumble at my door. I opened it up, and there was Roy and a bunch of his friends. They physically carried me down one flight of stairs.

THE SONG WAS "YESTERDAY WHEN I WAS YOUNG."

Yes. I gave that song to Roy Clark, and I have heard that it turned his recording life around.

WHEN YOU WRITE A SONG, WHAT ARE YOU AFTER?

One hundred percent communication with the public. When I was an in-house producer, I never let anybody know that I was a writer because it would intimidate them. So I didn't broadcast it.

Have you heard of Martoni's? It's an Italian restaurant where a lot of the record people congregate in Los Angeles, or used to in the mid-sixties. One night a guy came up to me, when I was working with Herb Alpert, and he said, "Herb Alpert is lucky."

I said, "You better rephrase that. Herb Alpert is a genius."

And he said, "What do you mean?"

"Because he communicated with millions of people. He didn't try to get over their heads. He's a nice person and he believes in what he's doing."

He said, "Yeah, but when the trend changes, what's Herb Alpert going to do?"

I said, "Don't worry. Herb Alpert will change the trend."

JERRY SEABOLT

Retired. Former record promoter with United Artists
Records and Capitol Records.

Retired. Former record promoter with United Artists
Records and Capitol Records.

**HOW HAS COUNTRY MUSIC CHANGED
OVER THE PAST FEW YEARS?**
As far as the popularity of country music is
concerned, I remember we went through the
"Glen Campbell Good-Time Hour." So
everybody became country. When I first got
into the business, everybody wanted to be a
rock 'n' roll star—complete with greasy hair,
Cuban-heeled shoes, silk suits, and skinny
black ties.

Then, right after that, everybody wanted
to be folk. All the girls looked like Mary, and
all the guys looked like Peter or Paul. The
guys either had a beard or they were bald.
And then, right after that, everybody wanted
to be black. That was a big thing. Everybody had to be black. Archie Bell and the
Drells were a big thing, along with the
Memphis Beat, the Atlanta Sound, and so
forth.

Then, the "Johnny Cash Show" made
CBS, I believe it was, and everybody was
country again for a while. We got the Country Music Awards broadcast, so everybody
came back again. Eventually, the country
radio stations in almost every market were

Number One in the ratings. They just came
in—they sneaked up on the pop stations,
they sneaked up on the middle-of-the-road
stations—and before anybody could realize
it, people had gotten to the point where they
were no longer closet country folks. They
came out of the closet, and they had their
bib overalls on; and you no longer went to
concerts and saw pickup trucks in the
parking lot. There were now Bonnevilles and
Chevrolets and Cadillacs—everything else.
When you pulled up at the stop light, the
guy next to you didn't roll the window up real
quick so you couldn't hear whether he was
listening to country music.

Then the country stations got a little bit
complacent and a little lazy. While the
country stations were sitting back on their
laurels talking about what a great job they
were doing, the middle-of-the-road station
across the street was going, "Wait a minute.
If he can play Merle Haggard, I can play
Merle Haggard. We're both going for the
twenty-five to thirty-nine audience." That guy
who used to punch the buttons back and
forth so he could hear Merle Haggard,

Johnny Paycheck, or Kenny Rogers no longer had to punch the dial because the middle-of-the-road station was playing the same thing the country station was. And he'd put up with Mantovani for three and a half minutes so he could hear the new Loretta Lynn.

Now country stations, staffed by smart people, are really redefining their music. They're filling a gap because a lot of the middle-of-the-road stations have actually become adult contemporary stations. Country stations are playing the same thing the rock stations are playing, 'cause now, see, they're greedy, too. They want that piece of that buck that the guy across the street gets who's playing all that kid music. So the country stations are now back to filling a purpose in life, filling a void that was formed by shifting formats. It's interesting, and it's a constant thing to stay on top of.

Then you've got the economic factors involved, too. There's only one dollar to be spent, and the advertisers are going to spend it with the top three or four stations of the month. There's a constant haranguing going on for that spot.

HOW DOES THIS AFFECT THE RECORD COMPANIES?

If you looked on the charts, you'd see the Top 20 is broken down between five record companies. The cost of doing business has gotten so exorbitant, so high, they cannot afford to have separate offices for everybody. Everybody can't do his own beautiful thing which doesn't make any money.

I made the statement one time that this business, since I was in it, ran high, wide and handsome—and very reckless—for a long time. Well, you had a situation where ABC Records lost $78 million over a three-year period and was bought by a company, MCA, that lost money. So somebody someplace down the line had to say, "Wait a minute. If this were any other business, we'd be out of it." You cannot consistently lose $10 million to $25 million a year.

I know one company that lost $42 million.

It's mind boggling. If a TV repair shop doesn't make money, it goes out of business. That's a fact of life. But the record companies are part of a conglomerate, and they make money. For instance, United Artists was at one time owned by Transamerica, which also owned the second largest rental car company, the largest insuance company, and the largest airline in the world. United Artists made them a lot of money.

You had a situation a few years ago where the record business had a boom year, a gigantic year—the best year in history. Record industry people, having the egos that they have, immediately rushed out and hired the world. That way, they wouldn't have to do any actual work. You hire somebody, and then you hire a secretary and an assistant. The secretary and the assistant have to have a secretary and an assistant, and so on. You give everyone a company car and give them all an expense account. So you have a $20,000-a-year employee who, with benefits, actually costs you $40,000 a year. So for everybody you add at that salary level, it's going to cost you $80,000 a year.

Now, that's all well and good if you've just sold $300 million worth of "Saturday Night Fever," but that only comes along once in a lifetime. The people in this end of the business are, first and foremost, business people. When other people asked me what I did for a living, I'd tell them I sold shoes. Basically, it's the same thing. The guy who works over at a car agency or the guy who works for any manufacturing facility, no matter what it might be—Xerox, a paper printing company, whatever—we're in the same ball game.

Record companies are in a business that sells to wholesale and, ultimately, to retail. It is a hard, cold, very fast paced, very greedy business; but you will survive. You may not have the money to be quite as flashy as you'd like, and you may find out that you won't be known as a clotheshorse, but you will survive if you take the right attitude. You say, "I get paid X number of dollars. I get paid for doing a job. I want to do a good job; therefore, I will go ahead and do it. And, it's not necessary for me to be seen at every cocktail party."

It's a big mistake that young people in this business make; people with expense accounts try to live up to that level. It's hard for a man to go out on the road and eat a steak dinner every night on the company, and then come home on weekends and have to eat meatloaf. He has a tendency to come home and want to do the same thing he did on the road. Well, companies frown on picking up your dinner tab on weekends, and they fire you. It's a mistake I made when I was very young in the business. I tried to live very high, wide, like I was a rich man. I think I was making eighty-five bucks a week. And you don't—you just don't—live that way.

IS IT A GOOD LIFE?

It's a frustrating and a very fulfilling life at the same time. The greatest feeling in the world is to have a record go Number One. You don't have to say it out loud, but it's great to sit back and say, "I did that. Yeah, the artist sang a great song, and the writer wrote a great tune, and the producer produced a great thing, but had it not been for me, nobody would have ever heard it."

That's what promotion people get paid for, and that's the thing that you take home at night. You go to bed, and you say, "I did good. Today I accomplished something."

IT MUST BE VERY HARD TO DO, TO KEEP IT ALL REALISTIC.

I looked at it from this standpoint. Our standard of success for a record is if it goes gold, which is a million dollars' worth of sales, or platinum, which is a million units of sales. I look at it from this standpoint. If we sell a million records, we have reached less than one-half of 1 percent of the United States' population. Where did we go wrong?

WHAT MAKES A HIT RECORD?

People. That's just pure and simple. Case in point, we put out a record by Kenny Rogers

called "Lucille." Everybody hated it but the people, and it was a hit record.

Aesthetically, we put out a record by another artist that everybody in this industry loved. It got Number One picks in Billboard, Cash Box and Record World, sure shots at every radio station in the United States, and nobody would buy that record.

ANY ADVICE FOR THOSE WHO WANT TO GET INTO THIS?

Yeah, my first advice is don't. That's for openers. And if I can talk you out of trying by saying don't, then you don't deserve to be in the business in the first place. If you ignore my advice and go ahead and take a shot at it, then you might have a chance of making it. You have to have that much stick-to-itness and that much drive to want to be in this business 'cause lawyers, plumbers, and almost anybody will end up making more money than you will over the next 25 or 30 years.

A very small segment in this business makes the big bucks. The rest of us make salaries commensurate with other management people in any other business. In many cases we make less money, because the people who set the salary schedules at the top feel that since we're in show business, we should be in it for the glory, I guess.

Basically, be prepared to serve an apprenticeship that may not have a pay-off at the end. Be prepared to work in a menial job. And you probably will get fired three or four times in this business before you finally settle down. I have lost several jobs in 22 years.

WHAT ARE SOME OF THE OTHER PROBLEMS?

The big problem in this business, particularly in promotion, is the fact that you get into a situation where what you're doing is very nebulous. This happens any time you're in public relations, promotion, or marketing—unless you're selling something directly on a one-to-one basis. If a guy goes out and runs a newspaper ad for shoes and the next day his store sells sixty pairs of shoes, he knows what he did. But when you're getting air play on a record, and I've said this many times, if there were ten things that you had to do to get a record played and to get it sold and only six of them worked, you'd still have to do all ten. Because you never know which of the ten will work.

It's more than ten. There are many, many things that have to be done on a day-to-day basis. And that's where the problem lies. It's so hard to look out and see the results. The results don't come for at least two or three weeks. Ultimately, they may not show up for months, because at the same time you're building this one record, you're also building the artist's image for the next record, the next record, and the next record.

If you don't put the problem in perspective, it can ruin you. It'll drive you nuts. 'Cause you sit back and go, "What am I doing here?" Meanwhile the salesman's out on the street, going, "I sold 2,000 records today. I sold $10,000 today."

HOW ABOUT PROBLEMS WITH STARS?

The bigger the stars, the more realistic they are. The people who have been in the business for a long time are the easiest to deal with. It's the know-nothings—those who don't know anything about the business but who have been told by everybody they've got a great voice—who are the hardest to deal with. I was in a fortunate position when I had a meeting with every one of our artists. We took the time to sit down and talk. I spent about a week meeting with all the artists. I said, "This is how I am. I want you to get to know me. I want you to know how I work. If you have any questions, here's my home phone number."

CHAPTER FIVE

RECORDING ARTISTS AND ENTERTAINERS

According to *Webster's New College Dictionary* the definition of fame is "a public reputation, a lofty reputation." The public demands to see an artist once in a while; they require a little personal contact to remain interested in you. That means concerts, personal appearances, interviews, photographs—and you've got to be nice through it all. Don't forget to live up to your image, whether it be a cute innocent girl, nice honest guy, macho, the weirdo freakish rebel, outlaw, or whatever you happen to be. The public expects it. Tear up a hotel, if that's what your image is, and watch the records sales increase.

Try to buy a hamburger if you're famous and easily recognized. Fans will tear your clothes apart. At the very least they'll stop and talk to you. Some artists will isolate themselves from the public, as Elvis Presley did. Famous artists meet people who want to use them. They want to push a song or themselves. That's one of the reasons why an artist's manager controls the circle of friends and people an artist associates with.

How an artist accepts the pressures determines whether his life as an artist is fun or not. It really determines how well he will succeed. Age, social pressures, the strain of long hours and hard work usually catch up. Only a few superstars have survived all the stages of success and enjoy the money and pleasures of old age.

Why do people do it? Talent, and believing in themselves. Larry Gatlin swept the floors of WSM television in Nashville for years while trying to make it in the music industry. There are countless other stories about the determination to be successful. Many people started in the music industry while working at below poverty level jobs. They didn't have much money—but they went for it anyway. Working as a musician on the road or sweeping floors in the studio, they still went for it. Tammy Wynette was a waitress in Memphis; the Beatles were from lower social economic families in Liverpool, England. Elvis's mom and dad were once dirt farmers in Mississippi. Chuck Berry was a beautician; Rod Stewart a grave digger; Elvis Costello, a computer programmer;

Roger Daltrey, a sheet metal worker; Chubby Checker, a chicken plucker.

Why did these artists and countless others make it in the music business? One of the reasons is their unique talent. Larry Gatlin is a great songwriter. Along with his brothers, he has mixed his experience from gospel singing with the current style to provide the public with a unique sound for today. That takes brains and talent.

Kris Kristofferson may not have the greatest voice in the world, but can he ever write songs that people relate to. It is a wonderful God-given talent that he has perfected.

The Beatles believed in themselves and their unique style so much that they refused to record anybody else's material for producer George Martin. It takes guts and talent to tell the one guy who can make or break you in the music business that you will only record your own material. Martin was already taking a chance on the young guys anyway. Why put up with egos and all the other problems that creative people seem to possess? One rumor suggests that the Beatles were signed because their manager, Brian Epstein, promised he would purchase a huge amount of records for his store. How could a record company lose money when it was guaranteed a large purchase of records?

But look at it in another way. John, Paul, George, and Ringo believed so much in their music and themselves that they wanted to record their music only. "Let the people hear us and our own music." If their own songs had bombed, that would have been the end of things. Producer George Martin was known for recording comedy albums with Peter Sellers. He had to stake his reputation, time, and talent on a group of kids from Liverpool, but they all had the talent to get the job done.

Elvis had a dream to be a singer. Really it was to be a somebody—somebody that people could look up to. He didn't follow the norms. He dyed his hair black, and he wore it long with sideburns. He wore pink shirts and black pants. You would have to be nuts to do that kind of thing in Memphis.

Elvis's sexual image knocked girls out. He was a nice guy and, at the same time, had a hard time with the pressures of success. He's not the only one. Elvis started his career himself, just as almost everybody does. He was unique. He had talent, and he got noticed by the right people.

Sam Phillips developed a talent in Elvis that he had been looking for—a white man who sounded black, one who could sing the blues believably. Colonel Parker, the ex-circus barker, took that image and sold it to the public. Once you get the public past the door, or to buy that record or tape, then the act must sell itself. Elvis could definitely sell himself. He wasn't afraid of being different from the people around him. It made him special, it made him stand out, and it made him a star.

The fans are the other side of the coin. They do almost anything to get close to an artist—some hide in garbage cans so the sanitation workers will carry them past the guards. Some use ropes and window-washing equipment to lower themselves from the top of a high-rise hotel to the penthouse suite. The frenzied feelings that a fan has toward an artist are real, whether it be a young Frank Sinatra fan in the 1940's, an Elvis fan in the 1950's, a Beatles fan in the 1960's, or an Andy Gibb fan or a Rolling Stones fan in the 1970's. The more frenzied the feeling, the more money the artist will make in record sales and concerts. But what are the fans so crazy about? The artists themselves or their image? The more the mystique (how little the public knows about the artist), the better the possibility of superstardom. Overexposure of personal information can hinder the building of an image or even retaining an image.

Mass hysteria, or the special hold an artist has on audiences, happens when the audience perceives that artist to be special. He may have a superior talent, look good, and be sexy. But the main reason for the artist's success is communication. The image he or she portrays allows the fans to include the artist in their lives. It's a personal thing. It's almost like a one-on-one relationship because of television appearances, records, talk shows, newspapers, and gossip magazines.

But the artists are human, just like you and me. Think of Elvis's pain in being forty-two years old and 250 pounds when his fans wanted twenty-eight and 180 pounds. Think of how difficult it is to be an artist performing on the road: You're away from your family and your friends. Fans are trying to get close to ask for an autograph, or to say who they are, or to push a bad song. The groupie has a dream of a one-night stand. What are you going to do? You can't refuse the autograph seekers because they will think you're on an ego trip. A disgruntled fan will not only refuse to buy your records but will also tell everybody they know that you're a snob. If you accept a tape from the songwriter, and he ever hears anything close to it on the radio, he'll sue you.

But artists really do love it; it's what they live for. They know that if they work hard and present the best show possible, then they've not only earned their money, but they've entertained you. They've helped you temporarily forget the problems of the world, of your day, and of your life for a few hours. The pleasure and happiness they supply by picking and singing is what's really important.

LORETTA LYNN

MCA Records Recording Artist and Entertainer; Country
Music Association Entertainer of the Year (1972), Female
Vocalist of the Year (1972, 1973), Vocal Duo of the year
(with Conway Twitty 1972, 1973, 1974, 1975).

HOW DO YOU SELECT YOUR SONGS FOR A NEW ALBUM?

I used to just sit in a room and listen to the things that were sent in but for a lot of reasons, that really didn't work. Jimmy Bowen, my producer, has a great system. He gets Dirt (Don Lanier) to make appointments for me at all the major publishing companies and then he (Dirt) and I spend a couple of weeks goin' to each publisher and listening to the best they've got. It really seems to work 'cause when *you're* going to *them,* the publishers know you're serious and you're not playing all those games that artists do if they own their own publishing company.

HAVING A GOOD BACK-UP BAND ON THE ROAD IS VERY IMPORTANT. WHAT DO YOU LOOK FOR IN ROAD MUSICIANS?

The first thing I look for is a good person who can get along with everybody on the road. Then I look for good musicians, and it's awful hard to find both.

WHAT DID YOU THINK ABOUT THE MOVIE *Coal Miner's Daughter?*

You probably better ask anybody but me! How can you ask someone to look at their life story on that big screen and ask them to make an honest judgement. I was probably in shock the first time I saw it. I was working at the Riviera in Las Vegas and Universal rented a whole movie theater for me and Doo to see it one afternoon. When it was over with I couldn't remember a thing except the part where I was hittin' Doo.

Right after that we went to New York to do promotion for the film. We did interviews all day and that night I thought we were going to dinner. I asked my manager, David Skepner, "Where are we going?" and he said, "We're going to see a movie." And I said, "What are we gonna see?" And he said, *Coal Miner's Daughter.* Reporters had been asking me questions all day about the movie and I couldn't remember a thing.

After I got used to it, I knew that they had done a real good job. Cissie got her Academy Award and I knew that was gonna happen; and I'm just sorry that Tommy (Tommy Lee Jones) didn't get more credit than he did. He really was Doo, but that's a whole other story.

HOW ABOUT THE PEOPLE WHO HELPED YOU?

Mooney—Well, what can I say? This was his idea. He started it all and he saw a lot of things that I sure didn't. If he hadn't had an idea, we'd probably still be up in Washington raising kids.

Patsy Cline was my friend. The first friend I ever really had in Nashville. She took care of me. When I think about it, I guess she showed me that it's okay to be different, it's okay to be me. Patsy was twenty years ahead of her time, both in her music and in her attitude toward people. I still miss her.

Owen Bradley was my producer on Decca (now MCA) for over twenty years. I always felt that I was the luckiest person in the world when Owen Bradley wanted to produce me. He'd done all the great country singers, Patsy Cline, Ernest Tubb, Bill Monroe, Kitty Wells, and I just thought I was the luckiest person in the world. If I had a second father, it'd be Owen. I could proba-

bly do a whole book about Owen Bradley but you haven't got the time.

David Skepner's been my manager for more than fifteen years and I think that we've learned from each other. We fight a lot—but that's good. A lot of artists have people around them just to tell them how good they are, but I don't need that. He may tell me he doesn't like something or suggest that I do it a different way, and I may not like it at the time; but when I get away and think about it, he's usually right.

He probably understands me better than I understand myself, and again, that's something else than an artist needs. One time we were fightin' about something and he said, "But Loretta, that's what you said to do." And I looked at him square in the eye and said, "You're not supposed to do what I say, you're supposed to do what I *mean*!" And to this day, that's probably the reason that he does things his way and we fight about it later.

Neither one of us is afraid of the other and when we each think we're right, we can really dig in and go to it, and that's the kind of relationship you're supposed to have with a manager—I guess you just call that respect for each other.

RICKY SKAGGS

Recording artist and record producer for CBS Records.
Country Music Association Entertainer of the Year (1985)
and Grammy Award winner for Best Country Instrumental
(1985). Songs include "Honey, Won't You Open That
Door," and "Don't Cheat in Our Hometown."

**HOW DID YOU PERSUADE RICK BLACK-
BURN AT CBS RECORDS TO LET YOU
PRODUCE YOUR OWN ALBUMS?**

I had talked to two or three labels in Nashville and played them a cassette of some
rough, unfinished cuts—songs like "Honey,
Won't You Open That Door" and "Don't
Cheat in Our Hometown." I was just out
playing recordings of my music because
after the "Don't Cheat in Our Hometown"
album was finished, I was free to get a new
deal. I was trying to make a major deal,
because the "Sweet Temptation" album cut
"I'll Take the Blame" had made Number One
in three different markets. It was very, very
"country"—traditional country—but still it
had something very new and updated with
an eighties sound. It turned on quite a few
people, and I felt that if it had been on a
major label, it would have had more of a
chance of becoming Number One in other
markets.

I was on the right track musically, but I
needed some help with a major record
company. I met this fellow on the plane to
Nashville. He was real nice; we sat and

talked a long time. I had been in Los
Angeles doing some work on the *Urban
Cowboy* album with Linda Ronstadt and J.
D. Souther. So we were flying in together
and he asked me what I did. I told him I was
working with Emmylou Harris and trying to
get a deal on my own. As it turns out, he
was Jim Mazza of United Artists Records.
When he said to send him a tape sometime,
I pulled my Walkman out.

As he was eating his dinner on the plane,
I let him listen to my songs. Boy, when we
got to "Honey, Won't You Open That Door,"
he really liked it. He felt the country stuff was
just too country, but he could "hear" "Honey,
Won't You Open That Door" and "Head over
Heels in Love with You." He made a point
that he'd like to have a meeting with all the
people in the Nashville office. They all
listened to it and everyone liked it. I was
thinking I may have a deal here; but they
sent the tape out to Los Angeles, and the
people there could not "hear" anything.

My friend Lynn Schultz of Capitol Records
felt so bad about the deal falling through
that he said, "Ricky, I'm going to make sure

you get a deal here in Nashville if it's the last thing I do."

SO ONE OF THE TOP EXECUTIVES AT CAPITOL CALLED RICK BLACKBURN AT CBS RECORDS TO GET YOU A DEAL.

He called Rick Blackburn at CBS Records, and said, "Rick, there's a guy here that I really think you would be interested in." Rick had heard of me because I knew Bonnie Garner, and she knew me through Willie, Emmylou, Waylon, and Johnny Cash. I met with Rick and played him my stuff. When he asked, "Who produced this," I told him that I had. Rick took me to lunch and we wrote a deal on a table napkin.

There were two bargaining points. One was that I would be allowed to record a gospel album. About 90 percent of the time, when you're with a major label, they've got you and don't want you to do a gospel album. He said, "That's not a problem; just don't come with one first or second."

The other bargaining point was that I would produce my own records. He swallowed real hard and said, "Well, I'm going to have to check you out." While he was checking me out, I was all over town checking him out.

We met again and he said, "I checked you out with Rodney Crowell, Emmylou Harris, Rosanne Cash, and people that you have worked with in the studio. They said, "Let him go and do his thing. Don't tie his hands; let him do what he needs to do." I said, "Well, great . . . because I've checked you out and you check out real good, too!" That is the way our relationship has been, very up front and honest with each other. I love my relationship with Rick. I wish every artist could have this type of relationship with a record company executive.

IT SOUNDS LIKE YOU CAN SAY ANYTHING YOU NEED TO SAY TO HIM?

If I don't like the way something is going, I tell him. I don't tell any of the other people at CBS and let it seep up to the top. I meet with Rick. If he has a burr in his saddle, he'll call me. As an example, I said something on-stage one time, as a joke, and some people took it wrong. He called me and chewed me out. I respect him for it and I understand. After he heard the context of my on-stage comment, he understood that I didn't mean anything by it. It was just one of those things.

DID YOU ASK FOR CREATIVE CONTROL OF YOUR PROJECTS BECAUSE OF THE "FEEL" YOU WANTED OUT OF THE FINAL MIX?

Well, I had to, because to me that is the final step. Marshall Morgan and I have worked together for a long time. He has been mixing my music and recording my stuff ever since I came to the label.

IS SUCCESS EVERYTHING YOU THOUGHT IT WOULD BE?

When I started with Ralph Stanley, I was fifteen years old. That was success to me—working with one of the top bluegrass groups in the country, and going to places like New York and Canada. Here I was, this hillbilly out of eastern Kentucky, still wet behind the ears, traveling all over the country. I got to watch him, listen to him, perform and work with him.

HOW DID YOU COME UP WITH THE BREAK-DANCING ON THE NEW YORK SUBWAY FOR THE "COUNTRY BOY" VIDEO?

Martin Kahan, the director of the video, had it laid out in his mind. We had a meeting in New York, and he told me that he had an idea I would be a banker or business-man and my grandfather would come up from Tennessee to see me. I began to throw some of my ideas at him and he liked them, too. I said, "Instead of my grandfather, let's make him my 'Uncle Pen'." It would work for the audience that knows me and the ones that don't.

Now the "Honey, Won't You Open That Door" video has some of my ideas in it. We had two or three rewrites before I got it the way I wanted. He wanted a lot of girls and drinking and I said, "That's just not me. That's not my image and my people know that's not my image."

WHAT ADVICE DO YOU GIVE TO PEOPLE WHO WANT TO BE STARS OR ENTER-TAINERS?

I usually tell people that you have to have something special and very unique, something nobody else does or has. If you've got the will, the want and the faith, and if you are willing to give up your home life and give up your time—in other words, if you are willing to give everything up except your music and to just work hard at that—then give it a real good shot.

You can't do this thing part-time and be successful. If you don't put that much time and effort into it, then it isn't going to produce any real results. It is just like a plant or tree. You've got to plant that seed and watch it grow. You've got to cultivate it, to keep the weeds from choking it and to let the plant get sunshine and water. The plant can be beautiful and produce wonderful fruit. But if you shut off the sunshine and rain and let the weeds get around it, it's not going to grow anymore.

STEVE GATLIN

Recording artist, musician, and singer with Larry Gatlin and the Gatlin Brothers. Manager of Gatlin Enterprises.

WHAT ADVICE WOULD YOU GIVE TO PEOPLE WHO WANT TO GET INTO THE MUSIC BUSINESS?

I think John Cash gave the best advice I've heard, something that we have lived by since we came to this town. He said to be true to yourself and do it your way.

First of all, I think you need to go to Los Angeles, New York, or Nashville. Your percentages are going to be far greater if you can get to a music center. Beat those doors down, you know, hustle.

What happens in this town is that they are struck by the fact that you might possibly someday become a star. That excites people. They go to a very important or powerful person and are told, "I will take your song, and I'm going to get Dolly Parton, or George Jones, to cut your record. But first of all, I want you to give me so-and-so." If you're some guy from the backwoods and don't know anything about it, that doesn't sound like much. In a moment of weakness, because the other guy's dealing from a position of strength and power and you're dealing from nothing, you give in. To me, that's being untrue to yourself and unfair.

That's not saying that it won't work. The song may turn out to be a Number One record and may make you a ton of money. You may become a successful songwriter or even a big star yourself. But, to me, that's not the way to do it. I couldn't live like that.

Look back at Johnny Cash's career. In the late 1950's, John, Elvis Presley, Carl Perkins, Jerry Lee Lewis, and all those guys, were rock-a-billies from Memphis. Look at all the flack that they caught when they broke into the country music field: "These guys are crazy; they've lost it; they've gone over the border." And, now, they are the biggest names in show business. Hank Williams was the same way. He was a rebel when he came because he did it a little different. But he did it his way and didn't sell out.

I was doing an interview on the phone with someone from West Virginia, and I told him that we were very happy with the Country Music Awards for George Jones. George is a good friend and a great singer. The interviewer said, "If you guys love him so much, why don't you try to sing like him?" I said, "Well, hell, wouldn't it be an awfully dull world if every record you hear on the jukebox was 'Here's Emmylou Harris imitating George Jones; here's the Gatlins sounding like George Jones.' " I said, "Different people do it different ways." You've got to have a little variety.

WHY TRY TO COPY SOMEBODY WHO IS ALREADY A STAR, BECAUSE THEY'VE GOT THE ORIGINAL.

When Larry first came to this town, he became known as a songwriter. We were cutting some albums. Kristofferson took a tape to Fred Foster, and we got started in the record business. At first it was just the Gatlins. Then we focused in on Larry because he was the songwriter and had some success as a songwriter. Kristofferson had cut a tune; John Cash had cut a song.

Larry, on several occasions, turned down hit records. People would hear him sing and say, "Boy, you've got the greatest throat I've ever heard. Here's a hit for you." Maybe he hadn't, in those early days, written a hit song; I don't know. But he had enough faith and belief in himself to say, "I can write them, and I'm going to stick by my guns."

So he really made the first decisions up front. A lot of his advice came from some of his songwriting buddies like Red Lane and Mickey Newberry—and people like Newberry who had always done their own material. Kristofferson did his own material. They kept advising him to hang in there, and he had enough guts to sit there. His wife was teaching school. He was working at WSM for $100 a week, sweeping floors, when he first came to this town.

Even though he wasn't making money, he didn't let that dollar or that star thing get in his way. He said, "We're going to do it my way, 'cause I know I can write hit songs. It may take me three or four more years." He grew and matured. He got a lot of bad rap when he first came to town about being arrogant. All it was, was a confidence in himself.

The irony of the whole thing is now, ten years later, it's all worked. I know there are a lot of people who are not all that thrilled with our success simply because we came to this town and did it our way. Our way is not the best way for everybody. I'm not telling people to sing only their songs, or that they should wear jeans on stage or only use their band. I'm just saying that the system we used is right for the Gatlins.

I WOULD LIKE SOME OF YOUR COMMENTS AND THOUGHTS ON THE MUSIC BUSINESS.

I think a lot of artists at times have been lax in running a business. We gross a lot of money; we spend a lot of money. We've got fourteen full-time employees who get a check every Monday morning whether we made a dollar or not. We own an airplane and a bus that takes us throughout the country. Our Master Charge bill is incredible every month, because you just can't move fourteen people throughout the country and not spend money.

All that stuff has to be set up. If you'll look at the top entertainers, you'll find that behind every one of them is a good, strong, solid business. There is someone that's taking care of homework.

You cannot sit there and have thousands of dollars running through your office, through your accounts—and thousands of dollars going out to band members, managers, agents, and all—without someone making some kind of good decisions. The people who have the overnight success, have a quick record, but don't take care of business are generally out of business.

We've got a lot of fans out there, and they're good and faithful and strong for us. We have been building these fans over the last three or four years.

WHAT ABOUT YOUR COMMENTS ON A MANAGER?

We had a manager who was a super nice guy and a good manager, but he just wasn't right for us. It goes back to being true to yourself, doing what you've got to do. If something comes up, the manager, unless you turn that control over to him, has got to come back to me—or some representative of me, Larry, and Rudy—and say, "I have this situation. What do you want to do about it?" Then we discuss it and tell him. He was a middleman.

We've decided that we want to keep the control of our career in our hands. That way, if we fail, there's nobody to blame but us. And if we succeed, there's everybody in our organization to share in the success.

Larry and Rudy have enough faith in me and our agency. They don't get involved in those one-night bookings quite as heavily as I do. I think the worst thing in the world would be to just get on a bus or on an airplane and start on a 30- to 40-day tour and not know what in the hell you're doing. Someone has planned your life for you for the next 30 to 40 days. You're just supposed to walk on-stage.

Now, a lot of artists are like that. A lot of them don't want to be involved in it. But I'm too business-oriented. I don't have a degree in business. I have a degree in Elementary Education, as a matter of fact. But I love the business aspect of it, and I want to know where our money goes. I want to know what's happening in our professional life and I want to have some kind of control over it.

I SEE LARRY AS A PERSON WHO DE-MANDS CREATIVITY OUT OF HIMSELF, WHETHER HE'S SINGING OR WRITING SONGS. AND I SEE YOU AS DOING THE SAME THING, ONLY BUSINESS-WISE. YOU WANT TO HAVE TOTAL CONTROL OF THE BUSINESS.

That's a fair statement. I do run our office to the degree that I manage day-to-day operations. Once in a while I get something that I can't answer. Then I go to Larry and Rudy. I have an idea, but it's some kind of a decision that I don't want to make by myself. I want to see how they feel.

Whether or not we should accept a date

next week in some particular town for x amount of dollars for some promoter—I can do that, because we have certain guidelines and things set up. I know if we need the work or don't need the work, or if it's an important market for us to work for the record company because they're trying to sell some records there. So we go in and do a deal. But, there are a lot of times when things come up that I haven't any idea what Larry and Rudy want to do. I have to check with them occasionally. I'm a liaison, so if people have problems or need to get to the Gatlins and want to know something, I'm the guy to do it. I'll get an answer.

HOW ABOUT EGOS? DIFFERENT PEOPLE HAVE DIFFERENT EGOS.

I'll tell you how we handle it. We try to take care of our people with bonuses throughout the year. Our guys play on all our albums. I gave them gold albums they can hang on their walls in their living rooms. When friends come over, they can say, "I played on that record and I helped that record sell 500,000 copies."

The other thing is that our guys make the same money. Our guys have all been with us within a six-month period of time, our band and our road people. Our pay scale is very fair.

They know that they'll never make as much money as Larry and Rudy and I. But we have 25 years invested in this. It is our responsibility to keep producing hit records, or we're all out of a job.

YOU ARE THE PEOPLE THAT PROVIDE THEM THE OPPORTUNITY TO WORK. IF IT WEREN'T FOR THAT, THEY WOULDN'T HAVE THE GIG.

But at the same time, I want to keep them happy, so that they want to stay. Mike Smith came in one time (about two years ago) and said, "I've been offered other jobs in town for more money." But he also said, "There isn't a better job in town." And that made us feel good. That makes us feel that what we're doing is right. We have a policy on the road that, when we do things, we do it together. We've been skiing two or three times. The camaraderie among our people is incredible. Everybody loves one another; everybody gets along. It all goes back to one thing that I have probably missed saying—the music. Every one of them is dedicated to the songs that Larry writes and to the harmony that Rudy and Larry and I are trying to do. I've sung "Broken Lady" two million times, probably, and I still get a thrill singing. I enjoy seeing those smiling faces.

FROM AN ENTERTAINER'S VIEWPOINT, WHAT DO YOU THINK ABOUT THE RESPONSIBILITIES OF A BOOKING AGENT?

The agent's main responsibility is to work as diligently as possible to do what the artist wants, to book the venues [localities] the artist wants to work. When we first started, we had to work a few clubs. We had $100 in the bank, and we made the statement one time, "No more clubs." Our agency did not balk, and at that time half of our income was coming from clubs. But we cannot work where people want to get up and dance. We are not a dance band.

I love to go to a good club, drink a cold beer, and dance just like everybody else; but there are certain acts and times and places to do that. We don't feel that our music is geared that way. We're a concert act. We are better in a civic auditorium, a place where people sit and listen.

I think the biggest responsibility of a booking agent is to book the kinds of jobs that the artist can feel comfortable with. Then think about the career moves that we need to make. Put us in places that are important for us to do in order to see the kinds of people that we need to see, to develop a career. We want to be here in fifteen years.

THIS IS A LIFETIME CAREER.

We don't want to blow in here, try to make millions of dollars, and then go hide away somewhere. We want to make good music

fifteen years from now. The Gatlin boys will retire when we stop cutting hit records, and stop cutting good records. When we feel like we're selling out and not making a contribution to the music industry, not being true to ourselves and putting out good music, that's when we'll get out. Let somebody else take over.

That's the way we were brought up and that's one good thing about being brothers. We were taught to give eight hours of work for eight hours of pay. That's the philosophy that we have; go that extra mile, whatever it takes. There is a lot of hard work involved in what we do, but that's the only way we know how to do it.

SOMETHING I WANT MY READERS TO UNDERSTAND IS THAT IT'S NOT ALL GLAMOUR. IT'S REALLY HARD WORK AND IT TAKES A LOT OF EFFORT TO GET THERE.

You know what is the easiest part of what we do? The hour that they see us on-stage. That's something that we've been trained to do, something that we've done all of our lives. You get up there, and you just be yourself.

The other day in Dallas, Larry and I spent twenty minutes talking on-stage, just talking back and forth and talking with the audience. We invite people to come into our "living room." We're going to do what God gave us talent to do. Listen with your ears and your heart, and let us try to move you. We'll sing something fast, something slow, and something funny, and something heavy. When you leave this place you've been entertained and we've touched you in some particular manner.

We've always tried to do that, but the hour that we work on-stage, that's the fun part. That's what we enjoy doing. We closed at the Fairmont, got in bed about two or three o'clock, and were supposed to catch the seven o'clock plane the next morning. Those are the things that are hard—getting up and packing after you've lived on the road for a week. You run downstairs to catch the bus or limo to the airport, you fly three or four hours, and you arrive in a strange city. Somebody takes you to another hotel. You check in, go to sound check, and do all that stuff all over again.

Behind the scenes, things are incredible. The hour we spend on-stage is a relief. It's back into the music. It's what all the other work is geared toward, to make that hour on stage the best it can possibly be. I never dread going on-stage.

AS AN ENTERTAINER, WHAT DO YOU FEEL ABOUT THE RESPONSIBILITY OF THE RECORD COMPANY TOWARD YOU AND YOUR PRODUCT?

We deal from a little different position than some new artists. Record companies have only x amount of dollars to spend on new artists and x amount of dollars to spend on proven artists. Our record company can take a chance on us. They can spend a few more dollars because they know that in the long run we're going to sell x amount of records and we may sell more than that. On "Straight Ahead," we knew we'd sell 200,000 or 250,000 albums with no problem. We did not know it was going to end up selling over 700,000, but we had some kind of base from which to work.

I HEARD LARRY SAY YOU SEARCHED FOR A NEW RECORD COMPANY BE- CAUSE YOU KNEW THERE WERE GOING TO BE FEWER AND FEWER COMPANIES IN THE FUTURE AND YOU WANTED TO BE WITH THE RIGHT ONE.

Monument Records was a good record company, but they did not have the national distribution. They did not deal from a posi- tion of strength. We decided to go with Columbia CBS. We had two or three other offers, but we felt we had a relationship with Columbia because they used to distribute Monument's product. We knew some of the people already, so it was like going back home. Also CBS is the biggest record company in the world and their country division is great. They had some money with

which to help promote us. If they're willing to take a shot on us, it's a whole lot better to go with someone like that than to go with some company that doesn't have anything and is struggling.

The only setback is that when you make that decision to sign with a big record company, with a roster of twenty people, you'd better have enough faith in yourself to cut some hit records. You can get lost in a big record company. We're competing— they've only got so much time and money to spend on people. They had Willie Nelson and Charlie Daniels over there; Crystal Gayle had just signed; George Jones had popped up again and become hot real quick.

But we felt that we were willing to take that chance because CBS believed in what we are doing. We knew we were going to cut hit records for them. They believed enough in us to say, "Come on. And we'll do it and make it work."

WELL, IF THE PUBLIC DOESN'T HEAR WHAT YOU'RE CUTTING, YOU'RE NOT GOING TO SELL MANY RECORDS. YOU WANTED TO MAKE SURE THAT YOU HAVE A RECORD COMPANY THAT CAN GET IT OUT THERE.

True, but even today you can't find our records everywhere. Each company has so many artists and there are so many record companies throughout the country. The companies do the best they can. People don't understand that it's not just the record company that's involved. Suppose you own a record store in Seattle, Washington. It is your responsibility to say, "I think Gatlin's records will sell." You have to go to CBS and buy those records and put them in your store. CBS does not just walk in and say, "Here are twenty-five albums; now sell them." As a record-store owner, you have the right to say what goes in there.

When a person can't find a particular record, he has to go to the record-store owner and say, "Listen, I want it, and I've got some friends who will buy some Gatlin stuff. How do I do it?" The store owner can always order it. Maybe the owner didn't think the record would sell. He's got to buy the copies and sell them to the public.

WHAT DO YOU SUGGEST TO A YOUNG PERSON WHO WANTS TO BE A SINGER, AN ENTERTAINER?

A new artist coming to town might be better off going to a smaller record company—to try to get in, and get a name established. When Mickey Gilley started his first deal, he went with a local record company in the Houston South Texas area. He had a couple of hits in South Texas that never did anything outside of Texas. Then he developed a base of people from which to work. People began to hear him, and he had records for fifteen or twenty years. But it wasn't until 1977 that he had "Room Full of Roses," which was his first really monster record. People said, "Mickey Gilley, 'Room Full of Roses,' " and associated him with that particular song.

Same thing with us. We had "Broken Lady" with Monument, but it wasn't really, I think, until we moved to CBS and came out with "Straight Ahead" that people recognized us. The distribution system at CBS is better. They're bigger, larger, got more people out there who honk and push it.

WHAT ADVICE WOULD YOU GIVE TO PEOPLE WHO DON'T HAVE THE TALENT BUT CONTINUE TO TRY?

It's hard to say what is and isn't really talent. Sometimes I'm amazed at some of the records that make it and some of the artists that make it. Some people in this business, I think, are more talented than others, sing better than others, or may have a better physical appearance. And let's face it, there is a physical attraction in this business.

The physical aspect does have a bearing on shows. Some people come for that physical thing—we get it all the time. When Rudy's introduced, the girls go crazy. They scream and holler because Rudy's a nice-looking guy. It doesn't matter whether or not Rudy can sing or whether or not Rudy can play the guitar. We try not to let that get in the way of the music and what we're trying to do.

As long as you are happy doing what you are doing, trying to make it in this business, there's no reason to quit. If you're spending every dollar you've got and your kids are going hungry—I don't think you can sit down and say, "I'm going to spend two years trying to make it, and if I don't make it, that's it." I think you'll know when to quit. I think the Gatlins will know when to get out.

Obviously, it's going to be easier to make it if you do have some talent. I admire people who have the stamina to go after what they want. Isn't it sad to see people miserable working at a job that they cannot stand and don't have a good time at?

It's not something that just happens overnight. We've paid a lot of dues. We've sung in a lot of places for very little money. It makes you appreciate success a lot more. We look back on our struggles and we laugh all the time, on the bus, talking about those things. Things are better now, thank God. The people have accepted us, and we love them and appreciate them for sticking with us. We had a lot of dedicated fans at first who knew we'd eventually make it. Now it's kind of nice to look back on it and say, "Thanks for your faith and understanding and believing in us."

CINDY SMITH

Recording artist and television entertainer.
Former member of Dave and Sugar.

WHAT ADVICE WOULD YOU GIVE TO PEOPLE STARTING OUT WHO WANT TO BECOME ENTERTAINERS?

I'd tell them to start at a theme park. People think that's wrong, but that is where I received my experience. For example, I was on-stage every day, four shows a day, in a theater that seats 1,600 people. A lot of people see you; you get more exposure than singing through a road band.

I WOULD ASSUME THAT BY WORKING AT A THEME PARK YOU WOULD MEET SOME OF THE RIGHT PEOPLE. HOW IMPORTANT DO YOU THINK THAT IS IN THE INDUSTRY?

It doesn't really matter how much talent you have, sad to say. You have to know the right people. To me, it is so political, not just in entertainment, but in anything.

Attitudes are really important. If you only halfway do your job, you're not going to receive very much. I think that is why I've gotten television work. I go out every single show and give 100 percent, no matter what.

You never know who is out in the audience. People will come backstage and say so-and-so producer from a big show is out there. That shouldn't matter. You should do the same show every single day.

DO YOU GET HIT ON VERY OFTEN BY PEOPLE THAT PROMISE YOU THE WORLD BUT NEVER FOLLOW THROUGH?

When I first started out at a local theme park, I was promised a lot. I really learned my lesson about what type of people to stay away from. I have not been "hit on" since then. I can usually tell who is on the up and up.

BASICALLY YOU HAVE FOUND PEOPLE TO BE NICE.

Yes, especially doing this television work. I did the "Nashville Palace," and I couldn't have picked a better crew or a better producer. The "Future Star" program was just incredible. Everybody was really nice and wanted to help.

87

DO YOU HAVE SOME SPECIFIC GOALS, OR ARE YOU JUST SEEING HOW FAR YOU CAN GO?

I would, of course, like to land a recording contract. My biggest goal is to do a sitcom on television. But for now I've got to go with the flow; take it as it comes. You do have to set a goal for yourself or you'll just sit in limbo.

WHY BECOME A RECORDING ARTIST?

It makes me happy. I'm at home with it. I feel I could be really good at it if I had the right people show me how to do things, take me around, and guide me. I like to make the audience happy.

WHAT ADVICE WOULD YOU GIVE TO OTHER PEOPLE SEEKING A MUSICAL CAREER?

If you want to do it, do it. Don't sit around and wait for it to happen. I have had every kind of job that you can think of outside of music—from renting baby strollers at a mall to working at a printing company. I've even dressed up as a clown, been a lifeguard, and been a Mouseketeer at malls. Anything to get money to set aside and do what I want to do. It might be a detour, but you have to do that.

You can't sit around and starve to death. I don't believe in that. Some people will say, "I starved. I'm a frustrated singer. I sweated it out." I think you can get a job and do that on the side and still have your music.

DID YOU LIVE ON A SHOESTRING?

Very much so and it got to me once in a while. I still worry about my money situation, but so far it's been real good for me. Too many opportunities have fallen into my lap, so to speak, and I feel like the Lord has said, "This is what you're supposed to do." Twice I was offered a job as a flight attendant, and I said, "No. I know it isn't what I'm supposed to do. I'm supposed to sing."

HOW ABOUT PRESSURES? YOU SEEM TO BE A VERY HAPPY PERSON.

I am basically happy. I do feel the pressure and sometimes wonder if it is really worth it. Then I'll see somebody in the audience smile, and I don't care who it is, young or old. It makes me feel good.

BROOKS HUNNICUTT

Recording artist and back-up singer. Television shows include "American Bandstand," "The Tonight Show," "Merv Griffin," "American Music Awards," "Mac Davis Christmas Show." Session and concert work with Rita Coolidge, Dave Loggins, Tony Orlando, Freda Payne, Helen Reddy, Kenny Rogers, Sam and Dave, Lynyrd Skynyrd, Rod Stewart, Three Dog Night, Al Wilson, and Bobby Womack.

HOW DID YOU GET INTO THE MUSIC BUSINESS?

I began to knock on doors as a single artist, which was extremely difficult, because I hadn't been in Los Angeles long enough to make a dent as an artist. I began to get some word-of-mouth recognition—a little bit of work here and there. My biggest break came when I went to work for a publisher named Richard Delvy as a secretary/administrator and song hustler. I began to learn about the publishing end of it and to do the demos for the company. As I did the demos, I learned about the musicians and how to put together really good backgrounds and leads, which began to, I hope, develop my own style. I was also doing other things here and there with different groups, but I was feeling very discouraged and actually getting ready to move home at that time. Richard asked if I would like to be the opening act and sing backgrounds for the first national David Cassidy tour. I didn't even know who David Cassidy was.

It was hectic, but very exciting because I "knocked out" his management firm and record company, and ended up with a recording contract for myself. I had a single released in nine days. That's the way it frequently happens. Actually, there are some intelligent moves you can make, but generally, and unfortunately, you usually get there and kick around as best you can.

AS A BACKGROUND SINGER IN RECORDING STUDIOS, DID YOU FIND A LOT OF PRESSURE TO BE RIGHT ON PITCH RIGHT AWAY?

I am fortunate because I have good pitch, and I've never had any pitch problems. However, most singers have pitch problems at one time or another. The cause could be a certain studio, the key the song is cut in, maybe one of the instruments is a nickel out of tune, or perhaps the part you are singing is difficult to hear. The vocal section is expected to arrive on time, write or read the parts promptly, sing in tune, have a good blend, and know about headphones, and how to use the mike. Most of the time we wrote our own parts. In other words, we came into the studio, heard the bare rhythm

89

section with a scratch lead vocal, and the producer pretty much left it up to us.

My reputation as a background singer in Los Angeles is based on the fact that I come up with tasteful parts when there are none. We memorize them on the spot and put them down. I had good training in the demo studio with no pressure, so by the time I made it to the big leagues, I had the studio down. There is quite a bit to learn about working with phones and mikes in the studio.

Now, the only pressure that I get into involves tracks for the television shows. There is a deadline, and they do have strict budgets. The biggest thing for them is the time factor, so that is a pressure date, and there isn't a whole lot of time to fool around. And, of course, it depends on who you are working for. The big rock acts generally have had enough money in the past, and we've been good enough so that there isn't too much pressure. Once in a while you get a stumper, and you just can't get a sound that pleases the artist or producer. Even then, I can't really remember a time when I have been treated badly. I always go in with really experienced, good-sounding singers.

Regarding pitch problems, I had a very interesting experience once. The Temptations were doing an album, and I was sitting in on their sessions. They were having astounding problems with pitch. There are five of them, and two or three seemed to be out at once. I began to sing their parts to them through the talk-back mike on one song, and finally all but one were singing in tune. All of us in the booth were baffled because, as you know, the Temps are renowned for their harmonies. We checked the instruments for pitch, discussed whether or not the studio was haunted, and on and on. We were all becoming almost superstitious. Finally, in an act of total desperation, I went out in the studio, donned headphones, and sang the part in his ear. It worked! Henceforth, I was known laughingly as "Coach." I saw the guys about three months later at a concert in Chicago, and they came

screaming down the hall yelling, "Hey, Coach!" They are really nice to be around.

HOW MANY POSITIONS ARE THERE FOR BACKGROUND SINGERS IN LOS ANGELES? ARE THERE A LOT OF JOBS OR ARE THERE VERY FEW?

I'm not an expert on statistics, but I believe that there are very few jobs compared to the amount of good singers available. There are so many excellent unknown singers. And there are a lot of good lead singers who don't know anything about backgrounds. Blending and phrasing in a background section is an art. It also tends to be handed down. The black girls have a dynasty on the head charts, and it has handicapped my income to a great degree. Not because there's a great deal of animosity, but mostly because they care for each other as a family. They have a lot of brothers and sisters and childhood friends. They are very musical and quite naturally sing a lot together and use each other on dates. I'm afraid they don't think of me first. They have always hired me when they ran out of singers to do a very difficult part, but, as a general rule, they keep it in the family. They're very proud of being able to do it and do it well. I respect that, but it sure does hurt my income.

WHAT ABOUT YOUR INCOME? DOES A HARMONY OR BACKGROUND SINGER IN THE STUDIO MAKE A DECENT LIVING?

The real famous black groups and the first-call readers make pretty darn good incomes. I don't know exactly what they make, but I would estimate between $15,000 and $40,000 a year when they are having decent years. It really can vary. That is the stressful thing about this business. There is no security. When the economy suffers, we background singers are many times considered a luxury and are the first to be deleted from the musical budgets. I've spent many months working secretarial jobs in the old days, and may again. The readers—the ones who do a lot of the commercials and most of the television work—would perhaps have more steady incomes. If you do a series or a commercial, you get residuals based on how often it is played. You do not get such large residuals on albums; we get a very small percentage. A good way for a background singer to make a living is to be on the road with a well-known artist. Unfortunately, it is exhausting, and it precludes you from working on your own career.

OKAY. LET'S TALK ABOUT THE ROAD. DID YOU LIKE BEING ON THE ROAD?

I've had some wonderful experiences, and each year there may be one or two places I go where I make friends, but those nice things are comparatively few. Overall, it's grueling on you biologically and mentally. It's really boring unless you are a featured part of the act or it's your own thing. When you're singing back-up behind someone of any magnitude, you do pretty much the same show every night, because the charts for an orchestra (for the hotels in Vegas, Reno, or Tahoe) are quite expensive. This gets terminally boring.

And even the best accommodations are very lonely. You try to be close to your group, but you live with each other so much that you tend to stay away from them off-stage. You end up by yourself a lot. If you're in a strange town and you're trying to conserve money, you don't go sightseeing, because it costs money to do that. You really have to keep your expenses to a reasonable level. When we did a week or more in one place, we girls usually tried to get a small refrigerator or insulate a trash can and keep tuna, and such. Then we'd go out to a couple of nice restaurants for a treat. The trick is you sometimes find yourself spending too much time in your room. When that happens, you get a bad case of the "sit-down-stomp, agoraphobic, hotel, wallpaper blues."

The artist gives us a per diem for food, say $20 a day. Now you might have a couple of days when you only spend $3 or $4 because you bought groceries. But then you may have to take a cab to a mall to buy something, and the cab will be $10. Everything adds up. If you want to go to a health club, you have to pay guest membership and so forth. It's hard to have enough to do and not spend a lot of money.

WHAT'S THE NICEST THING, OR THE FUNNIEST THING, THAT HAS HAPPENED TO YOU WHILE YOU WERE ON THE ROAD?

One of the nicest things that ever happened to me was really something I initiated. I was on tour with David Cassidy, and he always got a lot of fan mail which was left on the dressing-room floor. So I would collect and answer about ten letters from each concert. One letter was from the mother of a little girl who was in a wheelchair as a result of an accident. The girl wanted very much to come to the concert, but her doctors wouldn't let her. The mother said she hadn't told her daughter that she had written David, but if he could call, it would make the child's weekend and might help her get well. I went to the airport ahead of David and raced into a phone booth. I called them up and got the mother on the phone. Then I grabbed poor David out of the limousine and said, "Get in here," and I put him on the phone to talk to this little girl. She just couldn't believe it.

One other really nice thing happened when I toured with David. We had done a concert in Portland, Oregon. A year later David went back, but I was no longer with him. A little girl wrote me a letter and said, "You don't know me, but I saw you last year and thought you were great. I want to know why you didn't come back." We got to be pen pals. She came to visit, and she finally moved to Los Angeles. I eventually met her family, and we got to be super good friends. Now I have a family in Portland, which is just wonderful. These are the rare and wonderful things which I will always cherish.

I have good friends in many places around the world. I'd love to talk to them every week and drop by to visit more often, but there isn't enough time or money to do it.

Meeting people is one of the nice aspects of traveling. But, the thousands of miles that you drag through between those experiences—traveling on planes and in buses at odd hours of the night, eating jet-eggs and cheeseburgers—are soul shattering.

THE LONELINESS REALLY GETS TO YOU?

It's terrible for me. I imagine for a lot of the younger musicians, especially the guys, trying to score is a real fun thing. I used to enjoy going out, seeing and being seen. After you do it awhile, you begin to realize that there are generally few valuable results that happen that way. Going clubbing is expensive and boring, except for seeing a really good act now and then or visiting with someone that you already know on the road.

For me, it is extremely lonely. And when I'm lonely, I can't be creative and write because I'm too down to even express myself. One can only write so many letters, read so many books, watch so much television, do so many sit-ups, walk around the block so many times, or sit by the pool so many hours. Hotels all look alike after a while, even the nicest ones—they're all the same somehow. As long as I have a good bed, good air conditioning, and fair room service, it's the same. I have begun to get phobic about packing now and going to the airport.

HOW ABOUT POLITICS IN THE MUSIC INDUSTRY? DO YOU SEE A LOT OF IT?

I see some politics and some outright faithlessness. I believe that the business aspect of the recording industry is highly political with regard to executing contracts and making deals. Many a great artist has been lost in the old "new-president-record-biz shuffle." I once signed with a manager who later mistakenly thought I was having an affair with her hottest property. She dropped me and squashed my recording contract.

I just recently heard a sad story about studio singers. It seems that a very famous Los Angeles contractor did a commercial date, and the executives for the company weren't happy with the outcome of the session. So, a few days later, a new section was hired for another try. However, when the singers dicovered that the other contractor had already had a shot at the jingle, they refused (as nicely as possible) to redo the date, explaining that this man gave them a lot of work, and they wouldn't dare cross his path. Unfortunately, many singers are pretty neurotic, and their emotional insecurities seem to give them a lot of drive. Therefore, they are often found at the top, and you must play ball their way, or lose work.

I know that in the background "head session" circles there are girls who will come in behind your back when you hire them and say to the producer, "She's real good, but I can do better," and "I know so-and-so, and I sang for so-and-so." I have run up against a few really nasty people, but that tends to be individuals as opposed to a system. I looked long and hard to find very talented girls with no attitudes.

The faithlessness really hurts. You help make a great record for an artist. His album goes platinum, but the next time he goes into the studio, he runs into somebody else before calling you, and he hires that person instead. Many of my clients have been very faithful, but then they change their sound, go all male for instance, and there goes my work. It's debilitating never knowing where your next meal is coming from, no matter how good your reputation is. In Los Angeles I am pretty well-known as a background singer, but even so, I've starved a lot. I've done my share of straight jobs, and unless I want to stay on the road, it's hard to make a living.

And then there is the final insult. On the first album I did for Rod Stewart, a group name was put on the album credit as opposed to our individual names. The musicians' names were on there individually. And on the second Rod album I did, they misspelled my name. Ah, "Show biz is my life."

HAS LOS ANGELES GOTTEN CRAZY ON US?

There are a lot of nice people struggling. But it seems that when you get into the upper echelon, they think they have a license to be crazy. They do play with it, some to a greater degree than others. And, of course, the stress factor is amazing. I've had a lot of people say they met one star or another and the stars were creeps, had no manners, and so forth. People have no way of comprehending the physical and mental exhaustion that these people can suffer from. Say, for instance, they have been on the road touring for three months, and they come into town. They have to finish their album, so they go screaming into the studio. They have television appearances and magazine interviews in between. Finally, they can't come out of their homes or hotels because people will surround them. This stress is real.

HOW ABOUT THE PRESSURES THAT CAUSE PEOPLE TO TAKE DRUGS? THE ESCAPISM OR WHATEVER THEY'RE AFTER?

I know a little about those pressures, and as a rule, I don't take drugs. There have been times when I have been on the road doing one-nighters, and the sequence would be a plane trip, a two-hour bus ride, a little sleep, two shows, a little more sleep, and repeat the sequence for days and days. It doesn't take long to get real crazy when you mess up your body's rhythm by hopping all over the continent.

There have been times when people have said some little thing to me, and I've wanted to take out the nearest window—go through a wall. In the past I've exploded and hit things. It's probably taken seven or eight years for me to get my temper under control. When I feel a total irrationality coming on, I recognize it for what it is, and I try to calm myself down. Then if I still feel mad a couple of hours later, or the next day, I do something about it. There have been times when I'd go off on people simply because I was biologically miserable. I was so exhausted; I didn't know if I was walking or flying. There are the times when artists drink to feel a little better, do a little toot to be really hot on stage, and act like they feel great when they're half-dead. Then they get into a vicious cycle because when they do that, they're just fried the next day, and if they don't have time to rest, they've got to do it again.

THEY MAY HAVE THE FLU AND FEEL TERRIBLE, BUT THEY STILL HAVE TO BE ON WHEN THEY GET ON THAT STAGE. HOW IN THE WORLD DO YOU DO THAT?

Each person does an individual thing. There's a romance in performance for me. I learned to perform face-to-face with an audience, and it is a joy for me. I love to sing. If I'm singing lead, I tend to take my mood and use it in my performance, communicate it to the audience. I think people appreciate honesty.

I once went to see Katharine Hepburn in a play. She had broken her ankle, and before the performance, she came on-stage and asked the audience if they still wanted to see her perform. Of course they said yes; but she told them that if they didn't enjoy the play to ask for their money back! Wonderful, don't you think? I think that honesty is the thing. I don't enjoy watching an act that has the same slick smile, same patter, and same material every show.

When you're in a group, an "up" performance seems a little easier. If you're in a good close group, you help each other out. When I toured with Stephen Stills, it was the most wonderful tour experience I've had. I was a feature singer, and we were an equal family. We huddled before each performance, stacked hands, and said something about doing the show—not unlike a football team—and then ran out. If somebody was down, we all knew about it, and we'd pull for him. That was very effective. We only toured for a couple of weeks, but we managed to find a great deal of energy every night. We had a wonderful bus with beds, television, Betamax, fridge, electric piano. We also had superior tour management. This made everything much easier than the frequent disorganization I have experienced. However, even with all that, if you're going to be out touring for three months, you're all going to get fried and hate each other before it's over with. But if you know that it's going to happen, then you can manage yourself a little better.

WHAT KIND OF MONEY CAN THE AVERAGE PERSON MAKE WHILE ON THE ROAD?

It varies tremendously. If you have a poor economy, some of the best studio singers are willing to go out on the road for $600 a week. That is probably as low as anyone should think about, and that's too low unless there is per diem, rooms, and travel included. I would say $500 or $600 a week is what the mediocre acts are paying or acts that are maybe working the smaller rooms or opening for someone else.

In calculating a yearly income, you must remember that whatever you make on the road usually gets divided in half because most acts only work six or seven months a year. So you don't make much more than a well-paid secretary. Getting back to the pay scale, the headliners are paying between $700 and $1,500 a week. That's a wide range, but it really depends. If you pick up a big tour, like a top rock group or perhaps a John Denver, you may make a lot of money.

If you stay with an artist for years, a rare occurrence these days, you may receive a percentage of the gate as a bonus, but that is rare. The last artist I worked for was pretty well-known and a headliner. There were three show rates. One scale for two shows a night at a hotel; another for one show a night at a hotel; and the highest scale was for one-nights because they are the hardest to work. We were not on retainer, so if we weren't on the road, we had no income.

I worked seven months last year, and I had to budget my money over the other five

that I didn't work. It's difficult to learn, but if you're not going to be struggling all the time, you need to budget yourself and be aware of what the economy looks like. There really isn't a formula whereby you can work hard for six months, get a raise, and apply for a pension plan. Our income constantly fluctuates, and many times, what you make is a matter of how gutsy you are. There is no security and, at my age, I think about that with some degree of chagrin.

WHAT ABOUT THE GLAMOUR OF PERFORMING ON THE ROAD?

People say, "It must be so glamorous," but think about it. Inevitably, if you're doing one-nights, you have to get up early. Unless you have a charter plane, you have to catch an early enough flight to avoid problems. You may have to consider traffic so that you have enough driving time if you come in late, especially in the bigger cities.

In the meantime, the poor roadies are driving all night to the next location with the equipment. They drive because it's too expensive to fly all the equipment on the big tours. On the smaller tours, like Helen Reddy, we flew our instruments with us, and rented amps [amplifiers] in town. But the big rock 'n' roll groups have professional sound companies. They have to have a semi [van] take their equipment, and they have to schedule the tour so that they can get the equipment to the next gig in time. Those poor guys; I don't know how they do it. They work all day to set up, and all night at the gig, then they tear down and drive. I don't know when they sleep.

Since I'm a woman, I have to get my make-up together and hair curled. I have to figure out whether I need to take my costume to the sound check or whether I'll be coming back to the hotel before the show. The biggest part of a road gig seems to be hurry up and wait. You hurry to the airport so you won't be late, because you absolutely must not miss the plane. You leave the plane and wait for your luggage. Then you get in the limo or bus and wait to get to the hotel.

You get to the hotel and wait until you can be moved into your room, and then you wait for your luggage. Next, you wait until you go to your sound check, and then you wait for your performance. Then you wait in between performances.

It's grueling. You want your clothes to look neat, and you want a smile on your face. With a living instrument like the voice, you'd best not abuse yourself, unless you sound like Rod Stewart. Also, they're harder on ladies for appearance and attitude than they are on guys. A guy with an attitude is a guy with an attitude; a woman with an attitude is a bitch.

WHAT ADVICE WOULD YOU GIVE TO ALL THOSE PEOPLE WHO WANT TO BE SINGERS?

The first thing I would have to say is "Make use of all possible tools." Try to perfect your reading skills in order to get singles, television shows, and films; and try to make your harmony impeccable. Sing as wide a range of notes as possible. I can hear and sing all three parts, and I have a good falsetto, so I am not limited to just one range. Learn about your voice, how to control and alter it, the different qualities and tones it has. (When I arrived in California, I had a vibrato, and I knew nothing of the technique of singing in the studio.) Whether you sing solo or background, try to orient your voice as much as possible in the direction you are taking. For instance, country backgrounds tend to have a faster vibrato or no vibrato and very open, frequently falsetto-sounding tones. Gospel backgrounds have a wider vibrato, more chest tones, and full-voice sounds.

A LOT OF PEOPLE SAY THAT YOU SHOULD TAKE LESSONS OR YOU SHOULDN'T TAKE LESSONS. WHAT DO YOU THINK?

I'm reluctant to say this because it is not always true, but the most creative musicians I have met have either taken lessons later in life or have taken very few. It seems that the ones who have taken lessons from childhood, unless they have had very special, perceptive teachers, are handicapped within the bounds of their training. They are so confined by it that all they can do is sound like other artists. They can imitate everybody else perfectly, but they can't seem to find their own uniqueness. They frequently have tremendous technique, but very little style or taste. Now, on the other hand, those people with a tremendous amount of training tend to be wonderful orchestra or choral members because they can read.

I had classical training in high school and came out sounding like an opera singer. I retained the control training, but it took me three years to get rid of the classical sound when I decided that I wanted to sing rock 'n' roll.

HOW HARD IS IT FOR A WOMAN TO BECOME A MAJOR STAR TODAY IN THE MUSIC INDUSTRY?

I think it *may* be easier than it has been. Remember, the men tend to take the women where they want to go on a date, and women generally don't want to see other women. I think the degree of difficulty fluctuates, but right now I see more women stars—and the door open to more kinds of music—than I ever have before. Ten years ago, who did you have? Aretha Franklin and Dusty Springfield. Now you've got Linda Ronstadt, Emmylou Harris, Carly Simon, Dolly Parton, Loretta Lynn, Anne Murray, Barbara Mandrell. Perhaps the chances are better now than ever before.

Young singers need to go to a major recording center. That will probably be Nashville, Los Angeles, or perhaps New York, although there is a diminishing amount being done in New York. Detroit is finished, and Miami has a smattering.

When you move to a "music industry" center, you handicap yourself because you are in the biggest ball park, so to speak, but that is where the opportunity is. I went to Los

Angeles along with a million other singers. In this business you are basically selling yourself, and you, above all others, must believe in your product. It is really difficult to keep believing in yourself in that atmosphere—there is a great singer around every corner. Another important thing is to be persistent and methodical about trying to find work. You must meet other singers, meet producers and arrangers, and take your tapes and résumé.

Get experience any way you can—get in a group, get in a choir, get in anything. I sang in Watts in a black church for nine years, and it has been the greatest musical experience of my life. I learned to really sing there. When a riff came into my head, I opened my mouth and let it fly. I didn't have to worry about anybody judging my performance because they riffed all day long.

Rejection is not the exception in the music business, it's the norm. Don't take it personally. I did. Every time I was rejected, turned down, I'd sit down for six months. I'd lose all my equilibrium and waste a whole lot of time when I should have dusted off my bruised ego, regrouped, and gone out there and carried on. You need to tactfully stay in the streets. You don't want to be a gypsy, but you need to be in the right places. If there's a happening and you know somebody is going to be there that you'd like to see, stick your face in the door. There's liable to be a star there who needs somebody to go on the road. It's like musical bumper cars, you just don't know when or where something will click. Very exciting when you are young, very tiring when you're older. There just aren't any certain steppingstones.

WHAT ABOUT THE FUN SIDE OF THE INDUSTRY?

How about a description of the party to end all parties? The first year Paul McCartney did a "Wings over America" tour, he celebrated its close by renting the *Queen Mary* in Long Beach. Though I was supposed to go, I didn't, because I was called at the last minute to fly up to Lake Tahoe and work. The next year, we received an engraved invitation in the mail requesting the honor of our presence at the Frank Lloyd Wright mansion in Benedict Canyon. This estate is a seventeenth-century French provincial mansion on 50 acres. They requested that we wear white if possible.

We're getting ready, and I'm racing around trying to find white clothing. My old man said we had to rent a limousine, and I growled, "Why do we have to rent a limo? We've got a Cadillac."

"Well, because everybody rents limos for these things," he said.

I grumbled all the way to the mansion, but I rapidly became impressed as soon as we arrived at the gates. There were 200 or so fans there with cameras and autograph books. How did they find out about it? I wondered.

At the bottom of the cobblestone driveway, we left our limo, and we were sent to a white tent. There, our names were checked off the guest list. Then we were put in a white limousine for the trip to the mansion. The limo brought us to a big courtyard that had a fountain strewn with white flowers. All the guests were in white clothing, and I was beginning to feel like something from *The Great Gatsby*. It was quite beautiful.

At the front door of the mansion, a young man in full livery presented us with a printed program of the evening's events. The young ladies in antebellum gowns escorted us through the house, while the Nelson Riddle Orchestra was playing in the courtyard. The entire affair was catered by Chasens, the most exclusive restaurant in Los Angeles. The dining room was full of silver trays with every conceivable kind of hors d'oeuvres.

At 8:45, the Los Angeles Ballet danced a half-hour program on the lawn. They had a wooden stage, lights, and a huge PA playing a recorded program. Looking around at the guests, I saw Jack Nicholson, Tony Curtis, Linda Ronstadt, the Jackson Five, Olivia Newton-John, Peter Frampton, Rick Nelson, and everybody but God.

Another part of the lawn displayed a

miniature garden with miniature doll houses. Nearby, in two separate tents, two of the most talented airbrush artists in the United States were airbrushing the "Wings" insignia on the backs of the white shirts and blouses of the guests. A wonderful mime troup was performing on the lawn between the tents.

Then at about 9:30, dinner was served in a huge white tent that had a silver "Wings" insignia on top. The place settings were tied with white satin ribbons with "Wings over America" printed in silver. The match packs were also white satin with the same message. All the flowers and tablecloths were white, and the waiters serving coffee and tea were also in white. At dinner, I was seated with Tony Curtis and his wife. He was so very nice, and I was so very thrilled.

After dinner, there was a show on a stage inside the tent. During the evening they had had a real robot which rolled through the grounds paging people and telling jokes. The robot and a famous comedian emceed the show together. The comedian attempted a series of hysterically funny, unsuccessful magic tricks, and the robot did imitations of Ringo and John and recited funny poems about their careers. We were in stitches.

The entire cast of *The Wiz* sang "Ease on down the Road," and Chuck Norris gave a karate exhibition. There was a magnificent circus-quality juggler, and a magician performed two fabulous illusions, which Tony Curtis explained to me. As you probably know, he did the film *Houdini* and has a passion for magic. For the close, the late John Belushi did his famous imitation of Joe Cocker. We'd never seen it before and everyone just about fell over laughing— Cocker, too.

We were then invited down to the pool for swimming and disco. Now *that* is a party! There must have been 400 people there, and there was something to do every minute. It was the most elegant, fabulous thing I've ever been to, and I've never seen so many famous people. That was the party to end all parties.

GAIL DAVIES

Recording artist, record producer, and songwriter. Songs include "Good Lovin' Man," "Someone Is Looking for Someone Like You," "Grandma's Song," "You're a Hard Dog to Keep Under the Porch," and "I'll Be There."

WHEN YOU FIRST ARRIVED IN TOWN, SOME PEOPLE SAID YOU WERE HARD TO WORK WITH. WAS THAT TRUE?
The other day I did a show with Teddy Bart. Before we went on camera, he said, "Now, are you going to be completely honest with me?" And I said, "To a fault." As soon as the show started and the lights went on, he introduced me and said, "Would you say you are difficult to work with?" I said, "Well, that depends." He said, "On what?" And I said, "Well, if I had someone come into my house and do carpentry work and they did a poor job, I would make them do it over. They might think I was being very difficult. So in that respect, yeah, I have been hard to deal with because I expect people to do work properly for me, and I also do work well for others."

When I first moved to Nashville, it was hard, as a woman and as a stranger to establish myself as an authority on anything to do with music, or to gain the respect and command that I needed in order to make my albums. It gained me a reputation for being difficult. I really believe that anytime a person sets his mind on what he wants to accomplish, and then goes for that goal, there are going to be obstacles to overcome. Sometimes those obstacles include prejudice toward women. Some people just don't want to deal with an artist of either sex, period.

WELL, IT'S REALLY WORKED FOR YOU BECAUSE OF HOW WELL YOUR ALBUMS HAVE DONE. WHEN I TALK TO PEOPLE IN NASHVILLE, THEY TELL ME HOW MUCH THEY RESPECT YOU.
That is true. I've noticed that in the last few years I've gotten a lot of feedback, and I think that's great. I had to go through an awful lot of pain. I feel that when I look at my wrinkles, they carry clout. When I was younger, I would say things, and people wouldn't listen. I'm getting older now, and I've done a few things that have shown people that I do know what I'm talking about. Because of that, I've gotten the respect that also goes along with the reputation of being really tough and difficult. But,

you know, that just kind of goes with the territory.

WELL, YOU'VE BEEN IN THIS BUSINESS TWENTY-ONE YEARS, AND YOU'RE FI-NALLY ATTAINING SUCCESS. HOW DOES IT FEEL?

Well, pretty good. It's real hard, when people ask me about success, to define what success is—if success is financial security or records on the charts, or what. To me, I'm doing exactly what I want to do. My records do well; they always hit in the key Top 10. It's music that I'm proud of, music that I cre-ated, that I enjoy. I feel that is success. I would be happy if I had done a little bit better financially. I started in the hole with Warner Bros. because I had to buy myself out of a bad contract. That cost close to $250,000, plus points on all my Warner Bros. albums, and part of my publishing. So I started off very much in the hole, and it's taken everything that I have just to stay above water.

WAS IT WORTH THE GAMBLE OF SPEND-ING YOUR OWN MONEY TO PRODUCE YOUR SESSIONS, TO PROVE TO PEOPLE THAT YOU COULD DO IT?

It really was, and it was also dangerous. It was a learning process, and it cost me an awful lot to learn it. I always wanted to have a plaque made that said, "The tuition was high, but the school was great." I made some mistakes as I went along, but I feel very happy looking back on the things that I've done. I did press on and push hard enough to be able to produce myself. That's a very important thing. Now that I'm ready to do a co-production album, it's totally be-cause I want to. I admire the person I've chosen to work with, and I'm equally as excited about that as I have been about producing myself.

HOW DOES IT FEEL GOING TO A NEW RECORD COMPANY LIKE RCA?

It's very exciting. I feel a lot of respect for Joe Galante, and I feel a lot of support from him. We've only had two meetings, and it's just there. You can feel it when it's there. I'm going to RCA with a fresh approach, and we're going to make a terrific record. I look back on the songs that I have recorded over the last few years that have done really well, and they have been songs like "Round-the-Clock Loving" and "You're a Hard Dog to Keep Under the Porch," and songs that have to do with women. Women are basi-cally the people who buy country music records so this album is going to be called "Where Is a Woman to Go?" The title song was written by K. T. Oslin, who wrote "Round-the-Clock Loving." We're going to build the album on this theme of a woman's strength. It is not going to be offensive to men. We don't want to alienate anybody; we're definitely not anti-men. We're very pro-women, and just appealing to a market that has not ever been touched.

IS IT HARD FOR AN ARTIST TO UNDER-STAND THAT WHEN YOU HAVE A BIG-SELLING RECORD, YOU MIGHT NOT MAKE AS MUCH MONEY AS PEOPLE ANTICIPATE?

I don't think people ever imagine or under-stand what it takes to make money in this business. Every artist has to pay back what it costs to make his album. It costs about $100,000 to make an album these days—a really good quality, technically correct album. If you make three albums, and they don't sell really well, you're in debt for $300,000, not counting whatever tour sup-port or advances you've gotten from the company. I left Warner Bros. with a $500,000 debt. I've never seen a royalty check in my life! When you don't get royal-ties from your records, the only other way you can make money is on the road.

Another misconception people have is that when they hear your record on the radio, they think you're getting money for it. But you're only getting money for radio play if you wrote the song; you're not getting money from singing it. If BMI had not been supporting me on a monthly draw for the last two years, I would not have been able to make it. That's pretty much what I live on. I think people would be very surprised to know that I end up, after taxes, living on less than $30,000 a year. Somebody said the other day, "Wow, so-and-so got a million dollars to sign with some record company." So I said, "Okay, let's take a million dollars, just for fun. You're making a million dollars, so your manager is in the 20 percent bracket. Right off the top, there goes $200,000. Now you have $800,000. Okay, now you're going to have a lawyer on salary and an accountant. There's another 10 percent, so that brings you down to $700,000. And then of course you've got a booking agency, if you're working the road . . .

BOOKING AGENTS TAKE, WHAT, 15 PERCENT? THAT WOULD BRING YOU DOWN TO APPROXIMATELY $550,000.
Right. And then the government will take more than half of that.

SO YOU'RE DOWN TO $250,000.
And out of that, you're going to have to take all of your expenses—your overhead if you have an office, your employees that work for you—secretaries, and so on. So out of that million dollars, you'll probably see around $100,000. It is amazing. In fact, when I get albums—this has always irritated me—I have to pay $4.00 an album if I want to sell them on the road or something. Of course, your relatives and friends say, "Hey, give me one of those free albums." And I say, "Free, my fanny, honey, this cost me $4.00, and with freight, $4.50, and if you want one of the *new* ones, it costs $5.00."

I HAD NO IDEA THEY CHARGE YOU FOR EACH ALBUM.
They give you the first twenty-five. But then I send an album to everyone who performs on it, so there's my twenty-five albums. Then I have to start paying for them. It is incredible just trying to make a living in this business.

I WAS WATCHING THE NASHVILLE NETWORK, AND THERE WAS PAULETTE CARSON SAYING SHE HAD BEEN DISCOVERED BY YOU. SHE AND RALPH EMERY EXPRESSED HOW MUCH PEOPLE HELP EACH OTHER IN NASHVILLE. DO YOU FIND THAT TO BE TRUE?
I do. It's like a chain of events. Linda Ronstadt recommended that Warner sign Emmylou Harris; Emmylou, in turn, turned Andrew Wickum on to sign me; and I, in turn, recommended Karen Brooks to Andrew Wickum. So it does go like that. People get behind and support each other.

There is a hard side to the town, too. People are getting to be a little more competitive. People who are very secure in themselves continue to help others because they don't feel a threat. Emmylou Harris said one time, "You know, this is music; it's not a horse race." And there's no finishing line; I don't have to beat so-and-so. Maybe the promotion people feel that way, but I hope that the artists don't.

WHAT DO YOU THINK THE ODDS ARE TODAY FOR A PERSON TO BECOME A RECORDING ARTIST—AN AVERAGE PERSON WHO'S GOT THE TALENT AND WANTS TO MAKE IT?
It is very difficult because the play list on the radio stations has gotten so tight. It's very hard to break in. I know Paulette is a wonderful singer and a great writer. She's had some very good songs. But getting the radio stations to play them, to take that chance, when some of them only have a rotation of thirty-five or forty songs, is hard. Of course, they're going to play what their listeners will keep tuned in to—it's just very hard to introduce a new artist. It's really pathetic to me, because I see so much talent that hasn't been on the air, and then I hear a lot of stuff on the radio that really should not be there.

I'm really thrilled when a group like the Judds comes along. They're wonderful, they're raw and unique. Reba McEntire is fantastic; it's really nice to see somebody breaking through.

DOES SUCCESS HAPPEN TO PEOPLE WHO DESERVE IT?

Not necessarily. I have never found that talent is a prerequisite for success. I have always felt that talent would be a nice thing to have, but I have seen people without it do quite well.

A lot of my generation got drawn into the music business by the Beatles excitement. It was so exciting back then to be in a band, and many of them didn't have what it takes to make a living at it. They quit school and didn't have training for other work. All of a sudden they had children and a wife to support and hit age thirty without a vocation. I saw it happen to a lot of my friends.

WE SHOULD DO MUSIC BECAUSE IT'S ENJOYABLE AND FUN, BUT IF YOU WANT TO BECOME A RECORDING ARTIST, WE'RE TALKING MANY YEARS BEFORE YOU GET A SHOT, A CHANCE.

A lot of time and dedication. It doesn't go bam, bam, bam, bam. I have seen one person in my entire life where that has happened, and that was with Sylvia. It was just an absolute fluke. Sylvia came here and got a job with Tom Collins as a secretary. He took her in the studio, she had some minor hits, and then all of a sudden, bam, she went from nobody to just a monstrous star. So it can happen, but boy, is it ever rare. That's the only time that I ever heard of or saw it. A lot of it has to do with Sylvia being such an attractive person. Tommy did a very good record with her; it was just one of those things. If he could do it again, he'd be doing it with others.

Most of the time, people have to resolve themselves to the fact that they're going to dedicate their lives to music. In Nashville, I was buying some fabric and this girl started talking about her husband. They are songwriters, and he can't get any work. She ended up taking a job in a fabric store. Now she doesn't get to sing anymore. But I run into this all the time—waitresses and others who have come to Nashville to get into the recording business, but who end up doing other work. I guess they just didn't realize how hard it is. But I really admire them; they really should do whatever they have to do to stay here, stick it out, get a solid cut.

IT CAN HAPPEN, BUT IT TAKES TIME.

It's a tough little town, and you really have to persevere to succeed, to make it. I used to have a little plaque that said, "Luck is where preparation meets with opportunity."

I still have a picture of the children and people sleeping on the streets of India, with a little sign above it that says, "Cheer up, things could get a lot worse."

I would like to add, of course, that these are my opinions, and they are subjective. Sometimes I think people buy books, and they go, "Oh, boy, here's the answer." No book really has all of the answers, other than the Bible.

CASEY KELLY

Recording artist, songwriter, and publisher. Artists who have cut his songs include Kenny Rogers and Dottie West, Ed Bruce, Loretta Lynn, Jacky Ward, The Dirt Band, Johnny Rivers, The Vogues, Helen Reddy, Tanya Tucker, O. C. Smith, and Janie Fricke.

HOW MUCH MONEY CAN YOU MAKE ON A MILLION SELLER?

It's a phenomenon I've seen happen with recording artists and songwriters. They don't really know how much money to expect from the business. They just have that same feeling I had—you write a hit song and you can make a lot of money. They get a hit, and they go spend a lot of money. All their friends are saying, "Hey, you must be a millionaire! Wow! Hey!" And they think, "Yeah, I must be a millionaire." They stay in the biggest hotels they can find in New York and buy everybody lunch, supper, and new cars. And then, they don't have any money. They're in debt. And they say, "Well, what happened? I had a hit. My managers must have robbed me." Or they say, "My publishing company didn't pay me all my money."

Well, if you stop and figure out the number of units (records) sold times the amount that you get for each unit sold, you can find out that you're not a millionaire. A songwriter gets mechanical royalties of five cents per song for each record sold. Your song could sell a million records, which is an oddity in itself, but if it does, you can multiply that million times the five cents and you'd get $50,000. As a performer, you multiply the million copies times what you make per unit based on your points—maybe six cents per single and thirty-six cents per album—and you find out that the money is not as big as what you think it is. It's easy enough if you're very successful and if sales are high, but it's not the storybook vision that everybody has of how much money a hit's worth.

And it's the same with the songwriter's performance rights. Maybe you know a writer who's had a record played on the radio. Try to find out how much he got for the song—not how much he got in advances, but how much money he made on air play. Sometimes you make a lot, but if you have that dream of sitting on these stacks of gold because you've got a hit record, you really owe it to yourself to try to get rid of that concept. Figure out how much money you're really going to make.

HOW ABOUT ATTORNEYS?

The professional services—lawyers, agents, publishers, managers—are another one of these storybook things that I had to get over.

I always thought that Perry Mason was sitting out there and I would go in to him and say, "Look, I have this problem." He would know all the legal things and would take the problems out of my hands—just go out and whip all these people into shape and bring me back my money—and I'd have a great deal with the company. These attorneys are very knowledgeable. But they are tools to be used. They have the knowledge, but that doesn't mean they're going to use it all. *You* have to know what you want.

You have to know where you're going and where you're speaking from. These people know how to build any kind of house that you want to build, but you have to know exactly—and you have to tell them—exactly how big you want the rooms. They're not going to look at you and say, "I know exactly what you need here," which is the image that I had. I'd go in and say, "I want a record deal," and think that the attorney was just going to automatically get me exactly what I wanted. You have to know what you want, and unfortunately it tends to be a learn-by-mistake method.

You go in and do a publishing deal. Well, you have an attorney look over the contract. He might be aggressive on your behalf; he might see something that he wouldn't want you to sign and say something about it. But in the six to ten major deals that I've done, I've come to know exactly what I want in the contract. I know everything, including every clause in the contract. I might ask him, "Does this clause say what I think it says? Is there some reason that we have to have it worded this particular way?" They'll be up on the latest percentages paid by companies if you go to a big hot-shot attorney. But mostly you have to know what you want for yourself and what you want them to do.

Even after the contract's negotiated, or while it's being negotiated, they'll present it to you in various forms and you have the final say. You can't say to the lawyer, "Well, should I take this?" You've got to look at the contract and know whether that's what you want or not.

I learned things like what happens to songs that never get recorded or whatever. What happens to them after my deal is over with? I learned to say, "Maybe I should have a clause in the contract that says I'll get the songs back after a certain number of years." Or, "What's to keep the contract from just running on for 15 to 20 years or forever?"

WHY DOES THE COMPANY ALWAYS OFFER THE ARTIST A CONTRACT?

All contracts are always written by the company for the company's advantage. They're not going to put something in there to protect *you*. They're going to protect themselves. They're going to say, "We want to be able to extend this contract each year for another year, over and over again." They're not going to say, "You have the right to object at some point," or, "We have to do such and such to be able to extend it." And what I learned to put in the contract is that they'd have to either sell a certain number of units of songs, or they'd have to come up with a cash advance against the monies that they'd owe me, which makes them think a little bit before they pick up that next year. You don't sign with a company that isn't interested in you. They're not making any money for you. The point I'm trying to make is you have to learn everything you can. They're not Perry Mason.

A rule comes out of this that I've learned to live by, and that is "Nobody wants what you want as much as you want it." I don't care how much you pay them. Lawyers don't want what you want as much as you want it yourself. So you're the one who has to watch out, and you have to get these people to do what you want them to do. You have to tell them. Don't think you can just dump it in their laps. You still have to tell them what you want them to do.

DAVE
MADDOX

Music business attorney with the firm Maddox and Hicks.
Former executive secretary of the Nashville offices of
AFTRA and SAG.

WHAT IS AFTRA?

AFTRA stands for the American Federation
of Television and Radio Artists. We're the
collective bargaining agent that represents
people who perform on radio, television, or
phonograph recording, and on other non-
broadcast recorded materials, such as
industrial tapes, slide shows, store castings,
and so forth.

THEN YOU REPRESENT PEOPLE WHO WORK IN THE ENTERTAINMENT INDUSTRY.

That's right. Primarily in the broadcast
industry. Broadcast or recorded material
area.

HOW DO YOU REPRESENT THEM? WHAT DO YOU ACTUALLY DO FOR THEM?

Specifically, my job is to enforce our national
contracts. Our national contracts are collective bargaining agreements which cover the
various work categories that our people
perform in. I see that they're paid the proper
amount and that the pension and welfare
contribution is made by the employer. This
provides certain health insurance, life

insurance, and pension benefits to our
members. I see that they're not placed in
dangerous work situations whenever possible. I also participate in the negotiation of
national contracts and negotiate local
contracts that would involve people in the
broadcast or recording business. There are
a number of different categories including
announcers, actors, singers, dancers, and
news people.

HOW MUCH MONEY DO YOUR MEMBERS MAKE?

I don't have any statistics to back this up,
but probably 2 percent of our members
make extremely good money, another 2 to 5
percent make good money, another 10
percent make a living. Everybody else
cannot depend on their entertainment
industry income alone to live on.

MOST OF THE PEOPLE INVOLVED IN THE MUSIC INDUSTRY DO NOT MAKE THEIR ENTIRE LIVING OFF IT. WOULD YOU LIKE TO ELABORATE ON THAT AT ALL?

There was a study by the U. S. Department
of Labor several years ago that studied

unemployment in the performing unions. There's been some criticism of the study because there is some overlap, and by that I mean that it's not unusual for a singer to also be a musician, and therefore to be a member of the musician's union, or for an actor to be a member of several different acting unions, such as the Actors' Equity Association, the Screen Actors Guild (SAG), and AFTRA. Each one of these unions covers a different area of acting. So there may be some leakage in the statistics from one category to another. However, the study found that the highest unemployment was the legitimate stage. Actors' Equity Association had something like 60 or 70 percent unemployment. Next came AFTRA, then the Screen Actors Guild, and then the American Federation of Musicians, and so on. The lowest unemployment rate for the most employed union was seven or eight times what the national unemployment rate is.

In this country we think that if we have 4 or 5 percent unemployment nationally, that's reasonable and within tolerable limits. It means 96 percent of all our people are employed. The lowest unemployment figure in our unions was something like 35 or 40 percent. We also find, in doing a profile of our people in the entertainment industry, that they have a higher educational level than the average worker in America; yet for their educational level, they make less money. We found that they spend more money on continuing education, compared again to the national average. For their level of continuing education money spent, they do not get as good a return. So it is a business where there is a great deal of unemployment and where people have to continually scramble for jobs.

IN VIEW OF THE HIGH UNEMPLOYMENT RATE, WHAT DO YOU ADVISE YOUNG ENTERTAINERS TO DO?

In advising young people who come through my office, I have found that the most successful are those who are prepared to do a number of different things. Above all, the most important ingredient is, I believe, that they are willing to hustle and create opportunities for themselves. I think that that ability to find employment, or to generate a project that will create employment for themselves, is the single most important skill that they can acquire.

Let me give you an example of that. It used to be that singers grew up and maybe sang with a band in high school. They sort of gravitated into the entertainment business. They kicked around and worked on the road, one thing and another. They learned their trade the hard way. I don't mean to criticize that at all, but I have seen more and more people come to Nashville who are school-trained musicians and vocalists. They have degrees in music. They can read music; they know composition; they can arrange; they can do charts. While they're trying to break into, let's say, background singing, they go around and find out who needs some lead sheets done. They employ themselves doing lead sheets or arrangements, or they get a gig in a nightclub or a motel lounge to keep themselves going. They're continually trying to generate income for themselves by employing their different skills.

Suppose someone, a youngster of fifteen, came to me and said, "I want to be in the music business. I love music. I love to sing. I love to play." I would say, "Go bury yourself in a good music school somewhere and learn all that you can, because the better skills you have, the more employable you are." It's not that I think that practical experience and performing experience is bad; I think it's very important. But being able to do arrangements, write charts, and do lead sheets—being able to read music and being a quick study—comes from learning the discipline that you get through formal training. Being able to play two or three instruments well is important. There are some people here who are so successful that when singing sessions are scarce, they make money as musicians.

What I'm saying is you need to be a well-rounded performer. We're seeing now, in Nashville at least, singers branching out into acting, trying to acquire other skills in addition to their basic musical skills. And I think that's very good. They will be the survivors.

WHAT ABOUT THE STAR SYSTEM? WHAT DO YOU THINK ABOUT A SINGER WHO ACTUALLY BUILDS HIS REPUTATION AND SELLS RECORDS BECAUSE OF HIS IMAGE?

I think the star system is a fact of life. No two people get into the business the same way. It's not like going to college, then to graduate school to get a Master's Degree, and then going to work in the engineering department at Lockheed. There's no standard route into the industry.

I have been told by other lawyers that somehow they acquire a reputation for making a big deal with a record company for a particular artist. That word spreads around and generates other business for them. Other artists say, "Well, if that lawyer made a big deal with XYZ Record Company, then he/she must be able to deal with that record company. I can go to them and get what I want in a recording contract." Sometimes it's good and sometimes it's bad. Eventually, if you've got an unwarranted reputation, I think it takes care of itself. But because it's a fast moving industry, we depend on the gossip, the word in the street, and the visibility. I suppose there is some valid criticism that we're a surface industry, to a certain extent, and people go on surface images.

NASHVILLE'S LIKE A MAGNET. YOUNG PEOPLE COME HERE TRYING TO GET INTO THE ENTERTAINMENT INDUSTRY. WHAT ADVICE WOULD YOU GIVE THEM?

The first thing I tell everybody, because I've lived through it myself, is that if you want to do it, do it. I was twenty-eight; I had finished law school and had worked for a corporation for two and a half years. I was making good money and I had to take a cut to get into the business. But I was told that if I didn't do it then, I would wake up one day with a wife and two kids and a mortgage, and I'd probably be miserable for the rest of my life.

Secondly, I think you should do it as intelligently as possible. Gather all the background information that you can. It's very difficult, but not impossible, to do it long-distance. If you want to pitch songs, if you're writing songs and you want to get them recorded in Nashville, then you've just about got to be in Nashville most of the time. Once you're an established writer and have a relationship with somebody in Nashville, you may be able to handle it by mail and by phone.

Then you've got to be prepared for some period of initiation, some period of having to wait until a ship comes in or until you can get some employment in the industry. This alludes to what I said earlier. I don't think you can come here, pitch your tent, and expect to live off your employment in the music industry. In my experience, the industry is a business that is, at least in Nashville, a contradiction. While it's not quick to accept new people, it is very open to helping new people. I think maybe the contradiction is that you've got to spend some time acclimating yourself to the pace here. You have to find out who the people are who make decisions and which of those people are open to helping new people. To some extent, you've got to be willing to come in here and make some contributions yourself.

I encourage people to come here because I think the more creative people there are, the more creative things will happen, and that will make us a genuine entertainment center. So be prepared for some adversity. Prepare yourself economically, have a plan to find a job doing something that will enable you to spend some time getting in the industry, whether it's writing or pitching songs or singing or whatever. Come and do it.

CHAPTER SIX

ARTIST MANAGEMENT

Artist managers are people who manage an artist's career. Sounds pretty simple, but it's a little more complicated than that. A manager provides a guiding force in the artist's life. Unfortunately, entertainers lead more complex lives than most people do, and many of the decisions are also complex. Daily decisions involve thousands of dollars and sometimes the artist's entire career.

First of all, there is an image the artist must live up to. There's the possibility that the artist will make some type of public mistake, say or do something that will hurt or destroy his image. Falling out of public favor destroys record sales and means a loss of money from concert tours; in the long run, it means the loss of the record-company contract. For a recording artist, sometimes it's feast or famine. Most artists are on the famine trip all of their lives. Music centers—such as New York, Nashville, and Los Angeles—are full of taxicab drivers, waitresses, and short-order cooks who feel deep down in their hearts that it's only a matter of time before they're discovered.

On the other hand, when you're famous, everybody wants you. Television, record companies, promotion people—everybody wants your time. You have to do personal appearances, recording sessions, concert tours, talk shows, even interviews for books. All this creates an emotional stress; you're busy all the time without having any privacy. As Jerry Reed said, "When you're hot, you're hot."

It is life on a shoestring, or it's a life with all the riches that money can deliver.

As a result, the artist needs someone he can trust to help him with his personal and career decisions. Artists must make career decisions almost every day of their lives, so they turn over the decisions to their managers.

The manager will use his years of experience to make career decisions for the artist. He will help pick the correct songs for the artist's album or 45 rpm record. The songs have to fit the artist and his image; they have to keep the old fans and draw new ones. Radio air play and phonograph records must build the artist's image.

The manager will supervise the building

and the presentation of a stage show. A stage presence that fits the artist's image is essential. The show must be quality entertainment, or people leave disappointed and won't buy the artist's next album. Each personal appearance must fit the image that the fans and public have of that artist.

The manager will represent the artist in dealing with the record company. Besides overseeing the contract, the manager must fight for his artist in competing with the other artists on the label. He wants to make sure that his artist receives the proper amount of promotion and gratuities from the record company. The manager also supervises the recording projects. This includes the recording process in the studio and the design of album covers to fit the image of the artist.

The manager also represents the artist in all financial aspects. This includes the artist's payroll, taxes, and business with CPAs. It also includes supervising the booking agents who are selecting concert tours and other booking agreements for the artist.

In all of this, the manager's prime responsibility is to be fair with the artist, to always work as hard as he can to represent the artist to the best of his abilities. The manager should use all of his personal contacts and experience in the music business to further the artist's career.

Managers have been described as everything from being honest and sincere about building an artist's career to being outright crooks. You'll find some of the most decent people you've ever wanted to meet, or you'll find them full of hot air and baloney. It really boils down to how well the manager does his job. Is he going to get the job done for you? If he does, then you both have formed a successful team. If he doesn't, you may have been ripped off, or opportunities might be lost.

Managers can charge any amount of money that they want. Most charge between 10 and 25 percent of the artist's gross income. Colonel Tom Parker received 50 percent of everything Elvis Presley made, and a lot of people were outraged by that. But the Colonel may have been one of the main factors for Elvis's success.

DAVID SKEPNER

Manager of Loretta Lynn; President of David Skepner & The Buckskin Company; Executive Vice President, Loretta Lynn Enterprises; Chairman of the Board, Nashville Entertainment Association; an officer of the Country Music Association; a part-time faculty member for Belmont College's School of Business; and is a requested speaker for the communications departments of many colleges and universities.

WHAT ADVICE DO YOU HAVE FOR SOMEONE STARTING OUT?

Many young people, trying to get into this business, are reluctant to take the first step. They are afraid of being turned down or rejected or the're bashful. That's their problem! A person in my position looks for drive and motivation. All I can do is give a little guidance. I'll say, "Try this" and if it works, then keep going. But they're the ones that must put the effort into their careers. In the early stages I can't and no one in my position will take them by the hand, and walk them through each stage of the game. I don't have the time because I've got to put the effort into those people who have shown the interest, talent, combined with the drive and desire.

On the other hand, I do pride myself on being available to give advice. I talk to the Opryland performers, and people who walk through the door. I teach at Belmont College and lecture almost whenever I'm asked.

SO WHAT ARE YOUNG "WANT-TO-BE ARTISTS" LACKING?

They're raw talent looking for a place to happen. When you make bread, you can only do so much with it. You've got to let it rise by itself, before it can be baked into bread.

Look at the *Billboard* charts for the last ten years. With the exception of Tanya Tucker, and one or two others, there's nobody (male or female) on those charts under 30 years of age. Ask yourself "why". The nature of country music songs (material) is heartache, cheating, drinking, and "life is tough". You can't look at a young performer and ask the average country music buyer, (who is female and 28 to 45 years old), to believe that this sweet angelic face has lived those songs. When Loretta Lynn sings a song about cheating, drinking, and life, you believe her. When Conway Twitty sings a song you believe him! There's not a believability in young entertainers. But they still have to get out there, and put their time in on the rock pile.

Kids come in here and ask "What do I do?" I tell them to first get a demo tape that shows what they are and where they are in terms of developing their talent. Then they've got to get that tape to the people in positions that can be helpful. Sometimes the street contacts are more important then someone like me. The street contacts are friends, who may give you a call when someone doesn't show up for a session. Once you're into the group, you'll start getting regular calls. But first you've got to make the calls on your own, and get in with the people who are all trying to do the same thing.

YOU'RE SAYING THAT THE YOUNG ARTISTS HAVE TO MAKE IT HAPPEN THEMSELVES?

Yes, they need to get off their rear ends! No one's coming to them. Anthony Quinn was on the "Tomorrow" show, talking about his early years, and Tom Synder asked, "You mean it's a case of being in the right place at the right time". Quinn sat back in his chair and said "No Tom, it's a case of being somewhere at the right time". The translation being, they're not coming to you; don't sit at home wondering why you're not a star. Get out, you've got to do the scut work. The harder I work, the luckier I get. That's a basic premise. It's the only way I know how to operate.

Identity is another thing. A lot of people want to be singers because their mother, church choir leader, or someone else likes their voice. But there's a big difference between being "good" and being "commercially marketable." What I look for in that one percent, which is what it amounts to, is identity. When I'm driving to work in the morning, and I punch the button on the radio, the voice I hear, must have identity. I have people in my office all the time saying, "Listen, I have the next Loretta Lynn, the next Eagles, or George Jones. I tell them "Hey, I wish you luck, but I won't talk to you."

I want an original! You have to be an original, if your going to be a success. Loretta says "You have to be first, best, or different, if your going to get anywhere."

Many people in an executive position will not give you an honest answer. It's tough because they don't want to hurt anyone's feelings! Some young artists don't get honest opinions and waste a lot of time. If people would just say "In my opinion, I don't think you've got what it takes", a lot of lives would be made easier. On the other hand, it's that drive and desire that may win out over all the so-called "experts."

WHAT'S CORPORATE SPONSORSHIP?

The biggest single factor to hit the entertainment business since MTV. It can be the perfect wedding of the talent, personality, and image, with the corporate dollars, that want to tie in with the positive association of that image. At the same time it gives the event promoter invaluable advertising dollars. That allows him to alter his budget. The act gets more money and the corporate sponsor gets an association that he previously didn't have. It's wonderful, if you have the right elements in the package and know how to use everything correctly.

WHAT SHOULD A PERFORMER BE CONCERNED ABOUT?

A performer has only a few things they need to concern themselves with. Those are your family, the songs you write, your stage show, and cutting the right records. I don't care what order they are in, but those are the things that constitute your life. Anything that you get involved in, that takes you away from those things, is wrong because it robs you of the time you need. People come to me with get-rich-schemes. She's (Loretta) getting rich if she does the other things right. She doesn't need this other stuff.

WHAT'S THE MOST IMPORTANT THING A PROSPECTIVE MANAGER SHOULD HAVE?

Education! They have to learn the elements of the artist's career they are going to be dealing with as a manager. They have to know how record companies operate. They have to know how television operates, good and bad. It's a tool that they must learn to use. They have to know how a booking agency operates, and public relations firms work. You can't give direction if you don't know what you want and how to get there.

The manager must give direction to these companies on behalf of their artist. To go in and negotiate a record contract, you must know what it's all about. Otherwise, you're at the mercy of the company, who will give you a 56-page contract and say "sign here." That happens and it happens every day. Depending on the kind of client you have, you must spend five to ten years in the trenches learning how to make that contract work for your client. And then you still need the best attorney and accountant you can find.

You must be an expert in some areas and get people to back you up in the areas you don't know. I am not a lawyer or accountant, but I can get the best. I think I know how record companies, talent agencies, booking agencies, and public relation firms operate. That is my long suit. My job is to keep things happening and to make sure that all these people are in sync, all going in the same direction at the same time and with the same objectives. The only way I can get the best for my client is to know these areas as well as they do. That is not an ego thing, it's simply knowledge that has been acquired over twelve years at MCA and over thirteen with Loretta Lynn.

DO YOU HAVE SEVERAL THINGS GOING AT ONCE?

What the public and your client see is the success. What they don't see is what you're doing until success emerges. It's like juggling a handful of B-B's. Every time you throw them into the air, most fall to the floor and disappear and some fall back into your hand. The ones you end up with, in your hand, are the ones the public sees —success!

GENE FERGUSON

Artist manager of John Anderson and Charly McClain.
Formerly with Columbia Records
in promotion and management.

YOU HANDLE A COUPLE OF ARTISTS, CHARLY McCLAIN AND JOHN ANDERSON.
Charly is on CBS and John is on Warner Bros. I think both of them are very good success stories, but I have two great artists to work with, two very talented people.

I left CBS in July of 1978 and started with Charly McClain. In fact, she came to me and asked me if I would manage her.

HOW DID YOU MEET JOHN ANDERSON?
I was down at Warner Bros. because I had friends there. I was getting a soda, and I heard this voice through the wall. There was something in this voice that just woke me up, maybe reminded me of Lefty Frizzell. I knocked on the door, and I said, "Who in the world was that singing?"

Norro Wilson, whom I've known forever, said, "Oh, it's a boy we've got here on the label." I asked if they were going to do anything for him and Norro said, "I don't know."

I said, "It's unbelievable, Norro; that guy can sing that well, and you give me an answer like that." So he said, "Well, why don't you manage him?"

Time passed and finally I met John. I had no idea he would look the way he did because he sounded like he was forty. Here he was twenty-seven years old and had long, blond hair. It just doesn't sound like that voice could come out of that face. It's a big part of John Anderson's charm.

SO YOU BECAME THEIR MANAGER. WHAT DID YOU DO TO START?
Now this was the first time that I tried to manage anything on my own, to create something on my own, without the support of CBS. Suddenly it was just myself and one act who's a boy and one act who's a girl. So we started. Thank God for my twenty-three years of experience with CBS.

To me, the biggest thing you have to do is create a demand for the artist. The first thing I'd like to say about management is that. (I had always hoped I'd never be a manager. I never trusted them, didn't like them. I thought they were con artists, left and right. I never saw a manager until an act got big,

112

and all the years I worked at CBS, I can only remember two—Tanya Tucker's father and Barbara Mandrell's father. Those are the only managers I ever met, in all those years, who ever came to me and said, "What can I do to help this career?")

At any rate, I asked the people at Warner Bros. if I could use their mailroom. I was mailing out about 2,000 flyers on John a week. I designed them myself, Xeroxed them, folded them. Warners was good enough to let me use their equipment. I was keeping everybody informed about John's records, how the records were doing. This was to build his image and to give some identification to his face that went with the record.

HOW ABOUT CHARLY?
Charly already had a pretty good start. When I was at CBS, I was using CBS' facilities to help her. When I left, I was at a point where I could devote all my time to her. I can give all my time to John and I can give all my time to Charly because they're in different areas at different times.

Charly is beautiful. Quite honestly, I don't think there's a more beautiful country singer going, bar none. She's just it. She's one of the hardest-working people you'll ever see. She averages about 22 days a month working live dates. That may not sound like a lot to people, but you've got to remember you've got to get there, too. Some of the dates are hundreds of miles apart. If you figure the club work, say eight days a month basically (that's every Friday and Saturday), you can see how much more she's working during the week.

She is a tremendously hard worker. John's the same way. Charly's almost too business-like, but that's her make-up and her way of doing things. I think, as she comes along and gets a little more stable in what she's doing, then she'll learn to enjoy things more and not worry about so many things.

John's the other side of the coin. He likes to fish a lot and have a good time. So I have to rattle John pretty good to make sure that

he doesn't get in trouble for things he forgets. But he learns extremely fast.

THEY ARE BOTH GOOD EXAMPLES OF DIFFERENT PERSONALITIES OF ARTISTS.
The thing I like about both of my artists is their loyalty, their honesty, and their work. I'm sure my personality is plain weird to them at times. It's almost to the point where I don't feel that I have any identification at all. All I'm doing for them is reciting twenty-five years of what's happened. I'm going by the percentages. If we do this, the percent says this will happen. If we don't, the percent is low. Without my past, I couldn't figure the percentages.

IT NEVER REALLY HURTS TO GO WHERE THE CHANCES OF SUCCESS ARE BETTER.
I think you have to because too many new artists are coming up. We have to be very selective in the material that we pick. We have a lot of problems because we have a lot of friends who are songwriters. They're bound to get angry when we don't cut their songs. I have to avoid all of that and make sure my artist gets the best song possible.

YOU REALLY ARE IN CHARGE OF TWO PERSONS' LIVES.
Absolutely. We talk about records, but if an artist is big enough, the things that stem from a record career are phenomenal—commercials, television, movies. And it goes on and on as to how big you can be. It doesn't necessarily stop at records.

DO YOU DEMAND LOYALTY TO YOU AND YOUR JUDGMENTS?
We work everything out together. I don't think it's right for a manager to jump up in the air and say, "You can't do this, and you can't do that." Nobody should govern lives like that. I think managers who do that do it because they don't know the answer.

I can sit here and no matter what either one of my acts tells me—and they're both the same age—whatever they ask me, I can sit here and explain to them the percentage of going this way or going that way. I give them every option possible.

They should at least understand what they're doing and why they have to do that. Sometimes it may be short money to clubs; sometimes it might be leaving a club one night at twelve o'clock and catching the plane and going to Los Angeles to do a television show. I have to figure out how many millions of viewers watch, is it in prime time, and so on. It gets so complicated that if I were starting tomorrow, I'd probably quit.

WHAT ARE SOME OF THE FINANCIAL RESPONSIBILITIES OF A MANAGER?

When a contract comes up with a label, then you have to make the decision, with the artist, if you want to stay with that label. It gets down to business at that point.

It's not a case of loyalty. I wish I could say it was. When you don't sell with a label, you're gone. They have no loyalty toward you.

What do you need if you're going to sign a contract? Dollars up front are an important factor, but I wouldn't say it's the main factor. One label could offer you $400,000 more than another label, but it may cost you $2 million over a five-year haul because you took the $400,000. You have to be very careful. You must figure in the strength of the label.

You have to know their promotion staff, where they're located, how well they're governed. Who pays for the sessions? Is it charged back to the artist, or is the company going to pick it up? When you get into that, you really start flipping pages and writing a lot of notes as to what you want done. Today it's gotten to the point where, if it's not written down, you have no recourse whatsoever. You've got to have it down there, or they'll blow you off. It's unbelievable.

SO YOU'RE IN CHARGE OF YOUR ART-IST'S CAREER, BUILDING AN IMAGE, AND

THEIR FINANCIAL INCOME. IS THERE ANYTHING ELSE?

There's one thing that's really important to me. It might be a personal thing—and I hope to God it works in my favor—but it's that they come out of this business with *something*.

I've seen more artists have the big shot, take it, make a lot of money, and go broke. hardly feel sorry for them. I hope we have enough sense to decide between a rhine-stone fly swatter or a 100,000-acre ranch. You have to have the money because our country is built that way. I don't care what they say, it's a monetary thing. Everything you do is based on your monetary value. Security is important to me because I've seen so many people throw it away.

The two artists I have can stay in the business as long as they want, if things are governed right and if they cut the right product for the people. They may not stay as hot record-wise, but by that time I may have them into films.

IT'S REALLY HARD ON THE ARTIST, ISN'T IT?

It is, it's extremely hard. I give artists all the credit in the world for what they're doing.

IT'S NOT REALLY FOR THE MONEY FIRST. IT'S FOR THE LOVE OF WHAT THEY WANT TO DO.

No, I don't think it's money first. I hope it's money later, because I want them to be money-conscious. Every Holiday Inn, every club you go into has got somebody singing. The clubs can't pay much, but the singers like the atmosphere. They like the night life. It's their kind of life.

Ego plays a big part, too. They want to be somebody, which I think everybody does. I think that's great that you have that initiative to get up and want to be somebody.

I want to prove to them that I'm one of the first honest managers that's hit this town and done it right. I preach to them, quite hon-estly, that I have never been a money-conscious person. I can get along on what-ever it takes, but I want them to be money-conscious.

When an artist hits, so-called friends come out of the woodwork. We lost twenty acts one year to Los Angeles because everybody said, "You want management, booking agents? West Coast. Nobody in Nashville can handle it; they're goons. They're Southerners; they can't do any-thing."

I don't think what we do is magic, and I don't think it deserves any pat on the back. We get paid for what we do, and we work hard at it. But we don't waste any time, or we waste a minimum amount of time, going in the wrong directions. We know exactly where we're going, how to fortify everything we're going to do, and what action we should take at that point.

WHAT QUALITIES DO YOU LOOK FOR IN AN ARTIST YOU ARE GOING TO MANAGE?

If the person has the talent that I feel is commercial, then I want the person to be straight, honest, a hard worker—someone who wants the same things I want in life, someone who wants to progress.

I have so many people come to me and ask me how to get in this business. Before I ever answer them, I like to tell them to go home, because they have no idea what it's like. They think you cut a record and the record hits. You sign autographs, and they shower you with money. It does not work that way at all. On-stage is a small percent of the headaches that go with it.

HOW DO YOU, AS A MANAGER, SELECT A RECORD COMPANY FOR YOUR ARTIST?

You pick the record company based on the ones that are eating the charts up—the ones having the best track record at that time. They do turn over. You'll have companies who will suddenly lose a lot of people because of an austerity program. You'll have another company that will be building at that

time. If you're lucky, you can hit the right one when your contract's up. You may not want to leave. If the company is doing everything for you that you want, there's no point in leaving. For a few thousand dollars, it's really not worth it.

HOW ABOUT SELECTING A BOOKING AGENT?

As far as the booking agent goes, and I'll apply this to the record company also, it's the one who feels that your artist is what they want. Not to take him as a favor, or to do you a favor, but a booking agent that says, "Everything that I represent, or the large percent, loves that type of an act, and I feel I can book him. I can make money on him. If he makes money, everybody makes money." That's the thing. Somebody that's honestly interested in the artist's career.

WHAT ABOUT PRODUCERS?

Charly's a perfect example. She had a producer for four years, and—I guess I'll have to take the blame for it—I asked her to change producers. The key to the thing was I felt her producer wasn't giving her strong enough material. I noticed that a lot of the material was coming out of the same places; the publishing companies were the same. This told me that he wasn't getting the best for the act itself. I discussed this with Charly, and it took about two years to make the move. We weren't consistent with her prod-uct. We'd get a Top 8 record, then the next record would be a Top 17, then we'd go to a Top 7, and the next record would be 24.

SO YOU REALLY HAD TO TAKE A HARD LOOK AT THAT AND CONVINCE HER THAT SHE NEEDED A FRESH LOOK.

Nothing against her old producer at all. It could have been me. But they had done five albums, which is fifty songs. Within that span, I felt that we should have done much better. The better records we can get, the easier it is for everybody.

115

SOMETIMES YOU NEED A FRESH APPROACH.

The artists all change producers. They all change booking agents. It's like fresh life each time you do that. It's just so important to find the right combination.

HOW ABOUT SELECTION OF SONGS?

Selection of songs, that's an interesting one. In many cases the artist will come in and dictate, or the producer will dictate what he wants. We have sort of an unwritten standard agreement among the two artists that I work with that the artist, the producer, and myself will agree on the songs we do. Each one of us has to agree on a song.

WHAT ADVICE WOULD YOU GIVE TO PEOPLE WHO WANT TO GET INTO THE INDUSTRY?

I would say to know what you want to do and have some plans. Invariably, people come into this town, hang out in the bars, and ask the wrong people where to go. They don't get with the right people.

One of the quickest ways to get started is to cut your own record. If you can get it going in a major city, I wouldn't care where it came from. You take it to a label and say, "This record's doing great." They'll check it out and, if it is, they may buy that record and you can get on a label.

Other than that, it's going to be very difficult, unless your daddy owns a record company.

SO WHAT YOU'RE SAYING IS, IF YOU WANT TO BE A SONGWRITER OR A RECORDING ARTIST, YOU MIGHT TRY IT IN YOUR OWN CITY. SEE WHAT THE PEOPLE THERE THINK FIRST.

That's a good way to do it. I wouldn't come here under any illusions that you can get a label, that you'll be the biggest thing in the nation. By the same token, I guess if people didn't do it, we might not have any major artists.

HOW ABOUT ON THE ROAD? AN ARTIST MAY MAKE $10,000 A NIGHT. APPROXIMATELY HOW MUCH DOES IT COST FOR THE BUS, THE MUSICIANS, AND SO FORTH?

If they can net 30 percent, they're really doing well. You figure a manager, for instance, gets 15 percent of their earnings, and that's the low end. I've known some that have gone as high as 50 percent, but there's a lot of things entailed there, too. The booking agent gets 15 percent. Gas bills are unbelievable when you start filling buses, trucks.

PLUS THE SALARIES OF THE BAND MEMBERS.

Taxes on top of that. It's not what it looks like, at all. It's a lot tougher.

Ego helps keep everybody going a little bit. The bigger you get, the more you have to spend to get to the top.

A MISTAKE THAT I SEE PEOPLE MAKING IS HIRING TOO MANY PEOPLE FOR THEIR STAFFS.

This happened with another one of our artists just recently. I understand he had to sell his tractor trailers and let his lighting crew go. What it amounts to is the artist wants to perform well for the public, but what does the public want? Do people want to see the fire, smoke, and brimstone, or do they really just want to see the act? I think there's a fine line between underdoing it and overdoing it.

HOW IMPORTANT IS PERFORMING TO AN ARTIST?

When artists are on-stage, that would be 100 percent of the business. When they're off-stage, it's zero percent of the business. The singing is a very small part of the overall picture. But, to the fan, it's the only picture.

When you get off-stage, there's the harassment of the people; there's the traveling to the next place; and there are the contracts, the photo sessions, the studio recording sessions. When you go out to sing, you're talking about a 40-minute show.

Your whole life evolves around 99 percent of the music business off-stage and 1 percent on-stage, but that is the only part the audience knows about.

HOW MUCH DOES AN ARTIST MAKE ON A ONE-NIGHT GIG?

They vary in price, but they have a bottom figure, and they always say, "Don't go below that figure." You can go as high as you can get. But, again, that's based on their demand and what you can get.

DO YOU TELL THE BOOKING AGENCY WHAT YOU WANT OR DOES THE BOOKING AGENCY GET WHAT IT CAN GET?

Well, since they make 15 percent, it behooves them to get as much as they can. We do have to push them a lot of times. To be honest, sometimes they don't worry about how much an artist travels, as long as their money is coming in.

From my point of view, I have to protect the artist. Even though it might cost me a little, it's better for me to keep the artist healthy, and working longer, because we don't have thirty acts to turn to.

TANDY RICE

Chairman of the Board and founder of Top Billing International (a Nashville artist booking agency).

AS A MANAGER OF RECORDING ART-ISTS, WHAT DO YOU FEEL YOUR JOB RESPONSIBILITIES ARE?

We help the artists set business goals for their lives and make decisions with career advancement being the criterion. So we help them react intelligently to opportunities that come to them.

We also generate opportunities. We cause certain things to happen. We come up with publicity campaigns for them; we come up with campaigns for their albums that are out. We specifically come up with interviews for television, radio, print media campaigns. We specifically come up with cover costuming ideas, stage show ideas.

Every dimension of their professional life is what we're involved in. If we're successful, it's really measured once a year when the Internal Revenue Service says, "Fill out this form." That's the bottom line.

HOW DO YOU BUILD AN ENTERTAINER'S CAREER?

First of all, we analyze what we're trying to sell and what the sales points of this particu-lar artist are. Then we do everything we can to come down hard on accentuating the positive, eliminating the negative.

YOU HAVE A LOT OF CONTROL OVER AN ARTIST'S LIFE.

Oh, no question about it. The bottom line is, I handle 100 percent of all the monies that several million-dollar-income-producers generate. Oh, you can make mistakes, but you can't make too many of them. You can't make them too frequently. The one thing you can never do is violate a trust; that's the one inexcusable thing you just can't do.

If you ever breach a confidence or violate a trust, you're not worthy of managing anything for anybody, period. It doesn't matter whether they generate $5 million dollars a year or 50 cents.

SO YOU FEEL HONESTY IS THE BEST POLICY IN THIS CASE.

Oh, it's the only policy. The relationship between an artist and his manager has to be so special that they share a common bond of trust and affection. They have to share affection.

We share dreams with each other. If you can't share dreams and hopes and ambitions, then you don't have the cement that's necessary when those strong winds come. And they do come. That's the tie that binds; that's the bond right there.

SO THIS IS REALLY A TEAMWORK EFFORT.

Oh, it's got to be. No question about it. Of course, there are different kinds of teams. But this is a team, and one of the things I insist on is that I call all the shots. I don't want to be a manager in name only.

WHAT IS YOUR BIGGEST PROBLEM WITH ANY OF YOUR ARTISTS?

That's not an easy question to answer. Of course we always have personal problems. I would say hit records. Hit records are so important to us, and we're so totally dependent on somebody across town for that. You feel rather helpless. We hope and pray and do everything we can to get ready to capitalize on the hit records.

Our Creative Services part is our hedge against being totally dependent on hit records. And we're at a point now where we have seven or eight artists who have their own television shows. If we just had one artist who had his own TV show, that would be a blessing, but we've got a whole bunch of them that do. And that, very frankly, generates more impact than a hit record.

YOU MENTIONED PERSONAL PROBLEMS. WHAT KIND OF PERSONAL PROBLEMS? IS THERE A LOT OF EXTERNAL PRESSURE THAT CAUSES PROBLEMS?

The more successful we are, the stronger the pressures are. The stronger the demand to be gone from home, the stronger the pressures are on you when you return. And it takes a real, real mature attitude and a great sense of humor to be able to cope. I've read so much about coping with stress in the eighties. It seems we're all under such incredible stress. Coping with just the routine stresses of living is a problem. You add to that the stresses of being a celebrity and the high profile—you wouldn't believe the letters I get.

BUT A LOT OF PEOPLE WOULD LIKE TO BECOME STARS. HOW DO YOU HANDLE A PERSON THAT'S GOT A LOT OF ENTHUSIASM BUT DOESN'T HAVE THE ABILITY?

It's a very delicate thing because we don't want to be rude and gruff and painful. Those people never forget how that moment is handled. They come to you with a dream. I'm not trying to romanticize or dramatize what we do here. But I remember what it was like in 1964, when I wanted to be somebody so bad I could taste it. I'd go to see some of the big shots. I'd try to get help, and they'd laugh at me. Or they wouldn't have time to talk to me. That hurts. So we try our best never to hurt people, but we turn them away by the scores. I'd say we average between thirty and forty a week.

WHERE DO YOU FEEL COMPETITION COMES IN?

I think competition is a healthy thing. If you haven't got competition, you're in the wrong business. I don't care whether it's teaching in college or in the banking business.

My point is competition is vital and necessary. In this particular business, we are unique because we don't have ethical standards, codes of conduct, the way accountants or doctors or lawyers do. You can get out of the penitentiary after having slain fifty people and robbed two hundred banks. You can walk right out of there and put up a sign that says, "I'm a personal manager." There are no restrictions whatsoever.

WHAT WOULD YOU TELL YOUNG PEOPLE WHO WANT TO GET INTO THIS BUSINESS AS A BOOKING AGENT OR A MANAGER?

First thing you ought to do is go to Belmont College. I'm a backer of the school. I'm on the Board of Advisors over there. If they definitely want to get into the music industry, then they must go there or to Middle Tennessee State University and take advantage of that knowledge. The only problem, of course, is it's such a fun, glamorous, exciting course, everybody wants to take it, and there are too few jobs available.

A person must absolutely decide that's what he wants to do. I've got a theory that once somebody decides to do anything—and more specifically, makes a decision to get in the music industry—the logic, hardships, obstacles, and all of that is really secondary. You can get around the obstacles. You can live through the hardships. My theory is if they want to get in bad enough, you can't talk them out of it anyway.

JOE SULLIVAN

President of Sound Seventy Concert Promotions; artist manager for the Charlie Daniels Band, Dobie Gray, Jimmy Hall, and Nicolette Larson.

***LET'S TALK ABOUT ARTIST MANAGE-
MENT, BECAUSE I KNOW YOU MANAGE
SOME TERRIFIC ARTISTS. HOW DID YOU
GET INTO THAT?***
It's a good story. On February 10, 1973, I
had a concert at War Memorial Auditorium
here in Nashville. Quicksilver and Blue
Oyster Cult were the opening acts. I got a
call, about noon on the day of the show,
from Blue Oyster Cult's road manager. They
were snowed in somewhere in South Caro-
lina. No way they could get out.

I had to come up with a replacement fast,
and through a local agent here in town,
Bobby Smith, I got two bands—Charlie
Daniels and a group called Flat Creek. Flat
Creek opened the show and Charlie Daniels
followed. Somewhere during the show, I
came into the building, into the auditorium,
and everybody was up. I didn't realize that
there was a local artist that could get that
kind of crowd reaction.

I met Charlie backstage and we talked.
He's the kind of guy I felt like I'd known all
his life. One thing led to another, and I got
into management. I told him, "I don't know

anything about it, but I'm willing to learn. I'll
just promise you that I'll make some mistakes, but I'll never make the same mistake
twice."

The group Flat Creek consisted of Tommy
and Billy Crain. Tommy now plays in Charlie
Daniels' band and Billy, his younger brother,
plays in the Henry Paul Band, which I
manage. There's something about that night
that was meant to be, I think.

***AS A MANAGER OF ARTISTS, DO YOU
DEMAND 100 PERCENT BACKING OF
YOUR DECISIONS?***
That has to be. If I have to call the artist and
get his permission to make a decision, he
might as well be managing himself. Charlie
Daniels and I made an agreement when we
first went into it. He plays guitar, sings, and
writes songs. I do all the business. We've
both stuck to that pretty well.

***HOW DO YOU SELECT ARTISTS YOU
WANT TO MANAGE? IS IT A GUT FEELING?***
It's somewhat of a gut feeling and, of
course, there are so many more artists than

there are managers. I probably turn down half a dozen to a dozen a month. A lot of them, I know, are talented and could make it, but it's just a matter of how many you can do a good job for. We've limited it to six for the time being, although we might try to take on a seventh at some point. Basically, I don't go out to find an act; all the ones that I manage pretty much come to me. A lot of them, I had met through concert promotion.

THEY ARE RESPONSIBLE PEOPLE.

Yes. There are some groups that I could go after that are selling half a million albums, maybe, but I wouldn't touch them because they're just irresponsible. Drinking problems. Drug problems. I don't need those kinds of headaches.

WHAT IS THE NUMBER-ONE THING YOU DO AS A MANAGER FOR THE GROUPS?

Long-range career planning is the number-one thing. And then the execution of that career plan. I sit down with an artist. We put together a game plan to reach that long-range goal. Each year we say, "What do we want to achieve this year?" And we set down certain goals.

Of course, I do all the major contract negotiations and so forth for them. My attorney in New York also gets involved in that pretty heavily.

IS THERE A SHORTAGE OF BUSINESS PEOPLE WHO ARE QUALIFIED TO MANAGE ARTISTS?

Yes, definitely. I would welcome another three or four really qualified artists' managers in this town. It would take a little pressure off me, because I really hate to turn away an artist who has what it takes to make it. The town's full of them.

WHERE DO YOU THINK WE COULD GET THOSE PEOPLE? DO THEY NEED TO HAVE

A BUSINESS BACKGROUND, DO THEY JUST NEED TO HAVE AN UNDERSTANDING OF THE INDUSTRY, OR BOTH?

A little bit of both. I think you have to know business because it is a business. You've got to be able to sit down and look at a profit-and-loss statement and see where you can cut costs so that the artist saves some money and ends up with something.

Many times, a career blossoms after about ten or twelve years. The guy will have maybe a four- or five-year streak of making a whole lot of money. Then it levels off again, and maybe goes to nothing again. I like to think that for the artists I manage, if they ever make it big and then the bottom falls out for them at some point, they're going to have enough money to live the rest of their lives comfortably. So many don't. So many spend it as fast as it comes in. A manager has to be in a position to influence the artist to put away some of his money to invest it in various good investments.

WHERE DO YOU MAKE YOUR MONEY AS A MANAGER?

Generally, it's a percentage of the artist's gross income. I think most managers work that way. There are some arrangements where the artist and the manager go into business together. They're both working on a net profit basis.

WHAT ABOUT ELVIS PRESLEY AND COLONEL PARKER, THE 50-50 DEAL?

My theory is that 50 percent of something is worth a whole lot more than 100 percent of nothing. As talented as Elvis Presley was, without Colonel Parker in the early stages . . . I think the man was a genius. I think he masterminded a whole career plan that kept Elvis a superstar when a lot of other superstars in that era were fading away. In that particular case, I would have to say that the man was not overpaid for what he did.

CHAPTER SEVEN

PRODUCERS

A record producer oversees the production of records—not the actual manufacture, but the recording and engineering of the sound. He is usually responsible for assembling the recording team: the engineer, the studio musicians, and other personnel. He will work with the artists assembled to hopefully record a record that the public will want to hear—and buy.

A record producer must have years of professional experience, musical and technical knowledge, and a knack for knowing what the public wants to hear.

The producer must first select the right song for the artist. He has to know the vocal abilities and personality of the recording artist to find the song that fits. The artist must sell the song by how well he or she performs it. Sometimes a great song won't hit until the proper recording artist sings it. Take "The Gambler" as an example. Don Schlitz recorded it before Kenny Rogers, but it was the Kenny Rogers' single of "The Gambler" that really took off and became a smash hit. Sometimes it has to do with believability of how well the artist sang the

song. Other times it has to do with the feel that comes from the recording session itself.

Producers must have a thorough love and understanding of music. It's the understanding of music that allows a producer to be innovative and to tolerate all of the hype in the music business. He must be able to produce different types of music and go with the flow when the public demands a new style or trend.

Producers possess the additional talent of being able to get along with—and at the same time, lead or direct—creative artists, musicians, and engineers so that these people perform to the best of their abilities. Creative people can be and are unique. That's not putting them down at all. It's just a simple fact that creative people in any type of business can be hard to work with. In the music business, a recording session can resemble a circus if the producer loses control. Most recording artists realize that the producer is there to *help* them. Producers and recording artists rely on each other's talent to put together potential hit records.

Producers must have one more essential

talent—they've got to have "ears." Ears is the ability to hear a potential hit song. This is usually established through years of listening to tons and tons of songs. It is also the ability to hear the marriage of a song to a recording artist, and to hear a recording that is in the grooves. Judgments are always based on the producer's own personal opinion of what the public will enjoy. He's got to trust his "ears." Today many individual producers are recording music in innovative ways that may catch the public's ear and create a new trend of the future.

Almost everyone wants to be a producer. Unfortunately few of us have the talents, guts, or craziness to qualify. Audio engineers, artists' managers, and almost everybody else in the music business would like to produce. Few will make it. For those who do, they'll make a small fortune. But the work will drive them crazy. Successful producers are always hassled by everyone who wants to get into the music business. Believe me, they barely have time to produce the artist they are currently working with, let alone someone who is an unknown.

If you want to get into the music industry, a lot of people can honestly help you. Publishers, record company A&R persons, and even artists' managers are looking for talented people. If you're good enough, they can get you in to see a producer. Being referred by a quality person in the music industry is the best way to meet a producer.

There are legitimate producers who work on a lower level, cutting demo sessions. Many of them can be helpful in judging your talent and giving some direction to your career. Many have important contacts within the music industry itself. But remember that if you have to pay money, then you may be getting ripped off. Producers who really believe in your talent will usually incur the expense of the demo session in exchange for a percentage of your career. If they make you pay, question their sincerity. Better still, find a producer who believes in you enough to spend his own money. If you can't find one, maybe you should spend the money on a trip to Los Angeles, New York, or Nashville and try to meet the right people.

Producers may receive $1,000 to $2,000 per side (each song) they record. They also receive points (a percentage of the money the record company receives from record sales). Everything is negotiable—the more famous the producer the more points he can negotiate to receive. It is not unusual for the handful of top producers to make a million dollars a year.

NORRO WILSON

President of Merit Music Corporation.
Record producer for RCA Records, recording artist, and
songwriter. Former director of Warner Bros. Records,
Nashville. Artists produced include Charly McClain,
John Anderson, Mickey Gilley, Charley Pride,
and Reba McEntire.

**WHAT DO YOU THINK MAKES A
HIT SONG?**

That melody, that great little melody.
Whether it is simple or complex, it reaches
the emotions of the human being. Then you
need a matching lyric that is comparable. To
me, that's a perfect marriage, and it usually
works. I don't think we ever know the pure
secrets of what it would take, or we'd all be
very, very wealthy at this point.

To me, there is the music and then there is
the music business. Music is a commodity
we're dealing with. We're message carriers
of some sort. What we're trying to do is write
and record songs that sell to the public as a
reflection of human emotions.

When you can grasp those human emotions, put them in a little sack, shake them
up with some music and lyrics, and spill out
the mixture, if the mixture falls right, people
buy it.

Some people can hear commercial
material, and some people can't. Usually
great arrangers, people who have a great
deal of musical theory or musical knowledge, are never worth a damn at writing a
song or producing records. Some folks don't
have a clue about a hot lick. They don't have
a clue about a Major Seventh, about that
guitar taking that wild, screaming ride; they
just hear it, and there is something about it
they like.

**SO YOU'RE SAYING THAT MUSIC IS A
FORM OF COMMUNICATION?**

Yes. The record business is a communica-
tion business. It's music all over the world.
We still sing everything from "Jesus Loves
Me" to all our national anthems.

**WHEN YOU PRODUCE SOMEBODY, YOU
MUST TAKE INTO CONSIDERATION THE
HUMAN FEELINGS THAT PERSON HAS.
HOW DO YOU GET THE MOST CREATIVITY
OUT OF THE ARTIST YOU'RE
PRODUCING?**

I may work differently from most producers,
but I'd have to say that I get the most out of
people by being lighthearted. I just refuse to
let the artists and musicians come in and
feel bad. Music is positive; it's not a negative.

There are at least forty different reasons why they're not going to play my record on the radio, but if I went to record with that attitude, I'd never cut a hit or a good record of any kind. I try to establish an environment that reflects a feeling of excitement. We get excited about what we're doing and the music we're playing. I try to get the same thing out of the artists by not forcing them. A lot of people may say I'm too easy, but I've never gotten a good performance from an artist by pounding away or by forcing a song down the artist's throat. Artists have got to be made to believe in and have faith in the song themselves if they're going to give you a good breakthrough on it.

IN A RECORDING STUDIO IT'S IMPOR- TANT THAT YOU DON'T GET UPTIGHT AND NERVOUS. AS SOON AS THAT HAPPENS, YOU'RE GOING TO LOSE IT.

Simplicity is the ultimate complexity. It's true. In this industry today, all we do is suffer from paralysis of analysis. Everybody's got to sit around and analyze things. They can't just let something happen. If you think about it, all the flukes, all of the great giant hit re- cords, came on the spur of the moment anyway.

A new producer always overdoes every- thing because he wants to get it so right. When you're as old as I am, they're about ready to run you out of the business. They figure you don't know anything and youth is coming up behind you. I don't believe in that. I think you grow throughout your life, if you have your health.

An experienced producer learns that fine line of when to quit. If the singer wants to get mad and pout at me, he or she can, be- cause I'll say, "That's it. We've got the cut right there." We have the technical knowl- edge today to bring the artist back in and overdub. The best way to complete the overdub is to do it on the spot, and have time for the artist to be prepared and know the material. If it can be cut on the spot, it's great. Why? Our music is simple, not pro- gressive, not classical, just three chords in

most cases. How are you going to mess that up? Just let it lay there.

It happens in the studio. There's that little marriage, there's that little . . .

MAGIC?

Well, magic, but the word I'm looking for is leakage—leakage from one mike to another. We're looking for a live acoustic sound rather than it sounding like a lot of separate tracks stuck together. It's better to get that in our records. If it can happen that way, you do it that way. If not, then you've got to get the first priority—which is to get the best from the musicians. You can always overdub your singer. When it feels exactly right, that's the magic you needed to have a hit record.

WHAT IMPORTANT CHARACTERISTICS DO YOU FEEL PEOPLE NEED IN ORDER TO BE SUCCESSFUL IN THE INDUSTRY?

If you want to become involved in the music, then you need to have an understanding of the record business. It's beautiful that we have classes in publishing, recording, merchandising, and promotion. That's the business aspect. But there is also the creative aspect.

If you've got a producer who is pretty cool musically, you can bet your bottom dollar that he has tried to be a star or an artist himself, or that he has written songs. The thing moves a little bit better for him. He's got some feeling for or some insight into the art. But he must also have a good knowl- edge of what the masses want to hear, what they are really looking for. Did we write something today, did I produce something today, that will touch people's emotions and cause them to take a few bucks out of their pockets and buy a record?

If you don't look at it that way, then you're just pleasing yourself, and you're just lock- ing yourself into an area with no potential to broaden your scope in the industry.

IS COUNTRY MUSIC BECOMING MORE MIDDLE-OF-THE-ROAD OR MORE ROCK 'N' ROLL? DO RADIO STATIONS AFFECT

THE DIRECTION OF THE MUSIC YOU RECORD?

Each radio has its own marketplace. I have to get feedback from the promotion man. He may say, "Well, they don't like that record because they don't like the fiddle intro. It's too country." Or he may say, "They don't like that record because it has too many strings on it. It's not country enough." He may say, "They don't like that record because they're not playing middle-of-the-road or country now. They're going into funky country." Sometimes we have to conform; because otherwise they won't play our records. I've made a lot of "plastic" records. They weren't real records. They were plastic because I was taking care of a need of some sort, which is asinine. But, it's an obvious factor and has to be dealt with.

The radio station is constantly in a fight with the next three radio stations in the community and with those throughout the area. Each one wants to be the largest. The way to be the largest is to have the top rating. When a station has the top rating, it's got to be selling more ads, right? So stations operate on selling ads. They couldn't care less whether we sell records or not. If our record suits their air play, they'll play it.

YOUR NAME IS WELL-KNOWN. YOU'RE VERY SUCCESSFUL, AND I WANT TO COMPLIMENT YOU ON THAT.

I appreciate it. I don't feel that I've reached the top at all. I really haven't when I compare myself to several others in the community. There was a time in my life when I was trying to play "Keep up." The only person I'm trying to keep up with now is me. That's to say, I try to keep myself abreast of what's happening in the business and to have an effective foot in the door. I enjoy the community and the people. I want to be here, and I want them to call me old, crotchety, complaining, jealous, and everything else, because I want to protect this wonderful thing we have here for as long as it can be.

I have to thank the others. I didn't recognize, years ago, how effective some of the older people were as leaders of the community. I'm not saying I'm a leader, but if I could be, I'd like to lead us in the direction of keeping what we have, of being contented with what we have. At the same time, I think we should let it grow as close to being a fun business as we can. We've lost a great part of the fun to the business, and I expect we'll lose more. But as long as we think about it, it won't go to pot right away.

WHAT ADVICE WOULD YOU GIVE TO YOUNG PEOPLE WHO WANT TO GET INTO THIS BUSINESS?

Just get on the bus, get on the bicycle, get in the car, get on the airplane, and get to Nashville or some other music town. Get barefooted, and jump in the water. There is no other way in the world to do it, because it's that kind of an element.

We're not special people. It's an art form of some sort or other. You're dealing with throwing dice just about your whole career. There is a business element, and those who deal with it as a business do better than the others. But it's still a guessing game, and it's tough. But the way to go at it is just to jump in there and claw, scrape, pull, tug, and get in every door. Be persistent. Be fair. Try to know what in the heck you're talking about and what you're doing; have the knowledge.

I see all the young people coming here now. It's so refreshing. They're rolling into this town now, not only as pickers, but with an education of picking. You don't have to say, "Hey, I'm going to hum this tune for you," before they can play it. You can also lay a chart out before them and they can play that. That's admirable, and I think it's great.

IT TAKES A LONG TIME TO WIN OR TO BE VERY SUCCESSFUL IN THIS INDUSTRY.

I think so. Don't forget, once you reach a certain level, you have to keep up. You don't really want to go backwards. It's harder to stay up on top of the ladder than it is getting to the ladder. The ladder, that's hard; but once you get there—I mean, the first time

you produce a No. 1 record on an artist—
the most frightening thing in this world is
doing another one. It's just not that easy to
cut one. There is so much competition.

THERE ARE A GREAT MANY PEOPLE OUT THERE WHO'LL NEVER BE HEARD.

There sure are, unfortunately, and also a
tremendous number of writers who'll never
get a song recorded. I go to seminars and
workshops and try to tell the truth to these
guys, not paint a beautiful picture with all the
tinsel. I saw a lady the other day who came
down from New Jersey. She flew in on a
plane, and (bless her soul, she has the
money) she's just doing it. But there are
people like this who attend every single
function. They have no ability, and they
commit themselves. They give of themselves, go all over, all their life and try, try,
try. I know some in town, some people
who've been here so long that it really
makes you wonder. Some of them I've
known long enough that I actually have seen
them come up with some pretty good things
and some good work, and it still never
happens.

PEOPLE COMING TO NASHVILLE, LOS ANGELES, AND NEW YORK BRING A LOT OF DREAMS. VERY FEW OF THOSE DREAMS ARE GOING TO BECOME REALITY.

I think that they should be able to, in a few
years, recognize whether they have any
ability or not. It'll just come together. There's
no doubt about it.

SO YOU'RE SAYING TO GIVE IT A SHOT.

If you're going to give it a shot, give it a
shot. Just recently there was a young man I
was recording. I recorded him several years
ago, and then when I went to Warner Bros., I
signed him there. I tried to get him to make

a commitment. But he was comfortable in
Philly, making some R&B records. And I
said, "Look, if you're ever going to come
down here and do it, you've got to make a
commitment."

Well, pretty soon the company found out
that he's really not working the road or
making an effort to work the road. He's not
living here; he's not really doing anything
except recording. In a sense, the company
feels taken advantage of. The company is
investing the money, I'm producing the
record, and he's coming here to record. But,
then he goes home and cools it.

Now he's made the commitment. He's
moved down. He doesn't have a label deal.
We'll get another label deal. He's very, very
talented, a very good writer, a modern
country funky singer. He can already feel
the vibes and detect that the town needs
him.

DO YOU GET HIT ON ALL THE TIME?

I get eighteen calls a day here on an average, up until noon. I'd say five or six of those
calls are significant calls. The rest of them—
I don't have any idea who they are.

They get in their mind, I'm sure, that
there's a lot of money hanging around in
sacks. They're just going to come in here
and sing me a pretty song, and I'm going to
record them, put them on a label. So, you
have to be kind, and you have to explain
your position, if you're interested or not.
We're hounded day after day.

SO YOU GET A LOT OF PEOPLE COMING TO YOU WHO WILL SING A SONG TO YOU AND SAY, "YOU SPEND YOUR MONEY ON ME AND WE'LL GET RICH TOGETHER."

I don't blame them. That's great that they
believe it. But you have to shoot them down
just about all the time. How they could figure
that they could just come to town and do it
that fast blows me away.

FRED MOLLIN

Record producer. Artists include America and Dan Hill.

YOU ACTUALLY WERE PRODUCING HIT RECORDS IN TORONTO BEFORE YOU WENT TO LOS ANGELES.

My reason for moving to Toronto when I was seventeen was that it was fairly wide open. The music industry was in a fledgling state. I had doors open to me, whereas in New York every door was locked. I was able to learn while I earned. Toronto has always been good to me in that sense. It gave me a chance to experiment and to learn the craft while getting paid, something I could not do in New York. It is a smaller market, but it is still very satisfying, and it is a personal vindication.

After the hit "Sometimes When We Touch," we had lots of offers from the States. Clive Davis wanted us to be staff producers on label. I felt very strongly that Los Angeles was a wonderful place to be working. I told Matt McCauley that now was the time to go for it and move. Basically, for the most part, it worked out. We moved in the summer of 1978 and had tons of work. We were able to work with the finest musicians and engineers, all the top echelon in the world.

DID YOU REALLY ENJOY THAT?

To me, that's the biggest thrill in the world; to work with people I dream about—some of the greatest pop musicians that ever lived, like Gene Parks, Jeff Porcaro, Lee Squire, Steve Lycather.

HOW DID YOU FIND THOSE PEOPLE?

Because we were virtually the same age and had a lot of the same kind of energies, we got along fantastically. They loved working with us because we were not the run-of-the-mill type producers.

A lot of the producers in Los Angeles are what I call desk producers. They will sit behind the board, hire the arranger and everyone else, and all they will do is say if it was good or bad. It is very common. We were not like that; we arranged all the stuff. We were never in the control room. We were always out on the floor with the players, conducting and playing. We sang backgrounds. We did as much as we could to help. The players had a respect for that because Matt and I both are good musicians. We knew how to handle players and

129

knew how to get things done quickly. The players' biggest resentment is the producer who cannot make up his mind, or one who made them do thirty-five takes when they had it on the second one.

We went for spontaneity. We always went for feel. If there were mistakes, we fixed them. As far as players and background singers went, we got along superbly.

That feel is the most elusive but most satisfying thing when you get it. It is just chemistry. When you get the right players, the material is good, and you get a performance that has that excitement, that flair, you know you hit what you were going for.

To me, the excitement of a record ends after the basic tracks. I am a frustrated performer. I love playing and being with people who are playing. Everything else is boring to me, overdubs and background vocals. It is fun to hear things when they are finished or close to being finished. There is satisfaction and gratification in that, but mostly it is a tedious process. I am fairly picky in what I accept. Vocals may take longer when I do them than with some other people.

YOU ENJOY GETTING BASIC TRACKS DOWN TO SEE IF IT'S GOING TO BE THERE?

It's the combination of a lot of exciting chemistry. It's fun even though there is a lot of pressure.

The mix is the most tense of all because you have to combine all these great moments and make sure you don't blow it in the mix.

WHEN YOU GO IN, YOU'RE CONCENTRATING ON BASIC TRACKS AND GETTING THAT SOUND IN THE GROOVE THEN.

I like working with as many players on the floor as I can. I like to have three guitars, two keyboards, bass, and drum, and a lead vocal live off the floor to get the feel. I don't like to take in one or two and then add everything else.

WHAT ABOUT YOUR COMMUNICATION WITH THE ENGINEER?

Over the years, we built up relationships with engineers (in Canada) who kind of grew along with us. When we moved to Los Angeles, we had to find new people. Some of them fell by the wayside because of personality or stylization problems. It depends on the engineer. Some engineers do things exactly as I want them. Some guys I'm never happy with what they give me.

YOU TRY TO GIVE THE ENGINEER SOME CREATIVE SPACE SOMETIMES?

We try to. On the basic tracks, we are rarely in the control room, so he has that time to get the thing right and not be bothered by us.

The only other problem is with overdubs. We scrutinize them closely because we're in the control room more.

I mixed the Michael Stanley Band album *Heartland,* which is my most recent success; we had a Top 10 single from the album. I mixed that with an engineer. I manned the board with him. I was probably responsible for 60 percent of the sound on that album. It depends on the engineer as to what I do.

With an engineer like Bill Schnee, with his great talent and sound, sometimes I'm intimidated. At the same time, sometimes I want a record to sound more like me.

YOU KNOW IN YOUR MIND PRETTY MUCH WHAT YOU WANT BEFORE YOU GO INTO THE STUDIO?

I have a vision of it. Fifty percent of the time the sound is exactly as I envisioned it. Fifty percent of the time it's slightly different. It's never to the point where I'm unhappy.

The weirdest part about making a record in this day and age with 24 tracks and a good budget is that nothing has to be bad. You can always change the vocal part or the drum part. You can alter it and get a semblance of satisfaction on everyone's part. The artist has to be happy. I have an ego, but I'm much more involved when I make a record work for the artist. I do as much as he wants me to do or as little. The bottom line is it's his album. When it goes out in the marketplace, it's his name. I'm just a hidden personality with my name on the back of an album. I've come to some sort of grips with that situation. It doesn't help my ego, but it does pay the bills. I enjoy the satisfaction I get when I see my name on an album. I know what I did.

YOU LEFT LOS ANGELES AND WENT BACK TO CANADA. WAS THERE ANY PARTICULAR REASON?

It was based on health, believe it or not. We had been in Los Angeles for three years, and I loved working there. My wife and I found the lifestyle to be extremely phony. We didn't really fit into the party stuff. I never felt comfortable. But the main thing is that I was allergic to the air there. I became extremely asthmatic. My doctors said if I stayed for five or six more years I'd have emphysema. I said, "Forget it." I didn't enjoy the people, and we did miss Toronto.

THE CANADIAN GOVERNMENT PRO-TECTS ITS ARTISTS PRETTY WELL. DON'T THEY HAVE A POINT SYSTEM FOR PUB-LISHING AND AIR PLAY?

That is correct. CanCon (Canadian Content) was instigated about the time I moved to Canada in 1971. The Canadian record industry was viewed until then as a joke. There was no legislation. I think they were playing 3 percent Canadian music on the air in Canada, 97 percent American or what-ever.

Basically, CanCon provides for 33⅓ percent Canadian content played on the air. This started the Canadian record boom. When I moved up here, it was very good timing to be in the middle of this hunt for Canadian talent. Today, it is still 33⅓ per-cent, and they play it. If you're working on a Canadian act, you have a good chance of exposure. If you do a good record, a hit record, it will get that chance to become a

hit. If you do a mediocre record, you still may get some very good exposure. In a lot of ways, it's great. In some ways, it's bad because it gives people who are less tal-ented accolades which they would not get in the tough U. S. market. I believe in it 100 percent. I feel strongly that there should be at least 33⅓ percent Canadian music played.

WHAT ADVICE WOULD YOU GIVE TO PEOPLE WHO WANT TO BECOME RE-CORD PRODUCERS?

Five years ago, I would have said, "Keep at it. Something will break." Now, I'm a lot more cynical. If you want to produce these days, you had better learn to diversify, to do more things than just produce. I write songs; I perform; I sing, I do television music, film music; I produce records; I could engineer. Someone who really wants to become a producer must understand he has to broaden his horizons. It's all a survival tactic. If you can't produce the group you've been dying to produce this month, someone may call and ask for two songs for a televi-sion show. Matthew and I used to joke that it was a crap shoot. You had to do your best work, have the best songs and artists, and then it's all a crap shoot. But it was a fun gamble.

DO YOU HAVE ANY OTHER ADVICE TO PEOPLE WHO WANT TO GET INTO THE INDUSTRY?

As far as becoming a producer is con-cerned, you only get work from work. In this business, you can't knock on a record label's door and say, "Hey, I want to pro-duce an album." The greatest boon to anyone's career who wants to be a record producer is to do spec projects. If someone comes up and says help me do this demo, do it—even if you make no money. It might just be a way to get an album project. Courses aren't that much help in practical experience. It's all human experience, and you have to learn by doing it.

If you have any inclination for songwriting or if you feel you can pick a hit, then I say try to get involved through having your own publishing company. If you can get a song to somebody, that's a way to make money. It might not lead to the production, but it will give you some financial stability that will let you do some things on spec without worrying about how to pay the bills.

HOW MUCH DO PRODUCERS GET PAID?
I get $2,000 per side.

BUT YOU'RE A NAME PRODUCER.
I may be, but I'm not in the top echelon. I can also get points. Basically, it's a fee situation with points.

I get $2,000 per side, so on a 10-song album, I get $20,000—$10,000 in advance, $10,000 upon completion. I also get 4 points of retail; that's what I ask for. It's not worth it, because I lose sleep every night. I work two to three months solid for that money. If you knock it down to an hourly wage, it isn't that great. It's only great if I get the royalties.

JIMMY BOWEN

Division President of MCA Records, Nashville. Former President of Warner Bros. Records, Nashville. Former head of ElektraAsylum Records, Nashville. Record producer for Hank Williams, Jr., Bellamy Brothers, Eddy Raven, Dave and Sugar, Joe Sun, Conway Twitty, Kenny Rogers and the First Edition, Dean Martin, and Frank Sinatra.

HOW IMPORTANT IS IT FOR A PRODUCER TO UNDERSTAND THE "BUSINESS SIDE" OF THE INDUSTRY?

The price of records, the publisher's increase—everything affects the producer because you have to have x number of dollars to make the product. Those dollars are affected by everything that goes on in the music industry.

If you're going to be a record producer, you must have an overall knowledge of the music industry. From a business standpoint, you must, at all times, know where the industry stands. You must be able to read it ahead of time, businesswise.

The smart people, in late 1978 to early 1979, were those who saw the crash coming, who saw the big, big problems that hit this industry in mid-1979, putting 1,800 people out of work. Six labels closed down, independent distributors folded all over this country, and the independent retailers went out of business. If you're not aware of what is happening in the industry, it can hurt you.

An example, if you're about to meet with a label head to discuss producing an act, you're not going to blow yourself out of the deal by coming in too high right off the bat. You'll be a lot smarter to walk in and say, "Listen, I understand what's going on. I've worked out a deal with the studio for block rates for $80 an hour instead of $100 per hour. I've got a situation." In other words, you need to approach the labels knowing the state of the industry. If you come in high-balling when it's a low-ball world, you're in trouble. Several producers are out of work right now because they didn't recognize this. They went ahead and spent $200,000 or $300,000 on some new rock artist or some new pop artists. They're now looked on as high-cost, low-return producers. They can't control budgets; they're not good to hire during hard times.

Generally, you don't want to be a waster of money. If you do your pre-production properly, you won't waste money. It's important that you understand the business side. Unless you want to do these records free, you're in the business side.

133

HOW DO YOU PRODUCE A RECORD? WHAT ARE THE DIFFERENT STEPS INVOLVED?

We want to take production from step one to the completion of a record.

Step one of production is to find an artist or have an artist find you. You've got to have an artist to work with; that is the first thing. There's nothing more important than that or you can't produce. When you're first getting started, you will probably work with artists you wouldn't work with later on; but more than likely, you'll both be at the same stage. You're going to have to work with people who aren't ready, which is also of value to you.

At first, you'll produce some artists you probably shouldn't. You'll cause some marriages to happen that aren't the ideal marriages, but you must get some experience. When this happens, make sure that you always do the very best job you can. If you realize that it's a super bad marriage, get out of it as gracefully as you can. Save the artist's time, save the money, and save your own reputation. It will not hurt you as badly to walk away from a project, if you do it properly, as it will if you complete it and waste money.

Now, if you ever have to abort, go to whomever you made the deal with, and sit down and say, "This marriage is rotten." Try not to go in and attack that artist. That person you're speaking to signed that artist, either before you or because of you. If that's the reason, you explain that. You have to always have a cool head. Record companies aren't interested in having an artist who's going to be "squirrelly" part of the time. They don't really need producers who are "squirrelly" half the time either.

You always want to maintain a business approach. If it doesn't work, you're sorry it didn't work, but you'd rather not waste any more money. You can also discuss it in the same time frame with the artist, before you go to the label.

STEP ONE IS TO FIND AN ARTIST. WHAT IS STEP TWO?

Step two is to research your artist. The first thing that I suggest you do is to get yourself a discography of that artist. Get it from as far back in his life as he's on tape, to the present moment. He's known himself all his life, obviously. You don't. Don't try to come in after he's been singing for twelve or fourteen years, working at his craft, and hope you're going to jump on the train and ride a winner. It happens once in a while; that's the danger in it. Set yourself up so you never, never eliminate luck, eliminate lightning striking. Go at everything just as you would any other business. Go at it seriously.

Ask your artists to get you a discography in chronological order. None of them are going to want to do it because most of their tapes are embarrassing this late in life. Explain to your artists that they know themselves. You need to catch up, in a short period of time, so that you have knowledge of their development, what they are, what they have become, and where they came from.

If it's a home tape, that's fine. You need to come up through that period of time with them. You're not looking for hits; you're not looking for quality as much as you are hearing the voice.

There's so much you learn from researching the artist. You learn what not to do; you learn what to do. Beware of a producer who's ready to go to the studio a week or two after he's met the artist or has gotten the deal. He's looking for a miracle to happen; he's hoping it will all work out. It does work out just often enough in this business so that too many people get off on the wrong foot.

That history on your artists is so, so important. Fight them, make them give it to you. Promise to give it back to them. Promise it will never leave your house. However you've got to get it; just get it. It's one of the most important things that you're going to have on these artists.

STEP TWO IS TO RESEARCH THE ARTIST. WHAT DO YOU NEED TO DO BESIDES GETTING THE ARTIST'S DISCOGRAPHY?

The second part of your research is to have deep, relaxed discussions with this artist. Read your artist and find out what environment will let this artist open up, relax, and have the best rap with you. If it's at your house, go do it. If it's at the studio late at night, go do it. Find a place where that artist is most comfortable, so he will talk to you, so you can start to read him.

Being a producer, you've got to be a psychologist—not a psychiatrist, but a psychologist. You've got to dig into these people's heads. You've got to find out what makes an artist tick, what makes him give 100 percent sometimes, 80 percent sometimes, and 20 percent sometimes. Or you're going to be looking for luck, hoping the night you book him you're going to get the 100. You may not get it.

The whole trick is to figure out everything about the artist, so that when you go to tape, to make your record, you've got everything at max. You want everything at its best. The ones that break through are the magical records that happen that way.

When you get into these discussions, you want to get into the musical likes of an artist. Find what he listens to when he's home, on the bus, in a plane, or a car. It may not have anything to do with what you're going to do with him, but what does he listen to? Try to find out what triggers an artist musically.

Talk to your artist about the musicians that he likes or doesn't like. Never cast a session and have a musician on it that the artist has a bad vibe with. You're just putting a negative into your music that you don't need.

Get a rapport with him so he'll be honest. Sometimes he's afraid to say. He doesn't want to knock anybody out of work. It's your job to make sure that you find out which musicians he likes and which ones he doesn't like.

Now, another thing in that regard is that you don't want an artist to lead you into a session with bad musicians because he likes them. That's just as important. It's like casting a movie. If you put together a bad cast, you're going to have a bad movie.

You need to get a general feel of the artist as a human being and as a creative force. If your artist is not a good human being, you probably don't have a good artist. You probably don't have a one-of-a-kind. I'm not saying the artist should be completely straight; there's something about being one of a chosen few on this whole planet of millions and millions of people. You can count them in the hundreds, the ones who have been given a gift of musical talent. You've got to figure they're not going to be like your banker or your lawyer or like you. You've got to get into them as human beings, find out what that creative force is.

Usually in an artist, if he doesn't want it more than anything else in the world, he's not going to get it. If he has a part-time desire, I'd advise you usually not to waste your time on him. If he wants to record occasionally, if he wants to be an artist on the side, don't waste your time with him. There are only a few slots open at the top, and those are usually filled by people who want it more than anything else in the world.

HOW OFTEN DOES SOMEONE COME ALONG AND JUST HAPPEN INTO IT?

It happens occasionally, but if you luck out and get one of them, great. I think I told you about my first session with Hank Williams, Jr., when we did "Family Tradition." That was a very fortunate situation for me, as a producer, to walk into.

He didn't like his album and wanted me to do four more cuts just to finish it. I said, "What have you written?" He said, "Nobody wants to hear what I've written." I said, "Hey, what have you written?" and he played me "Family Tradition." We walked into the studio and cut it. My experience taught me to recognize magic in a session when it strikes and not to foul it up. I walked into the musicians and I said, "This is a simple song. I want the drums simple. I want everybody else to just stay out of the kid's way. I want to hear the song. I want to hear the melody. I want to hear the lyric and that's it."

That's happened to me a couple of times in my life, but it's not been the norm. Usually, it's work and sweat and going crazy, but luck does happen occasionally. Let those occasions be the exceptions in your life. After you've had a certain amount of success, you're more apt to run into fortunate situations.

In my opinion, you should always strive; and again, in the early stages, you've got to do what you do to get experience. But you should always strive to work with an artist who is one-of-a-kind. That is the only kind who can really, really break through. You can copy artists, and you can have success with them; but it's really not worth the effort.

Any time you take an artist who's like somebody else, you're starting off in second place, no matter how well you do. If you're doing a one-of-a-kind, you're doing something new. Music is all so similar that it's often hard to hear something new.

Sometimes a one-of-a-kind artist is not obvious when you first start with him. Usually, there will be a little something—you'll hear just four bars somewhere, you'll see the artist in person, you'll hear him with a guitar or piano someplace—and you'll catch that little moment of magic. You've got to hunt it, look for it. You're always hunting that gold, that one-of-a-kind. When you see the potential, it may be four years away or six months away from being developed. That's your problem. You've got to see if you can get the talent to the point of being valuable before you lose the opportunity to work with it.

Timing is an important thing in this industry. When we first signed the First Edition, Kenny Rogers was the last member to join. He only got in the group because somebody dropped out. As it turned out, in the first album, he got to sing lead on just two or three songs. One was "I Just Dropped in to See What Condition My Condition Was In."

The background voices were run through a Leslie Organ speaker, and there were all kinds of gimmicks.

Mike Post, who worked for me and produced that album, had a blowup after a couple more tries with Kenny and the First Edition. So I had to step in and work with them. During that period, just as I was taking over the production of Kenny Rogers and the First Edition, Kenny became very enamored with Donovan and the vibrato. I noticed it was starting to creep into Kenny's singing. The first session I did with him, we did a song called "But You Know I Love You." It was the first single that I produced with the First Edition. That's when he started putting that little vibrato in.

We learned something also in that first session. After we got the tracks down, I said, "Kenny, grab that guitar mike and let's throw down some test vocals." Every one of them was a master vocal. We learned that you've got to get him on as quickly as you can. The longer Kenny Rogers knows a song, the more he oversings it. He gets bored with it, and the less commercial job he does with it.

Look for flaws and negatives in researching your artist. Don't be surprised later. That's not to say you should be a doomsdayer or a negative person. You look for flaws quietly. The artist should never know you're looking. Sometimes your closeness to the artist prevents you from spotting flaws. There's a possessiveness that gets in there. You've gotten inside the artist's head to be a good producer. Next thing you know, all you see is the good. Now you're not a very good producer because you don't see the flaws. You don't see the negatives, so you're not dealing with them. You're not prepared for them.

Also, as the artist develops, when the time is proper, you've got to explain those flaws and negatives to your artist—especially ones that he is not correcting as you go along—so that he'll know what the flaws are and he can work on correcting them. If your artist isn't intelligent enough to have this kind of rapport with you, then again, you've probably not got a major artist.

There are exceptions to this. Nothing is a hardset rule. But, if you want to be successful in music and have a career in it, you'd better do your homework; do your research, so you know your artist.

You need to know what music the artist listens to for personal pleasure. What is he influenced by? What influenced him is still in there. You need to find out from him what turned him on, what stuck in his subconscious mind, because that's what's coming back out. You can use that in communicating with the artist.

You need to discuss writers, singers, and musicians with your artist. Find out what the artist likes in all those areas. Find out what musicians he likes. Maybe they're not in the city where you work, but find out. If your artist's favorite guitar player is George Benson, that should trigger you to consider that kind of guitar. You've also got to make sure that the artist doesn't copy current people he likes. That can be a danger.

When it comes to the songs, you need to find out what writers an artist likes if he doesn't write all his own material. The marriage of song and artist is very important. Don't let an artist die because his songs aren't good enough; use someone else's songs, and deal with the ego problem that doing this creates.

HOW DO YOU TELL A WRITER-ARTIST THAT HIS OWN SONGS AREN'T GOOD ENOUGH?

It depends on your position. If you're an independent and the artist is too, you take a bit softer approach and be a little more delicate with it. It's difficult for someone to be objective about his own songs. You're trying to get him out of the maze. You're trying to get him out where the people can see and hear him as an artist, so you've got to get into him and know him. Then, when he's writing, you've got a much better

chance at convincing him that his writing isn't strong enough.

You may have to say, "Not only is it my opinion, it's the opinion of Bowen" or whoever is at a label you are dealing with. Each artist is different. You'll read some totally wrong and blow it up; and you're no longer the producer. But it's a danger you have to face. If you're really going to do the job for the artist, you've got to be honest. If he fires you and you're no longer the producer, so be it. You shouldn't have been the producer, and you certainly don't want to waste his time, the label's money, and your reputation cutting songs that aren't going to have any prayer starting out.

The burden is also to know what's good and what's bad. Basically, you've got to have that instinct—have a gut feeling for the consumer and what he's buying now. If the instinct is not in there at all, you've really got a problem. You've got to try to get it. You've got to know what's selling and what the radio is playing, so you get more of a clinical approach to what works.

If you're going to be a successful producer, you have to know that when you say "don't do that" or "do that," you're right more often than you're wrong. Then people will listen to you.

You're better off breaking up a bad marriage by telling the truth than you are going forward. If you ever tell an artist the song isn't good enough, or if you pass a song somebody brings you for an artist, and it becomes a big hit for somebody else, don't worry about it. The only time you should worry about it is if somebody takes your artist and cuts that song with him and makes it a big hit; then you were wrong. You misread it, and you screwed up.

WHAT KIND OF DIRECTION DO YOU GIVE THE ARTIST?

If the artist has an obvious direction, that's great. If he's an artist who does just one kind of thing and that's all he can do, then the way you package that and showcase it will either work or it won't. That's the easiest situation. Most times, however, you find artists who are not quite fully developed in their own talent, whether it's the writing or the singing, the confidence or the presentation, the ability to pull it off on tape; so you've got to bring them along. You've got to work with them and get them headed in the direction they should go.

DO YOU EVER WORK WITH THE MANAGERS IN YOUR DIRECTION OF THE ARTIST?

Very seldom do you find managers at this point who can contribute much. Usually, they muddy the water. Basically, you'll find most managers can't be very helpful. When you do luck into a manager who can be helpful, use him.

I use managers to surround the artist, to get the artist to do what he ought to do. You always want to get a good rapport with the manager. First of all, the manager's with the artist all the time; you're not. If the manager hates you, he'll get rid of you. If you can't convince the manager that you're for his artist, trying to do the best for his artist, you've probably got a major problem.

The manager's very important in getting the artist to sessions on time, to rehearsals on time, to pre-production meetings on time. He can be helpful to the artist who's on the road, to make sure the artist is rehearsing or writing.

SO STEP THREE IS TO HAVE A KNOWLEDGE OF MUSIC AND SONGS. WHAT IS STEP FOUR?

Step three is music and songs; step four is finding the material. The two almost tie together. In fact, they could have been one step.

If you're working with a writer-artist, then you've got to cull through his stuff. You've got to send him back when he's got a great chorus but the verses aren't any good. You've got to find a way to get that across to him so that he fixes the verses and you don't lose the great chorus. Hopefully, if it's a

writer-artist, he has a good publisher who knows how to work with him on a writer's level. You, in turn, work with the writer-artist to get the best possible song.

If you work with an artist who is not a writer, the hunt is on for songs. You've got to find them. Always encourage both the artist and his manager to be hunting for songs at all times. I always suggest that as a producer, you don't let your ego get involved anywhere down the line, but especially in this area. You take a hit song if it comes from an ex-wife or from your biggest enemy. You owe that to the artist. Your job is to make hit records. He's paying you. It's his life and his money. Remember that at all times.

Go out and hunt those songs. Anywhere you get a hit song is great. The obvious place to hunt songs is your publishers, and you need to have a good rapport with all the major publishers. Usually a publisher will have a professional manager who casts songs. Your job is to figure out, in each publishing house, whom you lock up best with. If the publisher has two or three song pluggers, you try to find the one you think is feeling what you need best.

If there's no one in the publishing house who does that (and even if there is), I suggest you get to know the writers. Often the writer will think of a song for you and your artist that the publishers didn't think of. The publisher is pitching to a hundred artists a week and dealing with twenty or thirty writers. The publisher doesn't always have a clear head to try to figure it out. Often the publishers don't have a really good feel for what you want; to be quite honest, they lucked into the gig. Don't leave it up to them to find you a song. Get to know the writers they've got, and let them play it for you.

When I say the hunt is on, that's just what I mean. The song isn't going to come to you very often. You've got to create the relationships for the songs to be brought to you. You've got to go out and make yourself known. You've got to be reputable. If you tell somebody you want to hold a song, be honest. If the artist is on the road, don't say you want a hold on a song and that you're definitely going to cut it when you know that's not the case. Publishers and writers will find out about you. The next time you want to hold a song, they'll give it to three other people and tell you "yeah." They'll play the game back with you.

You've got to have a good rapport with those publishers and with the writers. Use honesty. Don't try to hurt anybody, but be truthful. It keeps you clean, and it makes your business dealings with these people much, much better.

We look for material all the time. There are certain publishers who are constantly sending in stuff for all our artists. About thirty days before you're going to record an artist, you also put the word out. Then the tapes flood in. The problem then is that when you're going through songs in that heavy heat, the last few weeks before a session, there's a tendency to take the best of the worst. So, when you have big, long listening sessions for songs, you cull about six or seven out of fifty. Get away from them until the next day. Then go back and listen to those six or seven. You'll probably throw away three or four of those.

After you've gone through two or three months of hunting songs, play your artist the best of what you've found. Sometimes you can take them off after eight bars and don't know why you even saved them. That cold reality of the meeting with the artist gives you a better perspective on what you thought you had found. With the great songs, you'll both just light up. If you miss the great ones, then I'd suggest plumbing or electrical work, because you aren't going to make it. There's only one other way to make it if you don't know a great song, and that's to hire somebody who does.

Also, research old songs. Many, many times, old songs come back as a brand-new song with different artists, different arrangements, different times. In that regard, you should try to get the catalogs of all the old publishing companies. You need to be a bit

of a junkie in that area so you get old songs. There's a wealth of hits in there. Some may not work again melodically; some may not work at this point in time lyrically; but a lot of them will work. Look back into the past.

You need to have a lot of meetings with your writers and publishers and go through as many songs as you can. If you get to two or three weeks before the session and you don't have any great songs, move the session. Don't wait for miracles or for your life to be saved at the last hour.

SO STEP FOUR IS TO FIND THE RIGHT SONGS. WHAT IS STEP FIVE?

Step five is setting your session. You've done all your pre-production on your artist. You've found your material or are in the process of finding it. You've got enough in hand to start so that you can book a session. Book your session as far ahead of time as you possibly can, because that guarantees the right studio, the right engineer, and the right musicians in every position.

Make sure you work in the best studio possible. The studio that gets the best sound is technically the best studio. Sometimes it's determined by your budget, but get the best. Get the best engineer available, all factors being equal. Don't settle for the wrong studio or for an engineer who just can't cut it. Move your session, put it off until you can get it properly set up.

HOW PARTICULAR SHOULD YOU BE IN SETTING UP THE SESSION?

The degrees in that area change as your career develops. When you're first starting, you might do a lot of 8-track work with musicians you know aren't quite right; but you're hoping that will lead to something else. I'm not saying you shouldn't do that; you need all the studio experience you can get.

You should hang out at studios and learn whatever you can to begin with. But try not to lose the quality, in the early stages. If you're an unknown producer and you've got a half-good studio and a half-assed engineer, then you haven't got it at all. But do the best you can. Once you get to where you're cooking a little bit and you're really a producer, book ahead. Get the right studio and the right engineer.

In a studio, the size is important for some music. The acoustics of one studio might be perfect for one thing but might not be for another. The studio I work in is fine for country, but it'll never be any good for rock 'n' roll. Don't try to do something in a facility that is unsuitable.

Now you've got to select your musicians. As I mentioned earlier, don't have any musician on your session who dislikes any other musician there. Don't have any musician who dislikes the artist or the engineer, or vice versa. Try to get an engineer who understands the music. It makes it a lot easier. Don't let the engineer run your session, but don't ever bluff in areas that you don't know.

Music should be made with care and love and good feeling. Everybody needs to like each other and like what you're into. If one man on the session is tired or doesn't want to be there or doesn't like the music, it'll blow the whole session.

When you're first starting out as a producer, you've got to bend in some areas, just because of the dollars you have. But, if you do your pre-production properly, you can still eliminate the quality loss. If you're going into a session as a new producer, and the guy only gave you four hours and wants three songs, then you've got to get your pre-production down. You've got to talk to the engineer; you've got to make sure your drummer's there well ahead of time. Figure out ways to make it work. Get the most out of whatever you get to work with. Later, when you get control and some track re-

cord, then there is absolutely no excuse for not doing it properly.

You've got to learn how to cast the band for the studio. You just don't get a drummer and a bass player, and so on. It doesn't work. The first key in casting your session is that the drummer and the bass player need to work together like one. That's your foundation. The whole house will fall in on you if you don't get a good foundation. If you get that foundation, you've got 50 percent of your studio music part covered. You can overdub anything else that doesn't work right, but it's hard to overdub the bass and the drums.

Try to find two or three teams for different kinds of music. Make sure that your electric guitar and your keyboard person work with the bass and the drum. If your keyboard and your bass player don't work well together, get rid of your keyboard player. Too many keyboard players play to another drummer. they don't even hear the drums and the bass; they're overdoing their own number. Use the kind of keyboard player who digs the music and who digs the other musicians he's playing with. Build your band that way. Usually, I'll use the same band for a whole album, but with some artists it's not as imperative as it is with others. It depends on the kind of music.

Don't blow up when you're faced with disasters. Keep your cool. Ask yourself what your options are. You've got to remember that musicians are artists and you've got to treat them right. You can't blow up if a musician doesn't show up on time, because the others will think, "Well, that could have been me." Producers, like doctors, have to stay in control. You've got the artist's life in your hands; his whole future is right there in your hands.

SCOTTY TURNER

A&R for Liberty Records. Producer of Willie Nelson, Waylon Jennings, and Del Reeves. Co-songwriter with Slim Whitman, John Marascalco, Mac Davis, and Buddy Holly.

WHAT DO YOU FEEL A PRODUCER'S RESPONSIBILITY IS TO THE ARTIST, THE RECORD COMPANY, AND THE BUYING PUBLIC?

A producer can't sit in an ivory tower and predict what the people out there want to hear. We'll take Slim Whitman as an example. He was appearing in England. He had sung everything he knew, and they were still yelling for more. He went on-stage and sang "Home on the Range"—just him and his guitar—in 4/4 time as opposed to 3/4. He came back and told us about it. We cut it in 4/4 time; and there's the gold album on the wall.

My job as a producer is creating harmony between the artist and the musicians. In the past, when I was a house producer, if the record company said, "Jump," I suppose it was my job to ask, "How high?" If they said, "We want a rock 'n' roll album on Sandy Nelson," what I used to do was to send a memo around to all the sales people, the promotion people. I listed 50 songs and I said, "Give me the ones you want." If the

record made it, naturally the promotion people were responsible. If it bombed, it was the producer's fault.

A producer is a person who creates harmony among the people who surround him or those he surrounds himself with. A lot of times producers are given credit for what they do; they're looked upon as gods. Absolutely wrong. When I cut a record, I'm working with ten producers in that studio; every one of those musicians is a producer. If somebody's got an idea, let him try it. It's the only way.

HOW DO YOU GET THE BEST CREATIVE FEELING OUT OF PEOPLE?

I don't know how other people work, but as far as I'm concerned, you have to consider the artist. If an artist doesn't like a song, you've got to think about that artist going out on-stage, night after night, singing a song he doesn't like. That's putting money in front of caring about the artist.

The most difficult thing for a producer to realize is that artists must have an ego. If they don't, I don't want to mess with them. But there's a fine line between egotism and arrogance.

I did a little survey one time, and I asked artists what number their record was on the charts. They told me immediately. I said, "What's the record above yours?" They didn't know. "What's the one below yours?" They didn't know. They knew one number, that's all they knew. In essence, we're working with people who are very, very touchy. When you're producing an artist, you are producing that artist and no other artists. It used to be very difficult for me to have Bobby Lewis in my office while Del Reeves was waiting in the lobby to see me.

Once the artist in your office leaves, then you must psych yourself up again to one waiting in the lobby. You treat each person as if he is the only one you're going to ever produce. It must be that way. You never spend 20 percent of your time and effort with one artist, 10 percent with another one; it's 100 percent all the way. If a great song comes in and it just happens that the song fits Del Reeves, you do that one song on Del, unless he doesn't like it. Then you show it to another artist.

Music is a difficult occupation to discuss or argue about. What you like may not be something that I like. When you're in a studio, you try to present something to the people that at least 90 percent of them will enjoy. That's why little ditties that become hits, like "Itsy, Bitsy, Teenie Weenie, Yellow Polka-Dot Bikini," could have been sung by anyone . . . maybe.

WHAT ADVICE WOULD YOU GIVE TO A SINGER WHO WANTS TO GET INTO THIS BUSINESS?

The best advice I can give is this. Find a producer or manager who will give you straight-from-the-shoulders answers. Find some financial backers you trust and have them checked out. Fly them in to see your act. If your producer or manager has a good reputation and says, "Yes, this act is going to make it," then the investors, if they decide to invest, shouldn't expect their investment back in 6 months, 18 months, or possibly 5 years! But if you're a really good singer and if you stay with it, then you may all make some money.

It takes an awful lot of money. The days are gone when you walk into a producer's office with a guitar and sing a song and the producer says, "Wow, you're great. We're going to go in tonight and cut." I wish those days were back. That's when making records was pure fun and excitement—not a job.

CHAPTER EIGHT

RECORDING STUDIO AND AUDIO ENGINEERS

Recording the song onto magnetic tape is the first stage in the concrete creation of the phonograph record. Placing the song on a phonograph record, reel-to-reel tape, or cassette tape gives record companies merchandise to sell. The song, the artist, and the recording will determine which piece of plastic is sold.

A song is recorded on tape in studio. This process must have the best artistic effort by the artist, the musicians, the producer, and the engineer. The producer is in charge of the entire three-hour recording session. Sessions are scheduled for three hours with a one-hour break. The producer is responsible for getting the best possible effort from everybody involved. Most producers have an image in their minds of what they want for the final product before the session starts. They know what the song should sound like, how it should be sung by the vocalist, and how it should be performed by the pickers. In most cases, the producer has worked with the artist and pickers many times

before—so he has a good idea of how well they perform.

The producer controls the creative atmosphere and the direction of the session. He will often start the session and then give the artist and musicians plenty of creative space to add their own personal insights to the song. This allows everyone to participate and to have fun. A sense of involvement and fun will really be evident when the song is recorded. You can hear that extra special effort on tape, and it adds to the feeling of the recording.

The audio engineer is responsible for the technical aspects of the session. He or she must make sure that all of the equipment is working properly. (A cancelled session can cost a producer or a record company thousands of dollars.) Most studio will provide drums, piano, guitar amplifiers, percussion instruments, and any other type of instrument needed beforehand. Sometimes musicians will bring their own drums, and they will always bring their own axes (guitars).

143

The engineer is responsible for the types of sounds from the studio instruments. The selection and placement of microphones will determine how certain instruments or vocalists sound. Proper microphone selection to match the vocalist's characteristics is important. Close miking of instruments will provide a more direct sound (sound of that instrument only). Moving the microphone back from the instruments a few inches or feet, depending on the loudness of the sound source, will provide a live sound. The direct sound from the sound source or instrument can be naturally mixed with the reflected sound. Also, sound from the other instruments will leak into the microphone and provide a live or ambient room sound.

The best studio musicians must be added to the session. Performing in a studio situation is much different than performing on-stage; in addition, the pickers must be able to get along with the recording artist. Personal insights and personal feelings have a lot to do with how well the song is performed and if it's in the grooves. "In the grooves" is the way the people in the music industry refer to that little bit of magic that is created. The recording artists, studio musicians, producers, and engineers must work together to create this magic.

Studios have been made out of everything from stores to barns. The size of the structure, its design, and the building material add to the type of sound the studio will provide. Special acoustical material and the placement of walls provide studios with a certain type of sound. The amount of direct sound versus the reflected sound is what makes one area of a studio sound dead and another area sound alive. Many engineers and musicians state that this mixture of room size, acoustical materials, and wall placement not only affects the way the instruments sound, but also affects the personal moods of the musicians.

The control room houses the majority of the recording equipment. All of the equipment in the control room and in the recording studio itself is for only one purpose—to get the absolute best recording of the song possible. Usually, the audio engineer is the person who operates the equipment during the recording session. Producers rarely handle any of the equipment during the basic session, but some producers will mixdown their own tracks.

Recording sessions are broken down into several stages. The first stage is getting the basic tracks—recording the rhythm instruments on magnetic tape. The second stage is overdubbing (or stacking)—adding an extra instrument or vocal to the tracks that were previously taped. The third stage is the mixdown; all of the tracks (there may be 16 or 24 separate tracks on the tape) are mixed down to a 2-track stereo tape. The stereo tape is later made into a lacquer master, a disc from which the actual records are made.

In the control room, the console (board) controls the signals coming from the microphones and assigns them to tracks on the tape machine. The console has faders, or volume controls; each fader controls the loudness and the amount of the audio signal from one microphone. Therefore, if you mike an instrument with one mike, you have total control over that instrument's sound. The equalizers on the console allow the engineer to increase or decrease the loudness of low, middle, or high frequencies.

The monitor system (the speakers) allows the engineer and producer to hear each microphone input at a different loudness level than the engineer is recording. The engineer's job is to put the maximum amount of signal on tape without distortion. Recording too low a signal will cause noise. Digital recording prevents these problems.

The producer is concerned with the performance of the musicians, and he'll leave the technical problems to the engineer. The producer wants to hear a decent mix. That is why the monitor mix in the control room is different than the amount of signal being recorded.

The cue, or foldback, is the amount of signal being fed from the microphones through the board and returned to the musicians' headsets (earphones). This allows the musicians to hear themselves and each other. It never seems to fail that the bass player and vocalists want more of themselves than the rest of the musicians. Echo and reverberation can be added through the monitors and cue system to make the performers more comfortable and to give the producer a realistic idea of what the final mix will sound like.

Through a patch bay, additional equipment may be added to create special effects. Compressors will reduce the dynamic range, which is the volume difference from the softest passage to the loudest passage of music, so the signal can be recorded properly on tape. For example, a singer or vocalist may sing softly, and then belt out loudly the next verse. The difference in the volume causes an increase in the amount of audio signal flowing to the tape machine. If the engineer doesn't reduce it by lowering the volume in the fader, the signal will be distorted on the tape. The other advantage of a compressor is that it changes the way an instrument sounds. As an example, if you have a bass drum, commonly referred to as a kick drum, and you want it to sound a little punchier, you can put it through the compressor.

Harmonizers will electronically correct the pitch of a vocalist who is singing out of tune. In addition, harmonizers can electronically double an instrument or vocalist. If you listen carefully to many of the records on the radio today, you will notice that the same vocalist is really singing the same words two or three times. Listen carefully the next time to a vocalist and try to determine if he is singing it once or twice, or if the effect was electronically created.

Noise gates will reduce the noise on the tape track. It is turned on and off automatically by the loudness (amplitude) of the signal. For example, take a snare drum. Besides the pop on a snare, you will always get leakage into the microphone from the cymbals and other drums in the room. An easy way to eliminate all the noise is to set the threshold of the noise gate to open when the loudness of the pop on the snare is above the threshold. As soon as the signal drops below the threshold, everything is turned off.

Once the audio signal of the instrument and vocalist has been altered to the desire of the producer and engineer, it is sent electronically to the tape recorder. The tape recorder in today's recording studios converts the electronic audio signal into a magnetic flux signal that is recorded on magnetic recording tape. Recording tape is composed of a plastic (mylar) base material with ferric or chromium oxide glued to its surface. The oxide is a metallic substance that can be permanently magnetized. An additional backing has been placed on the newer hot tapes (high-output, low-noise tapes) which have been created in the last few years. This special backing allows for an additional amount of oxide to be placed on the front of the tape, increases the strength of the tape itself, and a gives 3dB increase in signal.

A stack of 16 or 24 recording heads on top of each other will automatically divide the tape into 16 or 24 horizontal recording areas called tracks. Each track is a separate magnetic recording and allows for the engineer to record instruments on different tracks. As an example, the bass guitar can be recorded on track 1, the snare drum on track 2, the acoustic guitar on track 3, and the kick drum on track 16. Low frequency instruments like the bass guitar and the kick drum are usually recorded on the border or outside tracks of the tape, which are the tracks on the top and bottom of the tape. Some of the tracks are left open. These tracks will be used later during the second stage of recording which is called overdubbing or stacking.

After a song has been recorded, the engineer and producer will listen to a play back to make sure that it has been recorded properly and to eliminate and technical or creative problems. Everyone tries to help each other with respect for the producer's opinion. If the engineer finds a problem, he will ask the producer if he would like to listen again. Everyone must work together to get the best possible sound, performance, and feel.

To be honest, the song's performance will either be on tape or not. Good producers will hear most of the problems before the musicians or engineer speak up. Once the producer accepts the recording (basic tracks) he'll save that tape. Later he'll add additional vocal and instrumental tracks during the overdubbing process.

The recording studio is a very special place in the music business because it's the center where the creative, business, and technological aspects of the business come together. All of the participants (artist, musicians, producers, and engineers) are experts at their craft and work together as a team to create the product that is the foundation of the music business.

JIM WILLIAMSON

Record producer and audio engineer. Artists and clients include Bob Dylan, Loretta Lynn, Kenny Rogers, Dottie West, Johnny Cash, Don Williams, Waylon Jennings and Willie Nelson, and Gene Watson.

WHAT DOES AN AUDIO ENGINEER DO?
His responsibilities are to position musicians in a recording studio, mike [microphone] them properly, receive the signals through an audio console, blend it to the satisfaction of the client, and record it to date on an analog recording tape machine. In a remix situation, he'll receive the signal from this multi-track tape machine and blend or fine-tune it for the final product.

Let's try to divide this into three basic factors of engineering that I feel are the most important. First is the acoustical environment in which you place the artists and musicians.

WHEN YOU SAY "ACOUSTICAL ENVIRON-MENT," WHAT ARE WE REALLY TALKING ABOUT?
We're speaking of each musician's location in respect to one another so that they can hear one another play and perform with one another well. And from a technical stand-point, how well you receive the signal they play, with the isolation factor in mind.

ISOLATION MEANS THAT THE SOUND FROM ONE INSTRUMENT DOES NOT LEAK INTO THE SOUND OF ANOTHER INSTRUMENT OR INTO ANOTHER MICRO-PHONE?
That's correct. Control of separation, but not necessarily to supersede the musician's ability to hear the other musicians and what they play.

Let me touch on the acoustic factors of a studio. When we say acoustic, we mean surfaces of walls, partitions that would reflect or absorb—depending upon the desires of the engineer—the sound emitting from the instrument.

A HARD WALL OR A SOFT WALL IS GOING TO CHANGE THE WAY SOMETHING SOUNDS.
Exactly. The microphone has frequency response characteristics and directional pattern characteristics that are used in conjunction with baffles [partitions that can reflect or absorb sound] to obtain isolation as well as the proper sound of the instrument.

I ASSUME THAT THIS IS VERY IMPORTANT BECAUSE THE AUDIO ENGINEER IS IN CONTROL OF THE WAY AN INSTRUMENT OR A VOCALIST IS GOING TO SOUND.
Absolutely. It's as if the microphone were in an echo chamber, it will reveal certain frequency response characteristics and isolation factors due to its pattern selectability. The baffles in the studio will aid your microphone and its frequency response characteristics.

Second, let's speak of the technical aspects. The engineer is responsible for knowing his microphones and their response characteristics. In the control room, he is responsible for blending the signals received from the microphones through the audio console. He will add or subtract those frequencies that help a particular instrument to blend with all the other instruments. He knows and understands signal processing of peripheral equipment (such as limiters, expanders, digital delays, harmonizers, phasers, flangers, and so on) to enhance the signals received from the floor. By virtue of receiving signals from the microphones and processing them through the audio console, he should understand signal levels and the control of them, so as not to distort or have excessive noise that would diminish the quality of the product.

AN ENGINEER SHOULD KNOW NOT ONLY WHAT EQUIPMENT CAN DO BUT WHAT IT CANNOT DO.
Knowing what the equipment can't do is as important as knowing what it can do.

The third aspect of an audio engineer's qualifications, in my opinion, would be his ability to get along with people—to understand that it's not his way, but the way the client wants the product, that's important. He uses his ability to get the product the way the client wants it. He should be open-minded and accept input from the artist and the musicians, as well as from the client, when striving for the final product.

Public relations on the part of the engineer is a major aspect of his ability to do his job. He should be able to handle the musi-

cians, his client, and his artist from the standpoint of pacification that is necessary to achieve the proper technical effects. In essence, he has to roll with the punches; to know when to open his mouth or when to keep it closed; to have compassion, understanding, and patience; to have technical expertise and, hopefully, musical expertise; and, most of all, to enjoy what he's doing.

WHAT KIND OF QUALIFICATIONS DO YOU THINK A YOUNG PERSON SHOULD HAVE TO BE AN AUDIO ENGINEER?
One of the finest recording engineers that I've ever known couldn't find "middle C" on the piano. But as a mixer, sound engineer, he has an uncanny ability to do his job and he does it in an excellent manner. I feel that a formal education is not necessarily a requirement, but an understanding of the basics of what makes equipment tick is certainly an asset.

I think that having a good ear is a very basic requirement. An undying love for the job, I think, is a bound necessity. You can't have stars in your eyes, want to mingle with the stars and satisfy your ego, and do the job. You must love the job because, behind the scenes, fame and fortune is not necessarily a result of the job. Rather it is the self-satisfaction of doing a good job, knowing that others are going to listen to the product that you have been involved in and like it.

You have to be able to make a living doing it, too. Be satisfied with the rather low salary situation of a sound engineer. Some rise above that and some make requirements of clientele and achieve a rather nice salary.

WHY DO SOME PEOPLE BECOME FAMOUS?
Luck! Being at the right place at the right time has a lot to do with it. I think I always have the desire to learn. A person should have an open mind toward new and different things, while not forgetting the past or the beginning. You should enjoy putting it all together, making it work, not just for you but for the people you work for.

Some people say, "If I were engineering a product for a major client, my name would be associated with him. If I don't engineer a product for a popular artist, then I am not known as well." So that is part of the luck factor, being at the right place at the right time.

Some have put a high price tag on their work. What that does is eliminate a lot of the unknowns and the smaller acts from using that particular engineer because they really don't have the budgets to handle them. I have never felt that was a very good way of doing things; I don't condone that. I don't believe in doing it for me. I like to do an honest day's work for the proper amount of funds.

WHEN YOU WORKED WITH BOB DYLAN, WHAT WAS THE STORY WITH "RAINY DAY WOMEN"?

Bob had an idea that he wanted to do a Salvation Army Band-type situation. Without the opportunity to position microphones and musicians in the studio, we did a one-take, seven- or eight-minute cut of "Rainy Day Women." It was a sure challenge to engineering, but it was also a very rewarding experience, since the record did do as well as it did.

Those types of challenges are not uncommon to audio engineers. It's all your technical expertise and abilities that you've gained through past experiences coming into play. That and a lot of luck.

YOU CUT "COAL MINER'S DAUGHTER" WITH LORETTA LYNN.

After the live date acts, Loretta had suggested that she would like to add a couple of expressions to the fade choruses to make it a little stronger, more like she wanted it. So we overdubbed a couple of words.

IN HER SONG SHE SINGS ABOUT POVERTY.

This was her life that she was singing about. She wrote it, sang it, and it was about Loretta Lynn. She came from a coal miner's town and her family were coal miners. It

made her financially successful and known worldwide, not fearful of, or degraded by, her past. She sang it with great love and affection.

I totally respect musical artists. I feel that their life is not their own, that they give a tremendous amount of themselves to entertain the populace. They're on-stage all the time; they have to be. The public demands it. If they aren't, their popularity decreases. And that's something they can't have happen, or they lose their viability as an artist.

ONE OF THE THINGS THAT I'VE NOTICED WORKING WITH PEOPLE IS THAT IF YOU TREAT THEM LIKE A REGULAR PERSON . . .

I have a theory; I've lived by it and it works for me. I have never met a person who is better than I am. I'm not better than anyone else.

I aspire to do my job the best I can. I try to learn hourly, daily, monthly, yearly, how to do it better. And that's respected, or someone else needs to be in the chair.

IS THE INDUSTRY REALLY A BUSINESS?

I believe that any time money changes hands for service rendered, it's a business. But the music industry is different from most other businesses. We're dealing with the intangible, with the creative aspects of many people directed toward one end. Feelings, emotions, concepts, and attitudes, enter into play and are the product.

It's hard to have the clock on the wall and the dollar bill overcome the creative atmosphere, because ultimately I believe you end up with a bad product. Then you've spent the money and the time in vain. But there is a happy medium. You must secure a proper time segment and financial situation.

WHAT DO YOU THINK ABOUT THE MUSIC INDUSTRY TODAY? ITS DIRECTION, WHERE IT'S BEEN, WHERE IT'S HEADED?

I feel that record labels have become artist-oriented and manager-oriented rather than a creative outlet for artistry. Bankers, lawyers, and accountants—we need them, but not everywhere. There are some things that they can't do. It's my opinion that running a record label is one of them.

I feel that we need that creative aspect, the gut feelings, the sympathies, the feelings involved in the artistry of making a record. You can't do it by courting numbers and looking at bottom lines all the time. It should be a part of it, but not the total. And I think we need to get back to basics again. I think we've forgotten where it started, how it started, and who started it. Giving artists big bundles of money to sign with a record label is probably one of the most foolish, asinine things that a record label can do.

HOW CAN YOUNG PEOPLE WHO WANT TO BECOME AUDIO ENGINEERS GET STARTED IN THE MUSIC INDUSTRY?

Starve awhile and stay in and about the business. Maintain a low profile but be ready to leap upon any opportunity that's afforded you.

Some of our colleges offer opportunities for aspiring engineers to learn the basics of being a recording engineer. But it's become such a business that, when the recording engineer walks through that door the first day at work, he almost has to be a profit maker.

I've tried to talk with newcomers about what kind of a training program we have for aspiring engineers. We need to support our field of work by having places to help these kids learn what is required, so that they can make a decision as to whether they want to continue to starve and work their way into the recording industry or not.

TOM MAY

Retired. Former manager of A&M Recording Studios.
Audio engineer for the Carpenters, The Association, Herb
Alpert, Johnny Mathis, Andy Williams, Patti Page, Percy
Faith, Burl Ives, Tommy Roe, the Byrds,
and Buffalo Springfield.

HOW HAS RECORDING, AND I'M TALKING TECHNICALLY, CHANGED SINCE THOSE DAYS WHEN YOU FIRST GOT INTO IT?
The greatest change came about with musicians and the number of tracks. When I started in the recording business, I started mixing. We were mono, and we mixed straight to disc. Then we went to 3-track, and that was great because we had the orchestra or vocals in the center of the track. Then we got 4-track and 8-track, 16- and 24-track, and so forth. So people began to rely more and more on the flexibility of having all those tracks. I've done sessions where they put down drum tracks and that's all. Add this and that, I mean, that's kind of stupid. Now many of the studios are coupling two 24-track tape machines together. Most of the producers and arrangers have become rather crippled because most of them don't have the ability any more to write a full score and do a session.

IT WAS A LOT HARDER TO DO THE RE-CORDING BECAUSE YOU HAD TO PRE-MIX EVERYTHING.

Well, actually, I would say it's really easier. You hear the music in the room and you record it—it's all there. The conductor or the producer would make sure that everybody was playing their parts properly. They got musicians to play the way they wanted to hear it. You recorded it that way because you couldn't put everything off until the mixdown.

I think the guys today have a tougher job because they put it down a track at a time. They have no idea what it's going to sound like or what it's supposed to sound like. Even the producer doesn't know, because they come up and add all this crap as they go along. Some of them turn out good products, but others don't.

DO YOU THINK A LOT OF THE FUN HAS GONE OUT OF IT THEN?
It did for me; I used to do sessions live. You got goosebumps because you knew what you had. I had fun with some contemporary things, like "Sweet Pea" for Tommy Roe and a couple of albums with the Byrds. I did "For What It's Worth" with Buffalo Springfield.

All those guys were talented and proved it by going out on their own and making it. I enjoyed recording song material that was good and had some taste. Later, it wasn't really any fun for me to go in, sit down, and spend half the night with some guy trying to do a guitar lick that he couldn't do. Now the kids, they grew up with that sort of thing, and it doesn't work at them as hard as it did me. It's a young man's game now because, if you came up doing it the way I did, it's not fun spending six months doing an album that we used to do in three sessions.

I DON'T KNOW HOW THEY CAN AFFORD IT.

I don't think the people can afford it. That's one of the things that's wrong with the record business today. The studios were used to charging what they wanted to. The groups would go in and block book for three, four, or six months and spend half a million to do an album. Those days are just about gone because it's finally caught up, which I've been predicting for a long time. Too many groups were just too bad, and the few good groups that were spending a lot of money doing their albums were supporting all the failures. Finally, there came a day of reckoning, and when they regroup, they'll all be better off for it.

I'll tell you the strangest thing that I ever had to do when I started doing rock music. I'd spent half my life trying to improve the quality of the console to get better sounds, but I was asked to *distort* the sound. It was hard to deliberately do it. We would feed it back into a pre-amp to overdrive it. We'd get records back from the pressing plant because they were distorted, and we'd have to tell them that that was the way the producer wanted it. Now musicians have their own distortion boxes that can create distortion.

DID YOU ENJOY WORKING WITH A LOT OF THE STARS OR ARTISTS?

Most of them are very nice people. The ones who were scary to work with were the ones who were really not that talented or who had a very insecure feeling. Some of the new groups would come, and they would say to you, "I want to sound like so-and-so." Of course, the stock answer was, "Well, if you played like them, you would sound like them." But you could try to get a sound closer to it basically. There is really no great mystery about recording.

The engineers get a lot of credit for things that they really can't do. If it sounds good out there, you can really do a good job. If the musicians or artists are doing a lousy job, you know that, no matter what you do, you can't make them sound good. But the people that buy this stuff, or a lot of them, think that mixers are magicians and make everybody sound good. That isn't true. You can enhance the sound and a good mixer can make it a lot better, but you can't destroy what otherwise would be a good record by doing a lousy mixing.

WHAT ADVICE WOULD YOU GIVE TO PEOPLE WHO WANT TO BECOME AUDIO-ENGINEER MIXERS?

Take up something else.

HOW MANY PEOPLE APPLIED EVERY WEEK AS ENGINEERS AT A&M?

There were literally hundreds. One time I was there, there were a few thousand and that's not exaggerating. If a person wants to do it badly enough, they will eventually get the job. If they have talent, they may make it; but it is a relatively small industry when you look at the number of records that are sold.

There are a lot of people trying to get in. It's a great business, and I enjoyed it. I don't enjoy the way they record today, but the kids would because they have all grown up recording that way.

HOW MANY ENGINEERS IN LOS ANGELES DO YOU THINK MAKE OVER $20,000 A YEAR?

There are a lot of them that make more than that. All of my guys made more than that.

LET'S TALK ABOUT JOB SECURITY.

It's a fickle group of people you're dealing with. You can be a hero today and then things go cold. There are people that live off very poor mixes that have gained quite a reputation, but it's short-lived. It's a peculiar business. I've known some very good mixers that never really made it.

WHAT QUALITIES DO YOU THINK AN ENGINEER SHOULD HAVE?

The two things I think are most important— and I think they're equally important—are talent and the ability to get along with people. You've got to have enough talent to do the job, and you've got to be able to get along with other people. It's that simple. Artists and producers won't work with people unless they're compatible. Also, it's important to get the job done well and efficiently, not to waste time.

ANY ADVICE YOU'D GIVE PEOPLE WHO WANT TO GET INTO THE MUSIC INDUSTRY ON ANY LEVEL?

Let's assume you don't know anyone, and you want to get into the recording business. You have to be where the action is. You have to make the rounds to let the people know that you mean business, and you want to get it. Keep knocking on those doors. In the meantime, you'd better have something to do to support yourself. I know kids who just hung around and worked at other things for

three or four years, but they kept knocking on doors.

Eventually people will decide that here is an individual who is determined and really wants in. He'll get the job. And a lot is timing, being there at the right time. If you're there when they need someone, they'll give you the job. It's not easy, and if you really want to be a mixer, you should have music background.

HOW ABOUT DIGITAL? WHAT DID YOU THINK ABOUT IT?

Digital is a fantastic process, I think. It's unfortunate that the equipment is not more reliable. That, in my opinion, is what's holding up digital. It's not really the cost of the equipment; it's the lack of reliability of the equipment.

ONCE THOSE BUGS ARE WORKED OUT, DO YOU THINK THAT'S WHAT IS GOING TO HAPPEN?

I think so; I don't believe analog recording will ever reproduce music as faithfully as digital will. Analog recording is very good and, as a matter of fact, there are a lot of people who like the distortion that analog does. It sort of rounds off those edges. A lot of people like the analog better even though it's not as near the original sound as digital.

TRAVIS TURK

Record producer and audio engineer. Artists recording sessions include the Doobie Brothers, Ann Murray, Waylon Jennings, Ronnie Milsap, the Charlie Daniels Band, and Jimmy Buffett.

WHAT DO YOU THINK ARE THE PROBABILITIES OF GETTING A JOB IN ONE OF THE RECORDING AREAS SUCH AS LOS ANGELES, NEW YORK, NASHVILLE, OR MEMPHIS?

You have to be there at the right time, at the right place. I have heard stories where people have just walked in off the streets and said, "Hey, I would like to be an engineer," and it just so happened there was a vacancy.

Some employers want people who have all the background training and have experience; others want to train somebody from scratch. They want a person to know something about the business, but they don't want the person to have any practical experience. They want to train you to do things their way, so it depends on the place—and the situation.

An engineer should be able to know how to talk music and electronics. Sometimes he has to be ambidextrous. Of course, anybody can get that with physical training and be able to grab five faders, five different things, with each finger.

I believe that the engineer should be an all-around talent and know several types of consoles. If he doesn't know one particular kind of console, with just a little bit of working on it he can figure it out. That comes from electronic knowledge, being on top of what is happening.

DO YOU FEEL THAT THERE IS SUCH A THING AS MAGIC IN CERTAIN SITUATIONS?

This business is not a science; it's an art. If it were a science, then there wouldn't be certain classes of engineers; all we would have to do is open a manual, set the board, and record the song.

That's what science is. As an art, it is like a painter who takes a little bit of red, a little bit of yellow, and a little bit of purple, and he gets a new color. He didn't know that he was going to get that color. He did it by trial and error. He dabbled around. We do the same thing. There are so many combinations of knobs on a console. It depends on how you feel, how everybody else feels. But when everything is clicking, it happens and you know it.

TOM
IRBY

Studio designer and owner of Studio
Supply Company, Nashville.

HOW MUCH DOES A PERSON ON AVERAGE, FROM A LOW POINT TO A HIGH POINT, SPEND ON A BUILDING THAT HE WANTS TO MAKE INTO A RECORDING STUDIO?
On the low side, you are going to start somewhere around $60 per square foot; on the high side, as much as $150 per square foot.

LET'S TALK ABOUT THE EQUIPMENT IN A RECORDING STUDIO.
Low price on a 24-track console is probably somewhere around $25,000. For solid state, you could spend as much as $375,000.

HOW ABOUT TAPE MACHINES?
Most of the production-quality tape machines start at about $6,000 for a 2-track; a 24-track could go all the way up to about $90,000.

HOW ABOUT THE OUTBOARD EQUIPMENT SUCH AS COMPRESSORS AND LIMITERS?
That has been much the same for the past several years. For a good-quality limiter/ compressor, you are going to pay between $400 and $500. Microphones vary anywhere from $50 all the way up to $3,000 for a good stereo mike.

HARMONIZERS, MONITORS, SPEAKERS IN THE CONTROL ROOM?
Harmonizers range from $500 to $3,000. Monitors, speakers start at $75; for a complete system with the tuning and amps, the cost is around $15,000.

WHAT ELSE?
For a good 24-track room, you are talking about $150,000 for a console, and you are going to spend almost that much money for tape machines. You are probably going to spend $40,000 for microphones; $30,000 for gear; and another $15,000 for accessories. Generally, for a good, competitive, well-equipped studio, you are talking in excess of $300,000 or $400,000. That is for the equipment only.

CHAPTER NINE

MUSICIANS

Musicians are a strange breed. Some are off the wall, while others are straight as an arrow. Girls say, "Never marry a musician because he'll always be broke or living on his dreams." A musician will be on the road most of his life, playing in smoky old bars and at concerts. Most of the time, a musician is separated from his wife and kids and is playing somebody else's song to a bunch of people who aren't listening. The guys are at the clubs to meet the girls, the girls are there to meet the guys, and the owner hopes to make a profit. Wouldn't you know it? Money is the name of the game again.

Simply put, being a musician can be one of the best lives you can ever have or one of the worst. It's exciting to meet new people, to make a lot of new friends, to see new towns and different parts of the country. After a while, the excitement wears down to the boring bus ride from one town to another and to playing the same old songs for another five hours. After that, boredom can become numbness, and you don't even remember the names of the towns.

If the band gets its together, creates its own unique style and original songs, then it plays better clubs and hotels. Record companies are always looking for a way to make money, and that means finding a new act or group that is creating excitement in a local area. The record companies really do have people, or contacts, who listen to talent in nightclubs and bars. Each company wants to be the first label to sign a promising new talent. Sure, it's a lot of luck being discovered, being in the right place at the right time. But it's also preparing yourself to be discovered. You've got to get your act together *before* somebody takes notice.

So many people show up in music recording centers—New York, Los Angeles, Nashville, Memphis, San Francisco, Toronto, or Vancouver, and know how to play only one style of music. It's simply not good enough. Chet Atkins once said that the best advice he could give to somebody was for that musician to master his or her musical instrument. Know how to play it in any style from classical to country.

Few musicians make it all the way to recording artist. Glen Campbell did. He was a studio musician, but he also sang for the Beach Boys. If a musician has good talent, good looks, and stage presence (personality), then learning his craft in a band is a good start. There is always the possibility that he may become a recording artist in his own right.

If you're one of the few who becomes a recording artist, it's more than likely that you've got talent to burn and that you've earned every drop of the fame and success you receive. At each level, you've got to be able to cut the mustard or take a step backward. Only the very, very best survive all the way to the top. Some find happiness at a certain level (bar musician, concert musician, studio work) and remain there. Others dream of higher success. If you are pursuing success, don't forget the important things about life. Don't get caught up in the dream so much that you tend to miss the wonderful people and pleasures that life has to offer.

If you're one of the few who's mastered the musical instrument of your choice, then you must have the personality to go along with it. Who wants to work with some kind of an egotistical jerk? The number of qualified piano players in Los Angeles for session work alone could fill a small telephone book. You've got to be accepted and feel the vibes from other pickers. Maybe people have told you that you're the greatest musician they've ever heard. When you're playing session work with the pros, you've got to have your total act together—that includes your personal and social life as well as your musical ability. If you really want to be a studio musician, then go for it. But remember to prepare yourself in every humanly possible way. You'll get a shot to show your talents, but will you be ready?

LLOYD GREEN

Legendary Nashville steel guitarist. Recorded and worked with Charley Pride, Hank Williams, Jr., Charlie Rich, Don Williams, the Byrds, Leon Russell, Bob Dylan, Paul McCartney, and Peter, Paul, and Mary. Recipient of NARAS (Nashville) Award for Most Valuable Steel Guitar Player and the Most Promising Instrumentalist Award from both *Record World* and *Cash Box* magazines.

YOU ARE A STUDIO MUSICIAN. HOW DID YOU GET INTO THAT?

Like most of the musicians, I gravitated to Nashville. The magnet was the music. Very few musicians recording here are natives of Nashville. All have worked the clubs, worked the road, with various artists as a prelude to recording sessions.

SO THE OPTIMUM IS TO COME TO NASHVILLE AND GET INTO SESSION WORK?

It was, and still is, the premium area to be in if you want to make money. Otherwise, it is a much more difficult existence.

I ASSUME MOST MUSICIANS WHO WANT TO MAKE IT NEVER DO.

True. For every one of us that gets into the top echelon of session work, there must be ten thousand who don't.

WHY DO THE FEW MAKE IT?

You can never eliminate the factor of luck. Beyond that, the obvious prerequisite is being a good musician. Even more important are the personality factors that make up the studio musician. You have to learn to think quickly, learn to underplay. It is almost a relearning experience from what you've done in the clubs and on the road. Everything has to be sublimated musically. We have to play according to what the singer sings, not what we want to play.

Some musicians are a lot more opinionated and find it difficult to get along in the studio. They refuse to accommodate themselves to the situation and don't ever make it. Some are exquisite musicians who are not allowed to get into the upper income bracket because of personality flaws, at least flaws as far as recording is concerned.

ANOTHER INTERESTING POINT YOU TALK ABOUT IS THAT MUSICIANS HAVE TO PLAY DIFFERENTLY AND HAVE A DIFFERENT MENTAL ATTITUDE.

You can be a lot more flexible outside the studio. Most musicians who work in bands on tour—for instance, in country bands as sidemen—play what has been recorded by other people. All they have to do is to memorize what has been played; they don't have to be creative. They can probably play more loosely on-stage and get away with it, because it is not as obvious. In the studio, every little thing is magnified tremendously.

I've worked with bands who were exceptional on-stage and who sound lousy in the studio, because all the mistakes—overplaying, being out of tune and so on—show up in the studio. These are things you have to overcome as a studio musician. I've always contended it takes a year and a half or two before a studio musician is really worth his money.

DO THE ACOUSTICS KIND OF THROW YOU? HAVING TO WEAR HEADSETS AND ALL THAT?

Yes, that is a factor. Really, it's an asset. I've been recording since 1964, and the three or four studios we worked in then didn't require headphones, because of the way things were set up. There was more of a live sound and not as much control in mixing. But then we didn't have the sophisticated equipment. There were only 3-track and 4-track machines. Today the equipment is far more elaborate. We have up to 42 tracks in some of the studios. Everything is isolated, so that if they want to take any one instrument off, it is no problem at all. It is a little more difficult initially, adjusting to headphones and other acoustic things; but I suppose it is just another readjustment, another factor that goes into a studio musician's repertoire.

IS IT HARD WORK?

Sometimes, but it is fun work. When something is really coming off and you have a creative thing going—an intuitive sense among the musicians that something exceptional is happening on the tape—it is really a profound feeling.

YOU WORK THREE-HOUR SETS AND YOU MAY WORK THREE OR FOUR SETS A DAY. NOT ONLY THAT, ONE SET MAY BE COUNTRY AND ANOTHER MAY BE ROCK. HOW DO YOU DO IT?

Studio people have learned a little trick. I don't even know when or how I learned it. If I

do a country session from 10:00 AM to 1:00 PM, and then have to go to a rock session at 2:00, I'm able to totally erase from my memory what went on at 10:00. It just never comes back up in my mental processes. You have to do that and not have any overlap. When you walk out of a studio, that session is over, not only physically but emotionally, too. It's like erasing a tape. On the other hand, we use a great deal of concentration on most of the days we work because they are head arrangements where we make up or create the arrangement of a session.

WHAT ADVICE WOULD YOU GIVE TO PEOPLE WHO WANT TO BE STUDIO MUSICIANS?

Learn your instrument. You have to be knowledgeable because there are guys that play as well as you do. Know how to get a sound or an effect or a lick that somebody wants you to play. I just finished an overdub session this morning, and the producer had me do a really complicated thing that was unorthodox to the steel guitar. Because I know my instrument thoroughly, I was able to do it. If I hadn't had all the knowledge I had accumulated over the years, I probably wouldn't have been able to do it. I had to concentrate much more than usual because the producer didn't understand the steel.

HOW ABOUT WORKING WITH PRODUCERS AND ARTISTS?

You have as many different ideas from producers as you have producers. Each has his own little characteristics—some better, some less effective. After a while, it doesn't bother me; I've learned the different idiosyncrasies of each producer. I've adapted accordingly. Some producers honestly don't know what they are doing and they depend totally on the musicians and engineers.

YOU STILL HAVE TO DO YOUR ABSOLUTE BEST WHETHER THE PRODUCER KNOWS WHAT HE IS DOING OR NOT.

It would be irresponsible to do otherwise. Besides, you recognize that if you are on a big record, your work is going to be heard. Obviously, you want to play your best. You never know what is going to be the big record. Any time I've played on a big record, it has spurred my sessions.

YOU HAVE PLAYED A LOT OF SESSIONS. YOU HAVE MENTIONED THE SPECIAL FEELING THAT SOMETIMES COMES OVER A SESSION. WHAT IS THE FEELING?

It is totally intangible. It is just a magical thing that happens—a spontaneity that seems to pervade the studio. Everybody feels it and is aware of it. We know our craft; we know when that special moment is there. Without the reservoir of experience, I don't think people would be aware of it.

DO YOU HAVE ANY ADVICE FOR PEOPLE WHO WANT TO GET INTO THE MUSIC INDUSTRY?

Go to recording studios and see how they work. You can get a feel for the atmosphere, the environment of the studio. It is totally different from any other playing experience. Finally, the only way one can become a studio musician is through experience. That puts you in the classic *Catch-22* situation. People don't want to hire you without experience; but how do you get the experience if you don't get hired? Most of us got started by doing demo sessions. That way, you can get experience in the studio and also be heard by various publishers and record

producers. Beyond that, it just takes a lot of time.

HOW ABOUT READING MUSIC?

Probably about 90 percent of the dates we do are not reading music. I can read a little. We use the number system because it is more efficient. It is much easier to transpose with it than with chord tablature. Sometimes it is not as efficient with complex songs; I have to go to chords and symbols.

YOU HAVE CUT A LOT OF SONGS. HOW MANY OF THOSE DO YOU THINK HAD A SHOT AT BECOMING CHARTED OR BE-COMING HIT RECORDS?

I've been in on some that I just knew would be hits. I've probably been on more records than any other steel guitarist—something like 30,000 records. Freddie Hart's "Easy Lovin'," I knew would make it. I did all the early Charley Pride sessions. But he was such a gigantic artist that anybody could have placed bets and gotten odds that each would be a hit; and each record got bigger and bigger.

On the other hand, I've been in on some that I thought were magic, and they were never heard of again. It's not because the record wasn't there. The failure might have been in promotion or production, any number of factors. The record company can make or break a record once it is finished.

LARRIE LONDIN

Top Nashville drummer whose credits include tours, television shows, and recording sessions. Artists worked with include Floyd Cramer, Perry Como, Dave Loggins, Everly Brothers, Waylon Jennings, England Dan and John Ford Coley, Mickey Gilley, Bobby Bare, Roy Clark, Dean Martin, Eddy Arnold, Isaac Hayes, Minnie Pearl, Les Paul, Merle Haggard, T. G. Sheppard, Jerry Reed, Dolly Parton, Chet Atkins, Rosanne Cash, Olivia Newton-John, and Elvis Presley.

THE MUSIC INDUSTRY IS VERY COMPETITIVE. HOW DID YOU GET STARTED AS A MUSICIAN?

I started when I was almost sixteen. I always wanted to be a singer. That was what I was trying to be—delusions of grandeur, I guess. I thought I was Elvis Presley. I won a few contests for sounding like him and acting like him.

My actual start in the business came in Norfolk, Virginia. A drummer didn't show up one night, and I was in the back room cleaning up. A fellow came in and said, "Is there anybody back here who plays drums?" I asked how much it paid and he said "$75 a week." I was getting $50 for washing dishes. It seemed logical to play drums rather than wash dishes.

HOW DID YOU GET TO NASHVILLE THEN?

I was in Detroit. The group I had played with for ten years and our agreement with Motown—everything was breaking up; everything was changing, moving to Los Angeles. I sent out notices that I was looking for a job. I thought about going back to Florida (I was

raised in Miami) and getting a hotel gig, but Chet Atkins and Boots Randolph gave me a call. I had met them years before, and they were losing their drummer. They made me an offer to move to Nashville as their road drummer.

DO YOU THINK THIS WAS BECAUSE YOU HAD A REPUTATION?

More because I knew them. It had nothing to do with being good or whatever. Our group had played a few invitational golf tournaments, and they had been there. They saw that I played the kind of drums that could do their show. We got along at that time.

I had worked Nashville enough to know that I liked it, and my wife felt that she would. We picked up and moved there.

DID THIS GET YOU INTO STUDIO RECORDING ALSO?

When I moved to Nashville, it was as a road drummer. I had no eyes to be in the studio. I wanted to do the best job I could for them. Chet was unbelievable. I didn't know the stature of the man until I moved to Nashville.

I've always been the kind of person who wanted to do it myself, and I didn't want to use anyone's name. When people would ask whom I worked for, I'd say, "Nobody. I'm self-employed." Basically I was, too. Finally I had to give somebody's name, and I'd say Chet Atkins. It really opened doors for me. He did more for me than he'll ever know. He did a lot for a lot of musicians. I owe him an awful lot.

ATKINS HAS A WAY OF SPOTTING REALLY GOOD TALENT AND GIVING PEOPLE A BREAK.

He's so sensitive to people. It's one thing that he likes you as a musician. If he doesn't like you as a person, it doesn't matter how well you play.

Boots and I didn't get along too well. Actually I worked for him, part of his band. I decided to quit after two years. I was going to go back to Florida. Chet begged me to stay. He said, "Look, everything could really happen for you." All I wanted to do was to find people that I liked working with. Actually he is the reason I stayed.

WHAT IS LIFE LIKE ON THE ROAD? IS THERE LIFE AFTER THE ROAD?

I'm praying there is life after the road. The road is very lonely. It's always hard to leave your family, unless you have no family life.

I like short tours. Ten days is not bad—or two weeks. But three weeks or a month and you're ready to climb the walls, go through walls, to get to your family.

No matter how big the tour, no matter who it is the feelings are all the same. They can make it as plush as they want to, but you're still in that room by yourself. When the lights go out, there is nobody to talk to but you and your shadow.

DOES BEING ON THE ROAD CAUSE EMOTIONAL PROBLEMS WITHIN THE GROUP ITSELF?

Oh, sure. I'm out right now with Rodney Crowell who is probably one of the greatest songwriters in the world. He's an artist in his own right, but he produces his wife, Rosanne Cash. He produced a monster hit with her. Being out with her, you see her side of it; being out with him, you see his side of it. They can both handle it, but there's still the fact that they're not there together. I can handle it and my wife can handle it, but there are moments when all of us get hit with the feeling that we're here and our families are not. Sometimes that plays with how we treat each other in the group. We understand why these things are happening.

WHAT IS THE AVERAGE SALARY A PERSON CAN MAKE ON THE ROAD?

The bottom I have heard is probably $50 a day. The highest is $1,500 a day. It can be very good. There is great money to be made on the road, once you've succeeded in creating a name for yourself. I've been tremendously fortunate.

Nashville has a thing about road work. They figure that if you're a road musician, you can't do studio. If you prove that you can do both, then they don't frown at you anymore. It's just that people don't believe you are actually going out on the road. I can't go out without getting paid what I get, but sometimes I do it because of the music. A lot of times I'm fortunate enough to have both; that's having your cake and eating it too.

IN THE STUDIO, HOW DID YOU GET YOUR FIRST BREAK AT GOING IN AND RECORDING?

The first break was just being part of the group, being in a group that wanted to record. We were pretty young. Today the groups pay for a demo themselves. They do a demo tape and take it to record labels or producers. We weren't that bright. We did it the hard way, which was to let someone else come in and become a part of the recording session.

DO YOU ENJOY RECORDING?

I love recording. It gives me a chance to express things that a lot of people would love to express, but they didn't think of it at the time. I get a chance to say things on a record or tape and invent. You're like an inventor. That's the part that you hope for. You don't always have that and that's the frustration part of the recording. Sometimes they want what you played on the last record that was a hit or whatever. I like to have the freedom to be inventive, to take a song and do something to it that's not been done in that way before.

Even though the music is on a disc and the people can't see you, I think they can still tell if you're having a good time. Having a good time comes out in the feeling of the music. I think people can hear that; I think they know when it's from the heart. When you play music, you create, you give of yourself—and you do it for the love of it. If you can't do that, you shouldn't be in there recording.

HOW DO YOU LIKE YOUR DRUMS MIKED? DO YOU DO IT, OR LET THE ENGINEER DO IT?

The studios all mike differently. I tend to not say anything to an engineer as to how I prefer the drums to be miked. He generally knows the room; he may know what the producer likes or dislikes. I figure he puts them on tape and I play them. I prefer that he not tell me how to play drums, and I won't tell him how to engineer. All I mean is that I respect them as engineers. I'm not an engineer; I know how I like my drums to sound. If it's my project and I'm producing, if it's my neck on the line and I'm playing drums, then it's my say-so. As long as it's somebody else's, I'll tell them what I think when they ask me. I don't like to tell a man how to do his job.

WHAT KIND OF MONEY CAN YOU GET FOR RECORDING? IT'S ABOUT $220 FOR A THREE-HOUR SET. BUT CAN YOU INCREASE THAT MONEY?

Many people do. I'm double scale as a studio drummer in Nashville. Everywhere but Nashville, I get many times more than that. It can vary from $500 a session to $1,500 a session. There is miscommunication about what this means in Nashville. A lot of musicians and a lot of producers and record executives think that people who charge double scale think they are better than everybody else. That is not really what it is based on. For me, it was based on my health—I was working too many hours per day; I was sick and couldn't keep that pace. When you go double scale, you automatically get rid of people such as some smaller record labels. There are pros and cons about this. But I see it as creating work for other players. You're playing on hit records, and you have what the people want. You say this is what I have to get. They either pay it or they don't. I cut my work in half, but I end up making the same amount of money.

DO YOU FEEL FORTUNATE?

I'm probably the luckiest person you've ever talked to. Just the fact that I'm able to talk to you makes me feel fortunate. I've never really gone after anything or made plans about doing this or that. For me, it's either happened or it hasn't. The biggest dream of my life was to play drums for Elvis Presley. I never worked at it, but I got a call one day and there I was, playing drums for Elvis.

HOW DID YOU LIKE ELVIS?

I loved him. I didn't see what all these people see. He had his good and his bad, like anybody does; but I found him very sensitive. Everybody told me that he could put you down at the drop of a hat. What I found was a man who was lonelier than I was. His only real highlight was an hour a night on-stage. He came out there to have a good time. He liked to have people sitting behind him who gave 1,000 percent and did nothing but watch him. That's exactly what I did. Therefore no problem. If you didn't watch him, you got lost in the show. He and I got along great. He was very nice to me. I'm fortunate to have been a part of that.

YOU MUST ENJOY MEETING A LOT OF PEOPLE.

Some of them you do. Some of them you wish they hadn't burst your bubble. Sometimes the people who are paying you top dollar let you know it. Sometimes they have more respect for you than they do for the guy they're paying $50 a night. That's wrong. You're a human being first.

YOU'VE DONE WHAT A LOT OF MUSICIANS WOULD LOVE TO DO. YOU'VE PLAYED ON THE ROAD, MADE GOOD MONEY, PLAYED WITH THE BEST IN THE WORLD. WHAT ADVICE WOULD YOU GIVE TO PEOPLE WHO WANT TO BE MUSICIANS?

My advice is to be prepared. What I mean by that is to definitely be prepared technically for what you want to do. If you want to play big stage shows, be prepared to play a big stage show. If you want to do studio work, be prepared for that. But you also have to be prepared mentally and physically. So many times musicians and singers get hired because of their attitude toward the job. They're fun to be around. They're up, not just cut-and-dried or sitting around griping. If you've got problems, you handle them. Don't expect your boss or somebody around you to handle them. You need to be positive.

Younger players sit around and complain about the amount of money they make compared to others, or about the job that others get even though they think they are just as good. Who cares? Just sit down and do your job.

WHAT KIND OF EQUIPMENT DO YOU RECOMMEND?

I don't get paid to endorse and play equipment; I don't believe in that. I'm only as good as the equipment I'm playing. I've been with Pearl Drum Company for ten years. I play them because I've not played any others that have given me a better sound, that hold up better on the road, in the studio, wherever. If I didn't have that quality, I wouldn't be getting called. I use good equipment, and that makes me sound good. There are good drum companies out there, but these are the ones that work for me. Don't just accept equipment because so-and-so plays it—find it for yourself.

BILL
PURSELL

Conductor, musician, record producer, college professor,
and music arranger for recording sessions and
motion picture scores.

***THE RECORD INDUSTRY IS BOOMING.
WHAT KIND OF JOB MARKET IS THERE
FOR YOUNG PEOPLE WHO WANT TO BE
ARRANGERS?***

Well, if you are young and you want to be an
arranger and it's a good market, it's a
combination of who you know and what
you've done. And if you haven't done anything, it's who you know. I've seen more
"learn as you earn" type of people come
into this business who defy description. I've
looked at some of the scores: The strings
are in the wrong place on the score; the
brass are not transposed. The voicings are
incredibly encumbered, and I know that
these particular kinds of arrangers haven't
really studied scores. And yet these people
end up doing a whole lot of work.

The business welcomes people without
really interviewing them too closely to find
out what they can do. If someone has been
on a record session and the title comes out
"arranged by . . . ," a producer says, "Oh,
this is the guy we must have."

Arrangers would probably go up the wall
if their names weren't on the records, because they realize this is where their living is
coming from. That is why arrangers are so
uptight about getting their arranging credits
on the record. This is really their calling
card.

***ARE THERE MANY JOBS? WHERE ELSE
CAN AN ARRANGER WORK, BESIDES THE
RECORD BUSINESS?***

Well, he can start doing road-show charts.
He can do movies, if he's determined
enough to go and sweat out the Los
Angeles scene. Now, getting into the Los
Angeles movie-writing business is very
political. I know some people who have
gone out there and ghostwritten for different
people. They do scores, and they get a little
teeny-tiny credit at the bottom of the picture,
if they're lucky.

***WHAT KIND OF EDUCATION SHOULD A
PERSON GET?***

Look at a guy like Don Sabesky, one of the
best and more erudite arrangers in America.
I am positive that Don did not have the
conservatory training I did. On the other

hand, I am positive, from reading his book on orchestration, that he's been one of these people who's gone out and studied all the scores he could find. It's a matter of what you really want to do for yourself. A great deal of background doesn't hurt an arranger or a composer.

WHERE DOES THE MONEY COME FROM WHEN YOU ARRANGE FOR SOMEBODY?
It depends. If you're arranging for a record company, it comes from a record company. If you can get an independent production, it comes from a private backer.

EXPLAIN WHAT "DUMB EARS" MEANS.
Dumb ears has to do with recognizing what the public is going to buy. It is an evasive, mercurial ability that some people have. I've seen people without any musical education at all who can tell you what is going to hit. Look at Fred Foster. Look at all the work he did with Roy Orbison back in the days when they did "Crying" and all those big monster hits. There was this nice guy with a high, effeminate voice going out there and singing in front of a band. It was the craziest sounding thing in the world, and he was selling records like you can't believe.

WHAT WOULD YOU SAY TO YOUNG PEOPLE WHO WANT TO GET INTO THE ENTERTAINMENT BUSINESS?
Look at it closely. If you want to get into the entertainment business, go ahead and do it. I wouldn't tell my kids not to do it. My wife would; I wouldn't. I would try to help them. It's like any business today. In terms of the kind of thing we're talking about, it's risky at best.

DO YOU FIND TEACHING A STABILIZING FACTOR IN YOUR LIFE?
I realized that somehow teaching made more sense to me in order to understand what music is. It seemed important to try to dig as deeply as I could into the lives of other people who come from centuries before. I'm interested in getting inside of the music, almost as if I were watching the pencil move at the time it was being written. That's the way I like to understand music.

CHAPTER TEN

PUTTING IT ALL ON TAPE

In the previous few chapters we've learned about the various factors and people that make up a recording session. And we've learned how the producer is responsible for making sure that everything comes together and sounds right on the final mix. This chapter will explain step-by-step how the producer works his way through a session from pre-planning, through each stage of recording, to making the master tape.

Taking us through these steps is Jimmy Bowen, Division President of MCA Records, and producer of such artists as Hank Williams, Jr., the Bellamy Brothers, and Conway Twitty.

Laying the basic tracks
The session begins when the producer brings the arrangements to the studio. He has gotten together with the arranger beforehand, and the arranger has put down on paper what the producer wants. The producer has to know the material well—and so does the artist.

But the session musicians have never

heard the song before, and you want to get them into your tune so they'll all work together to give you something new. As producer, you have to lead the musicians into the sound. The best way to do this is to always keep a calm demeanor in the studio when working with the artist and the musicians. You can't shock anyone into getting the sound right.

Many producers will start a session by playing the artist's demo tape. But unless the demo has the same feeling that you're trying to achieve, it's better if the artist just plays it for the other musicians. If there are certain parts of the demo that you want repeated, let them get into the song, and then play them the demo and let them listen to what you want. Don't make the mistake that a lot of producers do by simply going into the session trying to make the demo sound more professional.

If you've done your pre-production properly, you'll know in general what you want the guitar to do on a song. I don't suggest you walk in and tell everybody right off the bat what to do. It's better to let them get into

167

it on their own. You should know, in your own mind, how it's going to sound so that you're heading toward it. But if one of the musicians has a better idea, or if they all have a better idea, go with them. Always try anything that the musicians want to try because they could very well be right. Listen to your engineer if he wants to try something—a time line, a delay line. If they want to try things, it's because something has triggered it in them.

Don't wear the guys out making tape number twelve, fourteen, twenty-two, thirty. Insecure producers will keep doing one more for safety, one more for protection. Somebody's got to know sometime when it's cooking. If you carefully plan your session, you'll get three to six super performances out of everybody, where all the energy levels are up somewhere between 90 and 100 percent. They'll get you a track in one of those six.

As soon as you can, after they've learned their parts really well, get it to a test track, a test tape. Get it down—mistakes, what-ever—and play it back for them. They'll hear what works, what doesn't work. Let them take the time, make the corrections, practice the chorus that you've just made a change in. Practice the intros, endings, the verses, get them down right. Then when you feel they're ready to make a master, you're going to get three to six super high energy takes.

Once you've got the best you're going to get this night on this one song, that's what you'll repair. If the bass and the drums are cooking and they're straight, you can repair almost everybody else if you do it right away. If you bring them back two or three days later, it's very difficult to get a musician back into the exact mood, get his energy up. That's why I stop and fix the mistakes. You can do another take quicker, but it's lost its peak and headed down the other way. All you're going to get is one without mistakes. You're better off to fix the one with mistakes if it feels right. It's that magic that's hard to recapture.

You hear about magic in making records.

That's when there's magic, when all those energy levels get up, and it's got that little something to it that's different than all the other ones. We want to learn to recognize that.

If you get to those three or six takes and you haven't got it, forget it. Do it again later. Sometimes, if it's your first time on the session, go back about four or five hours later and do that first song again. One or two takes, and they'll nail it. If they don't, play it again another day.

If you know you've only got this band for two hours and you've got to get another track, don't stop at that point and fix it. Know you've got it and know it's got to be fixed, but get your other track. Let the majority of the musicians leave and then keep the ones to fix that other track. If you have to lose them all, get them back as soon as you can, the next day or the day after, and repair that track.

It doesn't hurt, after you've nailed that master—especially the first one of the session—to play it back two or three times. Musicians may be getting coffee; they may wander in and out, but it doesn't matter. I let every one of them quietly know, "Super, man, that was great." Next tape they'll give you a little bit more.

You have to be very, very careful as the producer in a recording session; you can destroy it by the expression you carry on your face or the mood you're in. You're the focal point. They're all children looking to the teacher, the parent. They're there to please you. You're paying them money to do in a short amount of time something exceptional, so you've got to watch how you behave.

You've also got to watch your players as you're doing the session, especially when you're into that three to six masters. You've got to have your tentacles out. If one of them looks like he's about to faint or get sick or something, you're better off to take him out of the music than let him destroy it or cause it to be of lesser quality. Watch especially your drummer and your guitar players who have to do a lot of rhythm and picking and stuff. If they're exhausted and you say, "Give me one more," you are not going to get it. You're better off to take five minutes and let them rest.

With different musicians and artists, the pace is different. You have to learn to read that. Cast your band so that it moves at the same speed. If you've got one guy racing and one guy laying back, it can cause you a problem. It should be the artist's music, not the producer's. They should strive to get the artist's music on tape.

OVERDUB AND SWEETENING

If you've done everything properly to this point, you now have a basic track that you like and you've got to complete it. Overdubbing and sweetening of your product is an incredibly delicate process and very, very important. You have to be super careful that you don't blow your record from this point on.

After you've cut your basic tracks, and you've taken your rough mixes home and lived with them a few days, you'll often change what you were going to do—slightly or sometimes drastically. Other things will come to mind that you just didn't perceive when you were in your preproduction. Occasionally you'll make a complete left-hand turn and ignore all your preproduction. Something will happen in that live session, you'll go another way, and you'll have to reconstruct your record, in your mind, and know what you're going to do with it.

Just as you had to get all the energy levels up for the basic track musicians at the right time so that you get that extra magic, you've also got to try to do that in over-dubbing. It's twice as hard now because you've got one musician, a couple, or three singers standing there in a cold studio, with just you and an engineer. They're supposed to get to an emotional level that a dozen people got to a week before in a live session. It's very, very difficult, but it must sound like it happened the night you cut the basic track.

Make sure your earphones sound good.

When they put them on, you want them to go, "Wow! That's great." Now they start to get some energy, start to join your party that you've got going. You've got to do that. But it's just as important in the booth. If they come in and listen, it's also got to sound good and got to sound just like that earphone mix.

Too many people set up a monitor bal-ance, just knock themselves out, and kind of screw off the earphone mix, doing it in two or three minutes. Well, the poor musician's out there hearing one thing. He comes in the booth and goes, "Wow, I'm great. I don't sound very good, though." It's because you haven't turned him on.

If you can get across to the musician what you were trying to do with your lick or your chart, he can then take it, hear the track, and make it fit the music you've laid on him. Either that or come up with something new that does work. The key to it all is it's got to sound like you were in a great big studio, and everybody was there at one time.

You can't sweeten your mix ten times; money won't allow it. When it doesn't work, you've got to have the confidence in yourself to say it doesn't work—even if eight people in the control room think it's great. Be very careful about the volume you use in your control room. If a guy from the record company walks in, turn it up. You've only got him for three minutes; hype him. Rattle his heart inside his chest cage. But don't make any of your decisions that way. Get it down to whatever a reasonable level is so that you're hearing an honest thing. If you turn the volume up too loud, it'll sound brighter and better than it really is. Then, when you hear it on the radio, you'll say, "Oh, my snare drum sounds like it's under water. Why did I leave that vocal so dull?" It's because you've been hyping yourself for two, three weeks with that volume.

The order of sweetening is very, very important. This is an area where each one will develop his own style and own way of doing it. All I can tell you is the way I do it and what works best for me.

First of all, I think you should do any foundation sweetening first, the basics. If you think you're going to use two rhythm guitars, get that second one on as soon as you can, so you can see if that works. They'll wipe out the whole middle of a record if they don't work. If you're going to over-dub an electric piano and you have an acoustic piano on it, get to that early in your over-dubbing process, to see if the two keyboards clash or if they wipe out the rhythm guitar. Do all your foundation sweetening first.

The next thing that I try to do is to record the vocal by the artist. I prefer a live vocal. Those are almost always your best because there's another energy happening.

It's important that you find out from your artists when they like to sing the most. Just because artists work at 8 o'clock at night in their shows doesn't necessarily mean that's when they'd prefer to sing. They have no choice about that; they have to work at night. If you've got a group that likes to sing in the morning or in the afternoon, that's tough if you don't like to get up. If you want to cut that group, you've got to do them in the morning.

If you can't get the vocal on live, get it right after the session. If I get a track thats there but the vocal isn't—I try to put the vocal on right away again. I give the musicians a break, let the vocal sing it two or three times, and record. Now you've got your three vocals going with your session, and you got it recorded very close to the time the music all happened.

Now take your best of those three and/or your live, and do a vocal combination—if you think you've got a master out of those three, or a test vocal that's really, really close to what the final is going to be. The reason for this is because you're about to start sweetening a record. If you don't have the star on it, God knows whether your sweetener's going to work or not. The worst thing is when you sweeten the whole record and then record the vocal over-dub. He's trapped. He's got to sing exactly where you've sweetened him, in the corner you've boxed him into, or it won't work. Then he's restricted and can't quite pull it off like you'd want.

Sometimes—you'll get clear to the end of the record and you'd like to have that artist take a couple more stabs. Try not to ever lose what you've been working with before this. Don't erase it; keep that vocal. If they want to try it again, then let them. It's their music; it's their life. They should have the opportunity to do whatever they want within reason.

In whatever form it happened, you've got your basic foundation sweetening and you've got your singer on there. Now, you've still got a lot of sweetening to do at this point. I suggest that next you follow the foundation theory, come right on up out of the foundation. Any foundation instruments that are going to be doubled, any electrical guitars, get them on next. Make your strings and your background voices last because they can all be altered to fit what other things may have happened in the guitar over-dubs. Many times you'll go in and you've never envisioned a twin guitar part on your record, but it can work. However, it destroyed your string line that you were going to put down. If you already had the strings on, you'd have a clash or a problem and would have to give up or redo the guitars or strings. Strings are too expensive to lose! It's a $4,000 cost just to do one string over-dub, with arranger cost, copying cost, string players and studio. So get to that last.

Anytime you go to an arranger play him a good rough. Make it a good rough mix so that the man can hear the bass. More people foul up because in their rough mixes you can't hear the bass and the poor string arranger writes a cello line that clashes with the bass he couldn't hear. Be very careful about that. Always give your arrangers good roughs and always give them a 7½-inch tape. They'll all ask for cassettes. Let them make their own. Cassette players don't run true.

I always put the background voices on last. They can be altered to fit into everything else you've done. Plus, if you're using background voices, you almost always have harmony parts and you could wind up with clashes. If you record them too early, then the great string line you love might not work.

Let's assume you've got all your foundation sweetening. Now you're going to use horns, strings, and background voices on your record. I do the horns first, the strings second, and the background voices third. If I had to go back and do the horn parts, it's the cheapest of the three. Background voices take longer than horn players. Horns walk in and zap it right out, if they're good. If I have to redo anybody, I'd rather it be the horns. Or, if I'm going to lose anybody on the record, it's usually going to be the horns. That's just my own way of doing it.

Quite often, if you mix in stereo and you hear it on mono, AM radio, it's a completely different picture. I've done it to myself dozens and dozens of times. I thought I was so great until I heard it on the air. My suggestion to eliminate that kind of possibility is to mix everything in mono. I do my session in stereo. But when I'm working with my drummer, I do all that in mono. I do all my mix-downs in mono.

Mixing and Mastering

The mix-down is when you put together the puzzle that you've created. All the pieces are there; now you've got to put them all back together and make them work.

All during the recording process, you've been taking your roughs home, listening to them, digesting what works and what doesn't work. When you get to mix-down, you should at that point pretty well know what the end result is going to be. Before mix, you made your last over-dub session and you've listened to that rough or that cassette. You now know if there's something you're going to totally leave off during mix-down; if there are things you're really going to feather down in the music, something you're going to bring up, where things have to be together. Proportions are super important now.

The first thing I'd suggest is throw your twenty-four tracks up on the board without any E.Q., and get yourself, in thirty to forty minutes, a pretty decent little mix, just like you were going to make yourself another rough. Get a quick, total picture so that you can see what you've got. Listen to it three, four, five times. Now you're ready to put it together properly.

Now throw yourself back. Make sure you've got your board set up properly. Make sure, when you do that rough, you're doing panning. Get everything relatively where it's going to be and so forth.

If you're on a board where center could be questionable, like M.C.I. boards (they have a little pan knob that works loose) or any board that doesn't have a clip center, throw a tone up and make sure you have all your center modules dead center. This preciseness can really be important.

Sometimes you don't want, of course, an equal split. You want them offset here and there. But anything where you've got exact splits, do it by tone, off of the tracks you're coming from, and you'll be exactly left and right.

Leave the echoes off. Echoes should embellish, make it sound even better, but you'd better be able to make it sound good without any echo whatsoever.

Then go back and build your house from the foundation up again. Work on your drums. Get them sounding right. Check for phasing on all your drums, make sure everything's right. Some of these things you've done a couple of time already, but this is the last shot you've got at it, so check all your phasing. Get your drums sounding right. Drums don't have to be all the way left and right just because the possibility's there. Sometimes they'll sound better if you'll move them in a little bit. They may sound much better if you'll bring them in. Play around. Take your options. Get them where the drums sound the very best.

Then E.Q. (equalize) your drums some

within themselves. Make sure your snares sound the way you want. Get everything where you want it with that last E.Q., then add your bass.

Get your bass and your kick together, E.Q.-wise and balance-wise. You're building from the bottom up, bass and kicker together. Once that all feels and sounds good to you, remember, during this process, to go back and forth from mono to stereo, mono to stereo, always. If it sounds wrong in either one, you've got a problem.

You get your bass and drums in, then put your piano in. The piano's got to go with the kick and the bass. Get it in there where it belongs and listen to it and see if maybe the left hand needs to be brightened a little. Maybe it's muddying up the kick and you're losing both of them. More than likely it will interfere with the bass, or vice versa. E.Q. your piano, get it set. If you've got two keyboards, put the piano on the left, and the electric piano on the right—any combination that sounds good to you, mono and stereo.

After you've got your piano in, get to your guitars—your acoustic guitars. They're the next problem child in the midst of your records. Add your acoustic guitar; decide where you're going to put it. If you've got two, you may do the exact split. You may be offset, but get the acoustic guitars in and work on them until you can hear them, the piano, the bass, and the kick drum. Don't let any of these things you're adding in wash out themselves or anything else.

Now that you've got those things in, stay with your foundation instruments, go to your electric guitars. Find where they go; make them work in there. Next are any other electric instruments you've got, bring them in now. Get all your foundation instruments in.

Now, when you can hear them all, get them in proportion. This can take two, three, four hours just for the foundation instruments, going back and forth, back and forth. When you get them pretty much where you think they are, at that point, put everything else back in. Put in your singers,

everything. That lets you see right away if you've got your foundation instruments so bright they'll make your vocal sound dull.

Once you've put all this new stuff on top of your foundation, you see where that goes and try to put it where you think it ought to be. Get your horns set in stereo where you think they ought to be. Set your strings where you think they ought to be, your background voices where they ought to be, and of course, your lead singer's in the center. There's a big, wide spectrum there and there's room for everybody, if you'll work at it. If you just throw them up, it isn't going to happen.

You can find ways to create illusions. It's one of the reasons you have to have plenty of time when you're mixing down. You can't do it under a clock because you might find something great by having the time to experiment. But, if you're going to do that, you should have it in mind before you get to mix-down.

Now you've got your foundation and you've started to add your other instruments. You take them all back off, go back to your foundation instruments and add in. This gets down to personal taste. You may want to put your horns in next, you may want to put your low strings in next, all your strings in next. This gets into how you personally do it. From here on up you'll find your own way to build it. I do strongly suggest you get your foundation instruments in there first and add to it like a house.

However you do this, you get it all back in now, all except the singers.

Now what I suggest is to put the lead singer in. I may have to adjust all that E.Q. I've worked for two hours when that lead singer gets in. I get that working right, then I start adding. The last thing I add on is the background group. I usually add them last because they're the most flexible thing you've got.

At that point, after you've got everything else on, it's a matter of going back and forth, mono to stereo, mono to stereo. Stuff that's all the way left and right, when you put it on mono you won't have enough of it. Then when you get enough of them on mono, you open back up and it's way too much. It may cause you to bring them in some. It may cause you to compromise between mono and stereo, somewhere in there. It's not the ideal. The ideal is just to make great stereo, but unfortunately, you've got to make a living at this, so you've got to make mono and stereo. So then it's just back and forth, back and forth.

I do suggest that you mix mono, because your proportions will be better in mono for radio. Also, the tendency for stereo is to get the voices too far out in front. When somebody says, "I didn't hear all the words the first time," you tell them, "Please listen again." On how many hit records do you hear every word the first time through? Not always. Half the time, maybe, you heard every word the first time through. Pop, rock records—not country. Country, you do hear the words almost always the first time through.

When you're mixing, just be careful that you don't wad things up in your stereo. Don't clutter your own records. Learn to be able to hear everything on your record that you want to hear. If you don't want it, cut it off, or bury it. But if it should be heard, you want to make sure that you have a chance to hear it.

I suggest that when you can, dollar-wise, anytime that you get your masters and your 24-track done, that you make safeties. Don't keep them in the same studios; they may both burn up. Keep them in a different place. Once you've got your mixes, you should also have safeties.

Never send a master without a safety. It can happen—plane crash, lose it, spill gasoline on it. Anything you can think of has happened. Always make sure your tape boxes are clearly marked (Dolby, DBX), everything that ought to be on it.

We go to a whole other form when we go to disc and the mastering is just as crucial as any of the other phases. The mastering engineer can destroy you and he can save you. If you're wrong somewhere, many times he can make you come out smelling like a rose. When you get a good one, you stick with him. When you get a guy who can read your product, your deficiencies, or your extremes, and can deal with them and get them on disc for you, stick with him.

DENNY PURCELL

Master engineer. Artists' albums include Neil Young, Ronnie Milsap, Barbara Mandrell, Ray Price, Jim Reeves, Roy Clark, Jim Ed Brown, Conway Twitty, Gail Davies, Larry Gatlin, Ed Bruce, and Jerry Reed.

WHAT DO YOU DO AS A MASTER ENGINEER?

Here's basically what happens, from start to finish. When a client finishes his project, he ends up with a 2-track tape—either a ¼-inch or a ½-inch wide master that plays at 15 or 30 ips [inches per second] and has Dolby or DBX noise reduction. We schedule a time that is convenient for the client and for us. The first thing we do is set up the tape machine. The engineer in the studio has given me a reference tone (frequency), so that my playback will correspond with the studio's if I set my machine accordingly.

YOU'RE LINING YOUR TAPE MACHINE UP PROPERLY, SO IT WILL GIVE YOU THE BEST RESPONSE FROM THE TAPE. YOU WANT YOUR TAPE PLAYBACK TO MATCH THE TAPE MACHINE IN THE OTHER STUDIO.

Exactly. That's the whole reference point. Once we do that, the client (whether it be the producer or the artist) sits in the room with me, and we listen to the tape. We'll listen to it several times before he decides if he wants to make some changes.

At this point, several things happen. You have different relationships with each of your clients. Some clients will dictate changes to you. Some may be specific and say, "Add 3 dB at 15 kHz" or "Add dB at 100 Hz." Some may just say, "Add top end [treble]," and you'll try different top ends. You can also alter the bass and the midrange.

But other clients don't get technical or don't enforce their opinions. They ask you what you think, and then they either say "yes" or "no."

WHEN YOU ARE WORKING WITH A CLIENT, YOU HAVE TO TAKE INTO CONSIDERATION HOW CREATIVE HE IS. YOU HAVE TO FIGURE OUT THE BEST WAY TO WORK WITH THAT PERSON, AND MAKE HIM RESPOND, SO YOU CAN GET A GOOD PRODUCT—FOR HIM AND YOU.

What I love to do with people is give them an option. I like dealing with people in black and white, because then they know that they can respond to me in that manner themselves. The two of us need to relate to each other, and my job is to be his hands.

It's essential to remember that with any

one client there's not any one specific way that will work. Each client is an individual.

As the client listens to his tape, you suggest changes, he suggests changes, or we work together to come up with a sound that you'd want to put on a disc. Then you cut what's called a reference disc. A reference disc is to a master lacquer what a rough draft is to a term paper. When you finish with the client, he can take home the reference lacquer and listen to it. Then he can do one of three things. He can call us and say, "I love it. Keep it just like it is." He can say, "I love it, but I want to change these things." Or he can say, "I hate it. Let's start all over again."

We keep a record of exactly what we did; so when the client calls, it's simple to make the changes he requests. Unless the changes are drastic, he doesn't need to come in again.

LET'S SAY THE TWO-TRACK TAPE IS ON THE TAPE MACHINE. THE SIGNAL IS GOING TO BE TURNED FROM MAGNETIC FLUX ON THE TAPE INTO AN ELECTRONIC SIGNAL THAT IS GOING TO YOUR CONSOLE. AT THAT POINT, YOU CAN ADD HIGH, MIDRANGE, OR LOW FREQUENCIES.

Once the signal gets to the console, we add to sound what spices are to food. If a client needs certain spices that he specifically likes, we can add them. If he doesn't, we need not do anything to it. It's an option. The secret to good records is good tapes. I like to take credit for what we do here, and I think we do a great job—but the secret is the tape. Everything you do in this room, as far as equalization from the original tape, is a trade-off. If you gain one place, you lose in another; but lots of times, we find that the gains are worth the trade-offs.

WHEN THE SIGNAL IS AT THE CONSOLE, YOU CAN ADD HIGHS OR LOWS AND YOU CAN COMPRESS THE DYNAMIC RANGE. WHAT ELSE CAN YOU DO?

There are a lot of alternatives there, but that's pretty much it. From that point on, the signal path moves to the cutter rack. There's not much changing in the cutter rack, except that there are some little units there that control the de-essing.

EXPLAIN WHAT DE-ESSING IS.

De-essing is simply getting rid of the sibilance, the hissing sound that's caused when a person pronounces s. Most people know what popping is—p's pop on microphones. We have ways of getting rid of those and mastering s's.

It's very important to get the sounds right in the mix at the recording studio before the tape is sent on to the mastering lab. On a score from 1 to 10, if you're working in the studio, try to get a 10. If you don't, fine. Then maybe you can get closer to the 10 in mastering; but each time you give in, when you get to the end, you won't have a 10.

When people bring the tape to me, I try to get it to a 10. I very seldom get a 10, but I try. But if they bring me a 10 to begin with, and I don't get a 10, it's because I did something wrong.

SO THE SIGNAL COMES FROM THE CONSOLE AND TRAVELS TO THE CUTTER RACK. WHERE DOES IT GO FROM THERE?

To the cutter head, where you're dealing with two magnets. The signal goes from two magnets to two wires and then to a needle, the stylus.

Through those two electromagnetic coils, the signal is converted to mechanical movement. The stylus is going to try its best, by vibrating, to produce a mechanical version of the electronic signals that you're sending from the console and the tape machine. It's a whole different medium, though.

For example, if you put on a tape flat (E.Q.), have a perfectly flat (E.Q.) system, and cut that flat (E.Q.) on a disc, the disc won't sound the same as the tape. You try to fool the client's ears so that when he hears the disc, he thinks that it sounds like the tape. But there's no way to cut a flat disc and have it sound exactly like the flat tape.

Some clients know this to begin with. Some clients know that the loudest thing you can cut on the disc is the outer cut. Some clients know that as you go in on the disc there are fewer highs. Some don't know this, and some don't care.

SO THE STYLUS IS ACTUALLY GOING TO CUT GROOVES INTO A LACQUER DISC.

The disc is actually a sheet of Alcoa aluminum covered with a lacquer made principally from nitrocellulose.

I'VE HEARD THAT COMPANIES ARE VERY SECRETIVE ABOUT THEIR LACQUERS.

They're very secretive. We're also at a potential crisis situation. First of all, Alcoa doesn't like making little pieces of aluminum that are perfectly flat when they can make zillions of dollars on aluminum. Secondly, for the two major U.S. suppliers of the lacquer, there's only one source of nitrocellulose. That's a crisis situation.

WHAT YOU ARE SAYING IS THAT YOU HAVE A SHORTAGE OF LACQUERS.

We have a shortage because one of the components used in making lacquers is also used in making nail polish. The cellulose comes from cotton. It makes more sense to sell the same cotton to make nail polish because you'll make more money. The fact that lacquer also includes petroleum products contributes to the shortage, and we have to deal with that.

LET'S SAY THAT THE GROOVES ARE BEING CUT INTO THE DISC BY THE STYLUS. WHAT KIND OF PROBLEMS ARE YOU GOING TO HAVE WITH THAT DISC?

The things that a mastering engineer looks for, such as overcuts. An overcut is generally caused by putting too much signal [the loudness or amplitude of the music] on a disc, which causes one groove to spread into another.

IS THIS A HOT RECORD?

You're exactly right. Generally, putting too much signal on the disc causes grooves to cut through one another, or overcut. That causes a problem when the user puts his record on. The needle/stylus reaches an intersection, a crossroads in the grooves, if you will, and it sort of throws up its hands. It doesn't know which groove to follow, so it skips.

Another aspect of the disc, what to look for, is out-of-phase signals. Those are probably the two major things: signal and phase. Out-of-phase information causes the cutter head to actually lift up off the record.

HOW ABOUT ORANGE PEEL, RIMS, THAT KIND OF STUFF?

Those are imperfections that you notice in the actual lacquer itself. Before an engineer sets down the cutter head on any lacquer, he should inspect it. There is quite a high return rate on discs.

Approximately 25 to 35 percent of the discs that we receive are rejected. Before we cut on any lacquer, we inspect it. Even then, after you cut on it, sometimes you find something you didn't see. And even though you've spent thirty minutes on the side, you throw it away. And the client never gets charged for it. That's why mastering costs what it does.

Let's say it costs $110 for an album side, and about $50 for a single. That's for custom clients. Major clients pay the same rates, but they usually order 12 to 18 lacquers, plus tape copies; so it's different. Plus there is E.Q. (equalization) time. For example, we can make $200 to $500 an hour, if we are working in here by ourselves. But if a client wants to come in, we charge him $75 an hour. It's called appointment time. This means that he can come in, we'll stop our schedule, and we'll put his tape on and listen to it.

ONCE YOU HAVE THE GROOVES IN THE LACQUER, WHAT IS GOING TO HAPPEN TO THAT LACQUER? WHERE DOES IT GO NEXT?

This is assuming we've done the reference lacquer, we've gotten approval, and we've cut what's called a part. The master lacquer is generally called a part. For major labels we'll cut from 6 to 18 parts, meaning duplicates of the original reference lacquer with updates in it if there are any. Each part gets inspected to see that there are no faults in any of them. After that, they get packed in a shipping carton, which is picked up by an air-freight service.

We generally promise three-day service after approval, which keeps us quite busy. After we finish the project, it's air-freighted out of here in the afternoon or evening. Generally speaking, by noon the next day, it's at a pressing plant. They do a metal plating, a three-step process, at the end of which they come up with a negative of what I made. That negative, when used in a mold, produces a positive—a record.

CHAPTER ELEVEN

MASTERING AND RECORD PRESSING

Now that the recording session is completed and the producer is satisfied with the final mix, the stereo tape is sent to the mastering lab. Disc mastering converts the magnetic signal on the tape to grooves in a lacquer disc. The lacquer disc, which looks like a record, is sent to the pressing plant to be processed into stampers. The records are pressed out of vinyl, placed into jackets, shrink-wrapped with plastic, and sent to the distributors. The distributors place the record in the stores and everyone hopes for a hit.

Of course, this is a simplified version of what occurs in a record's final stages. The interviews that follow will detail the exact steps of manufacturing, but as you reach the upper levels of the industry, as much thought and work can go into a record jacket as is given to the recording of that record. Illustrators, photographers, and graphic designers are commissioned to create the right look for the jacket. This becomes part of the promotional campaign that surrounds the release of a new record. The bigger the image of the recording artist, the more money that will be spent on the record jacket. The promotion people want the image to be attractive, to jump out at you when you see that record in the stores.

It's all part of the process that makes the consumer want to pick that record out from hundreds of others on display, take it to the cash register, and buy it.

JOE TALBOT

Part-owner of Precision Record Pressing, United Record Pressing, and Peer-Talbot Music Group, MFP Inc., Nashville Record Productions, and American Fulfillment Corp. Former steel guitar player and performer with Hank Snow at the Grand Ole Opry.

WHAT DOES THE RECORD PRESSING COMPANY USUALLY GET FROM A RECORD COMPANY?

Normally we get a lacquer master. That's what we call the disc that has been cut from the tape. That then goes through a plating process. The lacquer master is cleaned very thoroughly. Nothing foreign on it—no fingerprints or anything. We use a mild detergent solution to clean it. After that, it's sprayed with a silver solution. Then it's put in the plating tank, and it's plated with nickel. When you separate that plating from the lacquer master, you have a negative.

Both the plate and the lacquer master have ridges and grooves, but they will be reversed on the metal part. The grooves become ridges and the ridges become grooves.

If it's a small run, you can stop right there, punch the center hole, trim the outer edge, and form that into the stamper that cuts the record.

HOW MANY RECORDS IS THAT STAMPER GOOD FOR?

On an LP record, 1,200 to 1,500 copies. On a 45-rpm single, maybe 4,000 or 5,000 copies. Usually, the negative metal plate will be put back in the plating tank to produce a positive plate. The negative plate is called the metal master; the positive plate is called the mother. The positive plate can be played just like a record. It's called the mother because it can give birth to additional stampers.

Usually the metal master and the mother are put into reserve, and the stampers (or negatives) are made from the mother. I don't know how many times that can be done; normally half a dozen times. That's essentially the plating process.

ONCE YOU GET THE STAMPER, IT GOES INTO A PRESS, RIGHT?

Right. The press contains two halves of a die. A stamper is mounted in each half so that each stamper creates one side of the record. Since our type of pressing is compression (as opposed to injection), a gob of plastic with a label on each side is placed into the press. Hopefully, the labels match up with the proper stamper so we don't have reverse labels. At the same time, steam has been going through the die and heating it up. Then the steam's trapped. When you trap steam and put pressure on it, the heat increases. The press closes and molds the record. After that, cold water goes through the die and cools it down. When it reaches a certain temperature, about 120° or 130°, the press opens and the record is taken out. At that point it's punched with the hole in the middle and the outer edge is trimmed.

IS THE VINYL SOMETIMES USED WITH FILLERS, LIKE STYROFOAM?

I don't think it is anymore. Years and years ago, 45's were made of inferior material. It had a lot of filler in it and was called Class 3. It had everything in it. The reason you could get by with that then was, first of all, the records were relatively short in duration, so you had a real loud level of volume on them. The record players were about $19.95 and didn't pick up all the noise on the records. As record players got more expensive, they could pick up those 12,000- to 15,000-cycle tones. The records got longer, so you had to pull the volume down a little bit. As far as I know, there is nothing but what we call pure vinyl in the entire industry today.

WHAT KINDS OF PROBLEMS DO YOU HAVE? FOR INSTANCE, IF YOU GET A RECORD WITH VERY LITTLE SPACE BETWEEN THE GROOVES, DOES THAT CAUSE PROBLEMS?

It can skip. Mostly it will skip on a less expensive record player where the cartridge has a poor compliance. By that I mean the needle doesn't have the ability to immediately follow the groove.

ARE THERE ANY OTHER PROBLEMS THAT YOU HAVE IN THE PRESSING PROCESS?

On our end, our three biggest problems are off-center, warp, and nonfill—where you just don't get a good molding in the process. There might be microscopic places in the record where it didn't fill properly.

SO EVERY RECORD MUST BE INSPECTED.

Usually there is a random sample. When we set up the press, a record is immediately played all the way through on both sides. Everything is checked—no noises, it's on center, the labels are right, and so forth. Then there are random samples as pressing is done. You can't detect minor off-center. Very major off-center is visible to the eye. If anything physically happens to that record, like a scratch on a side or a nonfill, you can see that. Of course you can see warp. Take a stack of 45's, turn them sideways, and roll them on a table, and warp appears immediately. Normally, you can simply look at a stack of records and see if there is any warpage. The spaces between them won't be uniform.

ARE THERE ANY OTHER RESPONSIBILITIES YOU HAVE IN GETTING THAT RECORD OUT IN THE BEST POSSIBLE WAY?

I don't think so. We use the best grade of vinyl available, and we make sure that we've got a good plating. We're on top of the machinery as far as watching temperatures and cycles and pressures are concerned. The records are inspected and handled properly.

Once we get through the plating process, as long as we do our part in mechanically molding that record and keeping a tight quality control on it, there is really nothing we can do to change it. Where it can really be changed is from the tape to the lacquer master. It can also be screwed up from the lacquer master to the plating, because you can induce noises and even some distortions. As long as we get through the plating process with good quality, then all we've got to do is to make sure the mechanics of what we're doing are right.

ONCE THE RECORDS ARE COOLED, ARE THEY PUT IN JACKETS IN THE PRESSING PLANT?

Yes. In our plant—and there are other ways of doing it—we choose to have the sleeve and the jacket right at the press. They're not sent to another section of the building. We find this eliminates a lot of quality problems, and it eliminates putting a pornographic record in a gospel jacket.

AND THEN THE CELLOPHANE-LIKE WRAP IS PUT ON.

That's right; it's polyethylene. It's called shrink-wrap, polybag, a number of different things.

ONCE YOU REACH THAT POINT, YOU SEND THE RECORDS TO A DISTRIBUTOR.

That is true. We box them in various ways, usually 25 to a carton. Some people want more or whatever. We've got various sizes for those instances.

WILL A MAJOR LABEL THAT IS GOING TO RELEASE A RECORD NATIONALLY SEND SEVERAL MASTERS ACROSS THE COUNTRY TO VARIOUS PRESSING PLANTS?

Sometimes they will go a step farther and send the metal mothers across the country.

In any case, they cut multiple sets of lacquer masters so that they all sound the same.

WHAT IS YOUR PROFIT MARGIN?

I'd rather not get into that. But I will say that operating efficiently and operating at a satisfactory level of capacity, the profit margin should be very satisfactory.

HOW MANY PRESSING PLANTS ARE THERE IN THE U.S.?

I'd guess that there are about 100.

WHAT ADVICE WOULD YOU GIVE TO ANYBODY THAT WOULD LIKE TO GET INTO THE MUSIC BUSINESS IN THIS AREA?

I got into it by being a salesman for a lacquer company. But I was as interested in the machinery and the process as I was in going out on the road. I was a typical entrepreneur; I just didn't know how to spell the word. I'm interested in every facet of the business.

CHAPTER TWELVE

RADIO STATIONS AND RECORD PROMOTION

The most important type of promotion available to record companies is radio-station air play. An excellent record is worthless without exposure, and radio offers the best and cheapest way to inform the public about a new record. Radio program formats are as diversified as the more than 10,000 radio stations now broadcasting. Every station in the country has programming that makes it unique. Yet when analyzing the multi-faceted approaches to radio programs, it becomes quite clear that stations do fall into basic patterns. In the realm of music, these patterns include hard rock, pop music, easy rock and middle-of-the-road, country, country-rock, classical music, religious music, and easy-listening music.

Trends indicate that programmers are always thinking in terms of who they want for their audience. They are in business for money. The five basic types of radio formats for programming a radio station are: (according to "Typologies of Radio Stations Target Audiences," by Robert Mooney and Roger Skolnik, *The Journal of Broadcasting*, Vol. XIV, No. 4, Fall 1970, pp. 465, 467.)

FOCUSED ADULT. These are upper income, professional adults whose social background mirrors what advertising agencies deem desirable from a marketing viewpoint.

FOCUSED YOUTH. This is a category that aims directly at the youth audience comprising sub-teens, teens, college students, and young adults.

DEPARTMENT STORES. The department store approach represents a concern with program contents categories rather than an adult's social characteristics. Programmers scoring highly in this category view their target audiences through the kind of programming they think will appeal to most listeners.

GENERAL ADULT. Programmers who place themselves in this category seek more than highly-focused type number-one audiences seen earlier. They welcome a broad base of men and women who are from all social strata and presumably tailor their programming accordingly.

YOUNG ADULT. Stations seeking adults in the 20 to 30-year-old category. Programmers here often combine the continuing appeal of the focused-youth format with the broadening tastes of young adults.

The catch-22 in all of this is: what makes a hit record? Is it the human need the record satisfies that makes it a hit? Is it the exposure it receives on the radio stations? The record companies like to see a wider variety of records played on radio stations. Radio stations play records that are already hit records, thereby increasing the audience and their profits.

Radio stations serve the public in a very special way. Sure, they receive money from the advertisements they air, but most of us listen because of the music. Even a disc jockey with a super personality may add only a little. It's the music we enjoy when we wake up, drive to and from work, that makes us select a certain radio station.

The program director or music director has a very powerful position. Most of them are honest, sincere people who love their work. Music and program directors' selection of what records their stations play depends upon their knowledge of the demographics of their community, and their freedom of choice to select any record they desire. The only limitation is the guidelines set up by radio station management.

Some stations are automated which means they play the same music as other stations across the country that use the same automation services. Automation is a pre-packaged music recorded on tape. The only thing that is inserted is the commercials, weather and time at the local station. In addition, many radio station chains use consultants to program their radio stations. It's not uncommon for a consultant in the Southwest to program radio stations across the United States. It is questionable how accurate a consultant can be about the unique qualities of a community several hundred miles away.

Many program directors simply play it safe by selecting the hits that are listed in the trade magazines. They use one of the trade magazines' Hot 100, such as *Billboard, Radio & Records, Cash Box,* or *The Gavin Report,* to select which records they play. It's always a safety-valve type of attitude because, if the radio station has poor ratings, the program director can always say that he has at least been playing the hits.

Records are sent free to some radio stations, in hopes that they will be put on the air. Playing a new record and having a radio announcer talk about it and the artist is the best way for the record company to inform the public about the record. The record companies want radio stations to promote the record through free air play. Because of the competition for radio-station air play, record companies hire national and local promotion people to get the record played. Hype, money, free meals, and just about anything it takes are sometimes offered to persuade the program or music director to play certain records.

GARY TAYLOR

Vice President and General Manager of Radio Station
KRPM-FM, Des Moines, Washington (Seattle). Former
program and music director for several top national radio
stations. Former vice president and managing editor of
The Gavin Report.

WHAT IS THE GAVIN REPORT?
It is a broadcasting publication subscribed
to by several hundred radio stations across
the U.S. Its function is to evaluate the success or lack of success of given singles and
albums in rock, the album-radio concept,
country music, black radio, and adult
contemporary radio.

**SPECIFICALLY, WHAT IS THE MAIN THING
THAT CAUSES A RECORD TO BE A HIT?**
That could be one of the hardest questions
that I've been asked. It has to be in the
grooves. You can take a record with superb
promotion, great marketing, and a lot of
money behind it. You can work it and get all
the right trades—*Radio & Records,
Cashbox, Billboard*—and you can take it to
No. 18 or No. 19. But if it isn't in the grooves,
it is not going to make it.

IS THE PUBLIC GETTING WISE TO HYPE?
The public probably never was aware of
hype, or the lack of it, as far as hit records
were concerned.
　A record promoter can tell the program

director that he has certain other radio
stations that are playing the record, and that
means nothing. The program directors don't
care. They want to know the record's demographics.
　The hype was more an "in" thing that we
spoke of in the industry.
　What you can do is to key off one good
cut on a bad album. If that cut is good,
people will go buy that album, then they get
mad because they find out the record isn't
that good.
　People can no longer go into a record
store and listen to products. They have to
buy by what they hear. So they're shooting
craps. It's really kind of risky to buy an
album in many cases. You have this incredible press, heavy advertising on the radio,
some television advertising, merchandising
to the point that it is on all the racks. They
have point-of-purchase reminders, and then
the person gets it home and it's awful.
　The music has to have a certain wonderful
ingredient that turns people on. You have to
push that excitement button.
　During my last year or so at *The Gavin*

Report, the music industry said, "Aha, punk rock is where it's at. We're going to do punk rock." The majority of people said that they hated it, and the radio stations didn't want to play it. The record companies got mad at the radio stations. Punk rock became a different kind of hard rock that only cultists are buying. I'm not questioning their musical ability; I'm not a musician. I'm not saying they are bad or good, but from a commercial standpoint, the question of what people like to buy, you're dealing in a fringe area. We deal in mass media; we want to appeal to a broad segment of society. People who make designer jeans aren't making the kind with ripped-out knees because that is for a fringe group. They are selling jeans to everyone who wants to look like Brooke Shields.

LET'S LOOK AT HOW YOU PROGRAM A RADIO STATION. HOW MANY RECORDS DO YOU GET A WEEK? OUT OF THAT NUMBER, APPROXIMATELY HOW MANY ARE YOU GOING TO PLAY?

We get from 100 to 120 records a week. On an AM soft-rock limited format, targeting to a 25- to 34-year-old listener, we'll probably select one. Maybe two.

WHY WILL YOU SELECT THOSE ONE OR TWO RECORDS?

Because it fits the parameters, the categories that have been established by a program director. The guy says that his core audience is women, ages 18–30. He'll play softer things that they like—Manilow, some Elton John, Doobie Brothers, Fleetwood Mac, some of Billy Joel's softer stuff, and some Neil Diamond-Barbra Streisand. He's not going to play the Cars, the Police, Styx. When a record fits the categories you have, you put it on the air.

On the FM side of the band, where you have the album type stations, there was a time when they used to play everything. That was programming to a very small segment, not a smart move. Radio stations cost a great deal of money to operate.

Hundreds of thousands of dollars are spent just in breaking even.

THAT IS IMPORTANT, TOO, BECAUSE YOU MAKE YOUR MONEY ACCORDING TO HOW MANY PEOPLE LISTEN.

Of course. We sell advertising. It's all right for everybody else to sell products, but it's not all right for radio to sell advertising. If we were subsidized by the government, as is CBC, the network in Canada, we wouldn't need the commercials. We have to be able to pay all the people who work for us. We have to pay for the music that we play; we pay musicians in music license fees.

We have to play to an audience that wants to hear certain things; we don't play a lot of Frank Zappa or Def Leppard. Middle America doesn't seem to have that particular taste. Can you imagine playing disco in Nashville or Memphis?

IT IS IMPORTANT THAT THE PROGRAM DIRECTOR AND THE STATION MANAGEMENT KNOW WHAT THE PUBLIC WANTS. HOW DO YOU FIND THAT OUT?

There is one method called a focus-group study. You bring people into a room and ask a lot of questions—about radio, about music, and so forth. It's part of radio's ongoing research to find out what people want to hear on the radio. It has nothing to do with record sales. It has been known for many years that 45's are sold to 14-year-old girls, not to 22-year-old men. Those men buy albums and they want Van Halen. A 24-year-old woman wants to hear Neil Diamond or the Eagles.

Record companies, in the meantime, have been putting out really hard, screaming guitar stuff and suffering from it. That type of music is geared to 12- to 17-year-olds. Most radio doesn't play to that group, and the advertiser doesn't want to reach that age group.

HIGH SCHOOL KIDS SEEM TO WANT TO LISTEN TO HEAVY MUSIC. THE AM JOCKS ARE OUT THERE PUSHING THEIR HEAVY MUSIC AND NOBODY IS LISTENING. THE

HIGH SCHOOL KIDS WERE LISTENING TO HEAVY MUSIC ON FM, AT NIGHT.
You must do your marketing to know your audience. Think about today's music and the music when you were seventeen. The music is different; the mentality is different. Since that time we have watched man take trips to the moon and walk on it. Satellites instantaneously beam a song from New York to Los Angeles to your home. We have incredible television cable programming. Field research people can get instant feedback by putting an electronic device in your home. Computers take in thousands of responses and display them on a television screen seconds later: 4,381 said they liked a movie; 2,817 said they did not like it; 461 were neutral; and the rest refused to respond.

We are bombarded with information. The number of magazines has quadrupled; we have videotapes, and so on.

Radio is sitting over here trying to compete. Radio has to know what its audience wants. I'll tell you what they want. They want instant gratification. They want to be comfortable; they want to hear something familiar.

WHAT WERE SOME OF THE MOST POPULAR RECORDS WE WERE LISTENING TO FIFTEEN YEARS AGO?
Led Zeppelin's "Stairway to Heaven" has been the singular most popular song available for the core group under forty. When that first came out in the sixties, nobody played it on AM Top 40 radio. Those who played "Whole Lot of Lovin'" by Led Zeppelin did so only after 10:00 at night. Some of the Chicago stuff was gargantuan and everybody played them until they burned them out. But none of us knew that the group was getting tiresome then, because we had no sophisticated way of doing research.

DOES REPEATED AIR PLAY MAKE A HIT RECORD?
It can make a record familiar. I've been working in the business for fifteen years, and

I'm not certain if I know what a hit record is. Debby Boone's "You Light Up My Life" was a hit record, but you never hear it on the radio now. Nobody wants to hear it, yet it's incredibly popular to the thirty-five plus group.

ON THE GRAMMYS, ONE GUY WON AN AWARD AND SAID THAT ALL THE RECORD COMPANIES HAD REJECTED IT TWICE.
That happens. I used to pick singles at *The Gavin Report*. I kept track and I did quite well, but I missed some incredible Number One songs. I could not hear them for the life of me.

Find a guy who can guarantee to pick a hit, and Columbia Records will give him a suite, pay him $500,000 a year, give him a big stereo system, and say, "Have fun. Just tell us which ones to release."

DURING THE DAY, DO YOU CHANGE YOUR FORMATS IN YOUR PROGRAMMING?
Yes. It's called day parting. You try to provide in the morning what people must have when they are busily going about other things while listening to the radio—the time, the temperature, the news, traffic reports, familiar music. So when they go to the office, or whatever, they are fulfilled. They know what has happened while they were asleep.

In the middle of the day, the audience's composition changes. People step down a pace. They are at work or working at home. The age-old philosophy has been to soften up a bit. Don't beat them to death. Play things that they grew up with or things they are used to listening to, like a lot of Beatles records. It depends on your target group. Later you are going to take them back home. You give them basics once again.

In the evening you have a different composition. Younger adults, male oriented, they want to go out with the boys and have a few beers. We give them music that coincides with their lifestyle. What you're trying to do is appeal to the audience's moods—not that of the program director or the disc jockey.

It's eye-opening to have people tell you

what they want. For years, twenty years, radio said, "They want to hear this," or "They want to hear that." For instance, people have been telling disc jockeys for years not to talk over the front of the records, but jocks still do it.

WHAT TRENDS DO YOU SEE FOR RADIO STATIONS?

Radio is finally catching up to the people at Procter & Gamble, Lever Brothers, and other brilliant marketing groups. As more signals come into being and the FM bias increases, the pie gets smaller. The giant radio stations that used to have ratings in the 20's now have 5's, 4's, 3's. In the 1980's, 3's are big deals. A 7 is a killer. In a big city if you have a 7 rating point, each point is worth a million bucks in advertising.

WHAT DO YOU THINK ABOUT SYNDI-CATED RADIO PROGRAMS AND AUTOMATION?

I have an automation unit and it works. I run it twenty-four hours a day. I can buy syndi-cated shows, but in my opinion there are few good syndicated adult programs avail-able.

WHAT ADVICE WOULD YOU GIVE TO MUSICIANS WHO WANT TO CUT A HIT RECORD?

As a station manager, I would not advise a musician as to what kind of record to cut. As a station manager, I am concerned with managing people employed with the radio station, budgets, revenues, and capital investments.

OK, WHAT ABOUT THE SAME QUESTION FROM THE VIEWPOINT OF A PROGRAM DIRECTOR?

I would say, "Swallow your pride and cut a commercial entity. Save your experimental concepts until a later time." A lot of people in the music business will not like that statement. They will say that I'm stifling the freshness or the newness of the music

industry. That is an excellent point, and they may be right.

Thousands and thousands of albums have been released that nobody ever played or bought. A couple of hundred have made it. Where are the rest? The groups all broke up; they're working in the post office now. The ones that made it were commer-cial entities. Make the commercial one first and then broaden yourself. Billy Joel used to do ballads. He's a hard-core rock 'n' roller; he's right into it. Christopher Cross has done a very beautiful piece of music, but who knows what he'll do next. But now he has credibility. He now has tons of followers, and they will support him financially while he seeks his next creative level.

IMAGE IS IMPORTANT, ISN'T IT?

It's killed some marvelous talent. There are many artists with a bad image who have never had a hit record and can't figure out why.

Wayne Newton has had an image prob-lem, but only with hit singles. Image hurt Elton John for a long time. It hurt Cher Bono. Peter Frampton was in a horrible movie, and it almost destroyed a marvelous talent. Image is incredibly important, and it is a very delicate thing to manipulate.

WHAT ADVICE WOULD YOU GIVE TO PEOPLE WHO WANT TO HAVE A CAREER IN RADIO?

Go to school and get a college degree. Study the facets of broadcasting, study management techniques and marketing. Then find yourself a little town, expect to be underpaid, expect to work long hours, seven days a week, while you learn what you did not learn in school. You can read every book out on how to hit a baseball, but you must stand in that cage for hours, learning to be a hitter.

WHAT ADVICE WOULD YOU GIVE TO RECORD COMPANIES ABOUT THE RE-CORDS THEY ARE PRODUCING?

A few years ago I was making suggestions, and it occurred to me that's like a record company coming to a program director and saying, "What record should I release?"

Those companies know what they are doing, and the producers are brilliant, talented people. I don't tell record producers anything except "Thank you."

HOW ABOUT PAYOLA?

It exists. It's there and it's ugly. A friend of mine once said, "You know when a man walks in and says to take $2,000 for playing his record, I'm going to take the $2,000. I'm not going to the general manager and tell him I was offered money. I love my wife and kid too much for that!"

Another person wrote me a letter. He said, "Do you know what it is like to be living in a city this size, where it costs so much to live, and you're not making a heck of a lot of money? Then some guy says, 'You don't have to play it. Just report it to the trades. Here is $1,000.' Do you know what that kind of money does? I can eat out once in a while and buy a suit. How do I say no?" He said, "I'm a good person or I wouldn't be writing this letter about these offers and things."

And I began to understand it. I don't endorse it, but I do understand it. Yes, it is a reality. But is it as big as we think it is? There are industry publications that are very much aware of it. If some guy is taking pay, they don't want him around. Both *Radio & Records* and *The Gavin Report* used to take active stances against payola. It's like business favors; it is an unfortunate part of our society.

YOU SAID IT DOESN'T REALLY WORK EITHER.

I don't think it does if the record isn't in the groove. You can get up to a No. 19 in the trades, and the record company will ship out all of those records, but a lot of times the returns equal the shipment.

THE PUBLIC ITSELF HAS THE LAST WORD.

The public is the one that says, "I like that." It doesn't matter what the music director says. The hard part is convincing him that he should or should not be playing it. That will be a continuous battle.

It is the public who decides.

SKIP STEVENS

Director of Skip Stevens Promotions, an independent record promotions firm. Formerly with Ovation Records.

WHEN YOU FIRST STARTED OUT IN PROMOTION WORK, DID YOU FEEL LOST WHEN THEY SAID, "HERE'S THE PHONE?"
I felt really lost. I didn't know what to say. The people I was working for didn't give me a lot of guidelines. They mainly said, "What you're trying to do is to get radio stations to play our records." I knew nothing about the stations. I started from scratch. I told everybody I was new, and I asked for information about them and their stations as a way of getting acquainted.

YOU WERE TRYING TO GET A PERSONAL RELATIONSHIP GOING, THIS BUILDING OF TRUST?
Trust and credibility. They are looking to play the songs on their radio station that will make their station sound good. If, over a long-term basis (anywhere from six months to years), you consistently present them with facts that are accurate, you don't try to over-hype, and you give them product that is good and that gets a response from their audience, you build a trust with them. After a while, you get to the point where you can

say, "Hey, this is a good record, and it will do well in your market." They'll say, "Okay, we'll give it a shot," without your having to wait until it's Top 10 in the national trades.

A PROBLEM YOU CONFRONT IS THAT A LOT OF RADIO STATIONS WILL NOT PLAY ANYTHING THAT IS NOT ALREADY A HIT. HOW DO YOU GET RECORDS THAT ARE BEING RELEASED SOME AIR PLAY?
There are about 120 stations that are what we call primary reporters—they report to the major trades. They are our main objectives. Of course, I want to get every radio station in the country playing the record, but you can't call them all. You concentrate on the primary reporters. Out of those primary reporters, I would say that 25 to 30 stations have a large play list. In other words, they play a lot of records and take chances on records that aren't established or in the Top 10. Depending upon your rapport, you may have 30 to 50 stations that trust you enough to go on a record that is not established. You work on those stations first. After you reach a certain point, then it's up to the

189

record. The record has to take off on its own and have enough credibility to get interest sparked and get an audience response.

DO YOU HAVE TO PROMOTE RECORDS THAT YOU PERSONALLY DON'T LIKE?

There are times when I personally have not been crazy about a song. The way I handle it is to just present the song and ask them what they think about it. I don't say it's great or a smash. I let them decide. That is really the way I try to treat all songs.

THERE IS A LOT OF HYPE IN PROMOTION, OR AT LEAST PEOPLE THINK THERE IS. WHAT DO YOU THINK HYPE IS?

I think hype is a very broad term. Most of the people in the music industry consider hype as information about a record that is not untrue but may be overglorified.

FOR EXAMPLE, SOMEBODY LAYING A LOT OF HYPE ON A RADIO STATION'S PROGRAM DIRECTOR MIGHT SAY THAT OTHER STATIONS HAVE PICKED UP THE RECORD ALREADY AND THAT IS WHY THIS PARTICULAR STATION SHOULD START PLAYING IT.

It would be very foolish; only a nonprofessional would lie about that.

Hype to me is more like somebody saying, "Hey, this is a smash. It's going to be Number One," with nothing to base that on. Unless it's somebody like a Kenny Rogers, the directors say, "Yeah, sure." Especially when it happens with every record out.

SO YOU LOSE YOUR CREDIBILITY AS SOON AS YOU START DOING THAT?

Sure, if you can't back it up and the record doesn't go. There have been records that I thought had Number One potential and have done nothing. Then there were records that I didn't think were that great that have done very well. It's a guessing game.

BASICALLY YOUR JOB IS TO GET THE RECORDS PLAYED ON RADIO STATIONS. HOW DO YOU DO THAT?

First, again it is credibility, your rapport with the radio stations. For a hypothetical example, you call them up and say, "I've got a record here. I think it's very good. We've had fifteen stations that have gone on the record out of the box (which means the first week). It looks like we may get ten more before the week is out. That would give us twenty-five stations in the first week and should get us on the charts at approximately 75 to 79." Again, you're getting back to the first thirty to forty stations that will play the record without having it in the Top 20.

So the first week you get twenty-five stations and come in on the charts at 76. The next week you have to get that next group. You need to get eight to ten more reports to move forward with a bullet (which means the record is moving forward with strength). The next week you call and say, "Hey, we picked up twelve stations last week, and we've moved from 76 to 65. Next week with a bullet. Everything is looking real good." By this time, you have to get to a certain point, say 60, before the next bunch of guys will play it. So now we're talking to stations that are looking for a little bit more; they're looking for things like response. How many phone calls are they getting at a station? How much sales are you getting in the market? You might call ten stations that say they're getting good phone-ins on it; the girls are calling in the afternoons. You can use that as another factor. So you get ten new adds and you've moved 58 to 49.

Now you're at the point where the record really has to be doing something on its own or you're going to lose it. The guy you're trying to get to add that record now is looking for some concrete facts that the record is doing well. You try to get together the stations that are getting requests, the stations that are moving it. In other words, on their individual charts, it's moving up. These stations will ask if it's getting any movement at the other charts. I can answer, "Yes. It's Top 30 in fifteen stations; it's in Top 20 at ten stations." As you move up, naturally the tougher it gets. When you get in the

Top 30, the national trades, at least *Bill-board*, is weighing the sales. The higher you get, the higher the sales are weighted. When you get in the Top 20 with *Billboard*, the sales are rated at 5 to 1. If you get it to the Top 20, it's going to have to be selling.

This is with *Billboard*. With *Cash Box* they do track sales for singles. So it's different systems for different trade publications.

In addition to moving records up the charts, as promotion director, I have independent people working for me. I have to coordinate their efforts, keep them motivated, and keep them aware of what's happening. You have to set goals for them. Make sure they are staying on top of things. That's part of it, along with mailing out records to people who need extra copies. Some people will ask for albums for give-aways, and we send those out. All of those things are considered legal favors. That increases your rapport with them. If you're nice to them, they're nice to you.

THE WORD PAYOLA MAKES PEOPLE JUMP BECAUSE IT IS ILLEGAL. BUT THERE ARE LEGAL FORMS—SUCH AS TAKING PEOPLE OUT TO DINNER, AND SO ON.

It happens all the time. Taking people to dinner, giving them albums to give away is common. If they can give away albums, it increases their listeners.

WHAT KIND OF INFORMATION DO YOU HAVE TO KEEP ON EACH RECORD?

We get play lists in from a lot of the radio stations, not all, but most. It tells their Top 40, or Top 60, whatever their format may be. We also get a thing from *Billboard* called Confidential Report, which tells by market how many stations are on your record, sales information. They call stores, distributors, one-stops, and ask them how they rate a record. That is the kind of information that tells us what's happening.

From that, you can know pretty well who is on the record. You should have a pretty

good idea anyway. At certain times the guys at the radio stations will get under pressure, and they make a mistake or even lie about it. They think they may pacify you by saying they're playing the record when they are actually not. It just makes matters worse.

HOW MANY PHONE CALLS DO YOU MAKE ON AN AVERAGE DAY?

I would say probably eighty. I have a heavier load than usual. I probably make sixty on Monday, ninety on Tuesday, eighty on Wednesday, and on Thursday it starts slacking off. Friday I hardly make any calls.

WARNER/ELEKTRA/ASYLUM DISTRIBUTES MANY RECORD COMPANIES' PRODUCTS AT THE SAME TIME. HOW DO THEY PICK THE RECORD TO PUSH OUT OF 100 RECORDS? YOU WOULD AGREE IT WOULD BE DIFFICULT IN THAT SITUATION?

I would hate to be in a position where I would have to work more than five records. First of all, it's so time-consuming to have to talk about five records, and then how do you draw the line? Of course, the company decides your priorities. As promotion director, you decide your own priorities for what the record should do. For example, an established artist will get thirty adds the first week without any trouble because he's established, done well at the station before, and had Top 10 records. With a new artist, you have to work much harder. The new artist would get the majority of the attention. When the established artist gets to the Top 20 and Top 10, that's when it really gets tricky. You really have to play your cards right, have everything clicking to get to the Top 10. That's where the work comes in on an established artist.

WHAT ADVICE WOULD YOU GIVE TO PEOPLE WHO WANT TO GET INTO THE MUSIC BUSINESS?

First of all, if they want to get into the music business, I suggest they make up their minds that this is truly what they want to do. It is a hard business to get into. But once you get into it, you can do very well at it.

I wanted it badly enough and lived through the poor times, and now it makes it all worthwhile. It's a business where people get hired based on their experience. If you're new and don't have experience, it will be tough to get that break. You just have to keep trying until you find somebody who is impressed enough with you or likes you well enough to give you a shot. When you get your shot, do your best. You don't get them very often.

JERRY SEABOLT

Retired. Former record promoter with United Artists Records and Capitol Records.

WHEN YOU, AS A RECORD PROMOTER, SAY "WORK A RECORD," WHAT ARE YOU BASICALLY SAYING?

I mean, make sure that it gets the absolute, ultimate amount of exposure that it possibly can, based on the fact that the record is or is not a hit. We would mail out in excess of 2,000 records on everything we put out. We'd call in excess of 400 radio stations across the country, on a regular basis. We'd call 400 retail accounts. We'd call the trade magazines constantly, getting a reading on what's happening. I was always in touch with the production department and the sales department to make sure that product was available once it was getting exposure.

If the need for an ad was there, we ran an ad. If the need for a giveaway was there, something to garner peoples' attention, that was done.

Once I had to get on an airplane and fly 1,000 miles. I walked into the man's office and said, "I flew 1,000 miles to see you because I thought it was important." And he said, "If it's that important to you, I'll put the record on."

I was no more persuasive than the regional man who was involved. But the fact that I spent about $600 of the company's money to get on a plane and go down there—that was the one thing we needed to push it over the edge, to get the guy to play the record.

Do whatever it takes because the return on the investment is there, if you can just get the initial exposure. And it's a crap shoot.

HOW MUCH ARE THE ODDS AGAINST A PERSON?

Well, there are probably, in the country field, about 150 singles a week released, and there are only 100 records on the charts. Normally no more than 5 to 8 records are added to the charts every week to replace those that come off the charts. That means there are 142 records on the average that are never heard of again.

THEN IT'S REALLY NOT REFLECTING ON THE PERSON'S TALENT?

There's no reflection whatsoever on the person's talent.

GENE FERGUSON

Artist manager of John Anderson and Charlie McClain.
Formerly with Columbia Records in
promotion and management.

HOW DID YOU GET INTO THE INDUSTRY?

About 1955, I was working in a gas station and a guy came in. He had this slick-looking white convertible Cadillac with wire wheels, and he said, "Do you want to get into the music business?"

I said, "Well, not really, but I need something that pays more than what I'm making now," which was about $38 a week.

So I went to work in a record store. That was in Washington, D.C. I worked for most of the retailers in D.C. Later I left there and went to work for Joseph M. Zomaski, who was the distributor for CBS products.

I was a territory salesman. I covered the Eastern shore, Maryland, around Hagerstown, and down through the Shenandoah Valley of Virginia, which is where I originally met the Statler Brothers.

I presented them to Columbia. Columbia Records didn't take them. We had another group on the label called the "Chuck Wagon Gang," and CBS said they didn't need any more gospel music. I introduced the Statlers to John Cash, whom I've been associated with since 1957. John heard them, put them on his show, and then everything became history.

I moved to Atlanta, Georgia, where I became field promotion manager, covering everything from the Mexican border to the East Coast, across through Tennessee. I later moved to Nashville in 1960 and became the national promotion manager for country, reporting to another national promotion man in New York. As a field promotion man, I covered all facets of music, not only country, but everything else.

DO RETAIL STORES WANT TO TAKE A CHANCE WITH NEW ARTISTS?

The record store—the buyer—is not that interested in taking a chance on a new unknown artist. They'll make him prove himself with a couple of records first, preferably wait for an album.

SUPPOSEDLY THE CHARTS ARE MADE FROM RADIO AIR PLAY AND HOW THE RECORD IS SELLING. THE RECORD'S NOT GOING TO SELL IF IT DOESN'T HAVE RADIO PLAY.

There are roughly 115 *Billboard* reporting stations, but there are about 2,500 country stations. Those 115 supersede all the rest. In other words, you could be played everywhere else and never get reported if it's not on a *Billboard* reporting station.

The trade papers report how many stations are playing your record per week and how many additional stations add your record each week. If it doesn't jump five places each week, then it will not receive a bullet.

ANOTHER FASCINATING THING IS, IF THE GUY AT THE RADIO STATION DOESN'T LIKE THE SONG, HE WON'T PLAY IT EVEN IF IT IS A HIT.
The public would create a demand and he would be forced on the record. It's opinions, and it's an unfortunate thing. I made a comment to fifty key disc jockeys that radio was more prone to take a major artist with a mediocre record and wear it out before they would take a new artist with a great record and give him a shot. I believe that to this day.

WHAT DO YOU THINK ARE THE RESPONSIBILITIES OF A LOCAL PROMOTION MAN?
He gets the record from the company to start with. You'll usually get a dub copy of it, an acetate that will last twenty to thirty plays. I may run that around the station.

Then, when the records come in, you have to deliver them to stations almost simultaneously to keep one DJ from getting mad that he heard it on the other stations before he got it. You try to keep yourself out of hot water in that respect.

With the major acts, there's no problem. When I started with CBS, we had the majority of country acts at that time. Flatt and Scruggs were hot with the "Beverly Hillbillies" and "Bonnie and Clyde." John Cash, Carl Smith, Lefty Frizzel—I could go on and on. We had about fifty acts at that time, and they were selling records. Everything I took in automatically got played.

If they're playing that much of my product, which is all big names, how do I slide anybody new in there? Let's say, for instance, I've got a new guy named Johnny Duncan. I used to tour with Duncan and go around with his records. It just took a long time to finally build his career.

I was always as honest as I could be with the program directors. There's no point in telling them it's a great record if we don't think it is. I get the same result if I ask for the favor. Then we let the public decide, which is really what should happen anyway.

THE PUBLIC HAS THE LAST WORD.
Always but a lot of times they never hear it to get any word in. In certain major markets, there is a lot of local talent going on, particularly in the Southwest. They do well. They may record here in Nashville, but they don't have a label. They just press their own stuff and put it out. There have been a lot of Number One records in Houston, as an example, which is not bad.

THE LOCAL PROMOTION MAN'S RESPONSIBILITY IS TO GET THE RECORD PLAYED.
He's the key man. Everybody else, when you get past that local man, starts the song-and-dance routine. I did a lot of it, so I can tell you about that firsthand.

As a regional promotion man controlling local promotion men, if I had a good local man, I always protected him. I would have some people that were very lazy. Promotion is one of the easiest things to dance around in the world. A lot of times, they don't have to go to the stations; they just call them.

The paperwork is phenomenal. You have to chart every record in every city, where that man's been, what he's doing, how many stations were called on, what jocks are on the air at what time. When I got out of that, after about seven years, and started doing the national promotion job, it got even worse. With the national promotion responsibility came the relationship with the artist.

An artist's ego is definitely different from the ego of the average person on the street.

Maybe that's why they have that little bit of difference. Some were very hard to deal with, and some were very pleasant to deal with. It's a difficult thing either way, because if you have a roster that's big, no artist wants one fiftieth of your time. Now it gets down to who gets what, when, and where.

One of the strangest things about promotion is that the big records you get credit for are usually the records you do the very least on. The small records that you work yourself to death on, nobody ever comes up and says, "Well, realistically we figured that record to die at 45 and you got it to 28, and I want to thank you." That never happens.

SOMEBODY HAS TO GET THE RECORD ON THAT FIRST BIG STATION.

There was a case where a record came to me by the name of "Big, Bad John." One day Jimmy Dean and I were sitting with the late Jim Denney. Jim wanted to borrow $125 on the song. He sat there, and he tapped it out on the chair, singing it. Dean said, "I don't like the song, but I'll give you the money." We cut the record and nobody had a publishing company for it. In the session Dean said, "Anybody got a publishing company?" Grady Martin said, "I've got one." Dean said, "You can have it." I think we sold 2.5 million copies of it.

Now the way it happened was a coincidental thing. Maybe this is the way life goes. Jimmy Dean was playing at a famous hotel in New Orleans, and Ron Martin (who is now a very heavy disc jockey on the West Coast) was the program director of WTIX in New Orleans. He called me and said, "I need an artist to do a Teem commercial."

I said, "I've got Jimmy Dean in town." He says, "No, man, I need an act."

I said, "Well, now wait a minute. Dean's had three CBS television shows." He was doing a morning women's show, and he'd had two or three others that had come and gone.

He said, "What will it cost me?" I said, "Well, it won't cost you anything. He's playing at the Roosevelt Hotel."

He said, "Will he be here Saturday?" I said, "He could be." He was working there for a week. So I talked to Dean and he wasn't too interested. I said, "If you'll do this, just appear and sign autographs, that type of thing, let him advertise it, he'll play the record."

That's really where "Big, Bad John" broke—at WTIX in New Orleans, which most people would never think about today, and Ron Martin is the man who's totally responsible.

I stayed with Dean, I think, two days that time before I came back. I called him back at the restaurant (I'd just left him), and I said, "Dean, the record's selling 50,000 a day." I could hear him crying in the phone. He said, "Ferg, I'll never forget you." I don't think I spoke to him for seven years after that. That's an idea of how a song will go.

IT APPEARS THAT THERE'S A LOT OF PRESSURE ON A PROMOTION PERSON.

Very much so. That's why the mortality rate for promotion men is about as bad as it is for executives at major labels.

THERE'S A SAYING THAT SOMETIMES AN ARTIST IS AS GOOD AS HIS LAST RECORD. DO YOU THINK THAT A PROMOTION MAN IS AS GOOD AS HIS LAST JOB, OR HOW WELL HE DID WITH THE RECORD?

I wouldn't agree with the first statement, to be quite honest. Mainly because I think when you talk about artists, you're talking about many different types. There are some truly God-gifted, talented artists. Then there are people who can sing on key. There's a difference.

There are artists, to me, who are so talented and so unique that even if times change, they still seem to fit in there. Then there are other artists who come and go, and if we get on that subject, we'd talk forever about those artists. Most of them mess their own careers up because they don't treat this business like a business.

HOW ARE RECORDS DISTRIBUTED?

Let's take it from the time it leaves the studio, when a record's cut. At that time, it's pressed and sent to radio stations.

The first records run are called promotion copies. That's to create a demand so it can be bought. There are fifteen days before you can create a demand.

I would call on people who owned the store. I'd walk in, open up a catalog, and say, "Would you like the new John Anderson or Charly McClain record?" They'd either say yes or no, depending on the demand of that artist.

That no longer happens because the one-stops and the rack jobbers moved in and said, "There's no point in being called on by a CBS man, an RCA man, a Mercury, on down the line. You don't need it. I'm going to come in here, and I'll show you the Top 10 pop, country, R&B. That's all you need."

If the store owner says, "What happens if customers ask me for so-and-so," the jobber says, "Well, if you don't have it, we'll special order it for you. This way, we cut down on your inventory, we cut down on your over-head, your cost factor."

I know a couple of rack jobbers who have 700 outlets. So if you don't sell that specific piece of product to that rack jobber, there are 700 outlets that don't get that record.

The company sends records directly to the stations. They're sent by mail and there are back-up copies delivered by the local promotion men in all the major markets.

The record club is what killed the mom-and-pop record stores. The record club is an independent profit center from any label. CBS might have one, but you'll see other labels in there. Whoever doesn't have a record club will be in there because they evidently cut a business deal with CBS.

CHAPTER THIRTEEN

MUSIC TELEVISION

What do you do if your business is in trouble? Sales are down; people have stopped buying your records. What's the problem; and better yet, how can you solve it? That's what a lot of people in the music business have been asking themselves the past few years.

Music television is the new way of getting people excited about the business. MTV doesn't solve all of the problems, but it has created excitement that means an increase in sales. MTV is a new form of record promotion.

Music television videos are really minimotion pictures. They are shot on film and they cost between $20,000 and $50,000.

That's a lot of money for a 3- to 5-minute film clip. The story line of the visual may or may not be the same as the original song. The average MTV viewer is between the ages of nine and eighteen, but some people from all age brackets watch.

Music television has created some excitement and record sales are doing better. Are the two tied together or is the public just starting to buy records again? Record companies are releasing new product, and—for the first time in a long time—radio stations are playing new artists and a better selection. Is that the reason for increased record sales? Or is it a combination of everyone working together. Only the future will tell where music television is headed.

RICK BLACKBURN

Senior Vice President/general manager of
CBS Records, Nashville.

IS COUNTRY MUSIC GOING IN A DIFFER-
ENT AND/OR NEW DIRECTION?

We are finding two businesses under the country-music umbrella. One is the contemporary side and the other is the traditional side. The fans who subscribe to one do not necessary subscribe to the other, and they are either active buyers or inactive buyers.

The older group, or traditional market, tends to be a bit more inactive in their purchasing habits. Country music is still their absolute favorite form of music. They listen to it on the radio and watch it on television. They do not necessarily buy records, cassettes, or albums on a regular basis. They make a good audience for television. I've had this debate with television people. They say the market share is strong, and I say, "Yes, but it's an inactive buyer."

The active buyer tends to be younger; he incorporates music into his lifestyle, and he likes all forms of music—not just contemporary country music. In a given week, this person may buy Ricky Skaggs, a fusion jazz record by Grover Washington, a new record by Bruce Springsteen, and a new Judd's record. He buys music, and he buys it whether it's country or jazz or classical or pop. This country music fan is more urban than rural.

HOW DO YOU DETERMINE WHICH OF
YOUR ARTISTS WILL GET TO DO A VIDEO
AND HOW DO YOU BUDGET IT?

What do you want a video to do for you? What do you want it to accomplish? What kind of statement do you want your video to make? On the Ricky Skaggs video, we wanted to take a traditional sound and incorporate it into an urban lifestyle. We filmed it on the New York City subway. We didn't want to do it in Nashville or Dallas. In that video, you've got break-dancing to traditional country music! That is absolutely unique.

RICKY SKAGGS CAME UP WITH THE
CONCEPT.

Yes; he said, "Let's get Bill Monroe and let him be my grandfather." Monroe later became the Uncle Pen in the video. We got some cameo appearances from David Keith, the actor from *An Officer and a Gentleman*, and even from the Mayor of New York City.

HOW DO YOU DETERMINE THE BUDGET ON A VIDEO? DO YOU ASSUME A VIDEO MAY STIMULATE THE BUSINESS ITSELF, BUT MAY NOT SELL THAT PARTICULAR SONG OR RECORD?

We give the song to four or five producers and wait for the storyboards. We don't give them much to go on except "Here's the song, and how do you see this?" The Ricky Skaggs video is different because the artist had the idea.

When we get the storyboards back, we and the artist select which one is the best. We sit down with the producer and director and ask what it will cost to get the job done. They submit budgets. In other words, we talk in terms of needs before we talk in terms of cost. We've taken a page out of the advertising agency book. Our product managers are account executives in charge of video.

YOU'RE LOOKING FOR JUSTIFICATION, AT ALL TIMES, TO MAINTAIN YOUR BUDGETS?

Yes, we talk in terms of needs. Sometimes we get a video idea back that is fantastic, but the cost will not let us do it.

DO YOU HAVE TO TAKE INTO CONSIDERATION THAT THE COST OF THE VIDEO MAY NOT BE COVERED BY THE SALES OF THE RECORD IT'S PROMOTING?

Right. "Poncho and Lefty" was the Number One video last year. I can't tell you how many records it sold, but it raised the image, and whatever we spent on the video, it was worth it. It was cost-justified.

We have found that unlike the appearance of young rock groups on MTV, a video cannot break an artist in the adult market. VH-1 is playing the hits and I don't blame them. If we did a video on an unknown artist, the adult buyer wouldn't respond

unless it was a unique song. In that case, you are breaking the song first and the artist second. A song like "Elvira" or "Short People" may allow you to break the song, but you may never break the artist.

IF THE CONTEMPORARY SIDE OF THE BUSINESS TAKES OFF IN THE WAY YOU'RE PREDICTING, THEN THE TRADITIONAL SIDE OF THE BUSINESS MAY GET SMALLER AND SMALLER.

Yes, it will, unless the younger contemporary buyers switch at a later age to the traditional form of country music. That is what happened in 1979 and 1980. The contemporary country music attracted the old rock buyers, 28 to 30 years old, who felt that the current rock music was too hard. They were exposed to the more traditional country music along with the contemporary, but didn't particularly like it. But Ricky Skaggs, who was younger and more energetic, came out of the traditional. As a result, some of the younger people have adopted traditional country music.

WHY DO YOU SIGN A NEW ACT?

You sign acts in terms of your needs. Before we signed Exile, we looked a long time for a group that would build our contemporary business. We've got legends: Nelson, Jones, Haggard, and Cash, but I wanted to build the more contemporary side. What we needed was to capture a type of sound to balance the rosters. Usually, you make a signing after you know what you're looking for and not on an impulse.

HOW DO YOU MOTIVATE YOUR STAFF?

Our goals are well-known by everyone because we all share in the goals. Every quarter, we sit down and see how we're doing. People like to be a part of that. You don't always have to give incentives or bonuses; you have to give people credit. Delegate responsibility, delegate authority, and let them do their job. If you have good people in place, that's the key in any business.

PAUL CORBIN

Vice President of Programming,
The Nashville Network (TNN).

ARE YOU GOING TO EXPAND YOUR PROGRAM FORMAT TO INCLUDE DIFFERENT TYPES OF MUSIC?
No, we have a unique, individual market that we have identified. It has been unserved, up to this time, with the kind of programming we can provide. Having a varied music package—putting on pop, switching to jazz, switching to big-band music, switching to Dixieland, or to something else that is foreign to the country consumer—would seriously damage what we are creating.

YOU'RE ON CABLE TELEVISION IN THE U.S. AND CANADA. DO YOU WANT ANY ADDITIONAL MARKETS?
We are currently exploring the foreign marketplace, taking a look at what opportunities we might have. We are the leading foreign service in Canada. We are a pay service there and have more households than any other foreign service. We're delighted with that because the Canadian marketplace is very strong for country music.

DO YOU HAVE A PROBLEM WITH THE CANADIAN CONTENT LAWS?
No, that was not a requirement imposed by the Canadian Radio and Television Commission.

IS YOUR DEMOGRAPHIC OF TNN CONSUMERS IN THE $25,000-AND-OVER RANGE?
It seems that we have upscaled viewers because they are the people who are hooked up to cable and who are taking varied services. Eighty percent of our coverage is in the A and B counties or the urban centers. Country music is traditionally strong in the B, C, and D counties. The C and D counties are not really wired for cable because of the expense. What has happened is an increase in the number of satellite dishes and we have a feeling that we are very strong in the satellite direct broadcast area.

ARE YOU LOOKING FOR PILOTS?
We are still very fragile as an organization in terms of the ability to pay the dollars that the

marketplace demands in order to acquire product and to hire top-name people to work for us. We have to take other approaches in order to be creative in the marketplace. One of our main approaches is that we are very serious about our cost control.

We're not competitive in the television marketplace for the purchase of materials. We're very unique in that we ask for a lot of rights and we pay very little. The range for acquiring a sixty-minute special, for example, is up to $15,000. But we have been quite successful in spite of our low fees.

HOW WOULD YOU LIKE TO CHANGE YOUR PROGRAMMING?

We would like to be able to do some programming that would be geared for daytime audiences. Our prime time seems to be doing quite well. We would certainly add some other formats to the prime time and not do as many repeats. Eventually we'd have time-zone delays instead of serving all the time zones in a single feed. On weekends we have been using sports programming that is unique for television. All programming on TNN is created by and for us and is not seen anywhere else. We are not interested in looking like the other services. As soon as we do, our audience would begin to perceive us as a less valuable service.

HOW MANY PEOPLE WATCH YOUR MOST POPULAR SHOW, "NASHVILLE NOW," ON ANY GIVEN NIGHT?

During a given week, there are 6½ million people tuning to "Nashville Now."

IT WOULD BE HARD TO DETERMINE A MARKET SHARE?

Yes, researchers tell us there are serious questions about the numbers we are getting, although we have to use them for advertising. They think that we are at the end of the stick in terms of consideration from the broadcast television numbers. I can tell you that based on consumer interest in the Nashville Network, we have a country card program that is in excess of 340,000 members. Artists are feeling a tremendous response from concert dates and announcements. Our figures show that we are in one out of four U.S. households.

HOW DOES THE NETWORK HELP THE RECORD COMPANIES AND VICE VERSA?

It's a "you scratch our back and we'll scratch yours" situation. We determined early on that, in the country music business, there are really only about 125 acts. So you have to define formats that enhance those acts. If, for example, you put on a special with a major star and the format is the same as the road show, you have cut the person's concert bookings. What you have done is say, "Hey folks this is the act; you can see it on television free, so why go to the concert?" This has happened to a number of acts that have sold their shows to some other services.

But if you create a format in a special program that doesn't expose the entire road show, you have the ability to enhance the artist's career. An artist appearing on "Nashville Now" can perform his current songs, talk about his tour dates, and then we all win. "New Country" was designed for enhancement of the record industry and promotion of albums and new releases. Those artists are requested to do a half-hour—four songs out of their new album, plus two other selections that the public would identify with, and they host the show. That is the record industry touch. Then add to that the video business, which seems to have taken off, and we have met that demand with our new series "Video Country."

On other formats you still might see a George Strait, but he would be fishing on "Country Sportsman." He's not performing or singing; you're seeing a different side of the artist.

So what we're hoping to do is create a presence. We're introducing the new material to the public and hoping that they get to know the artist and identify with the personality. In country, the personality is first and the music is secondary. Rock is the opposite. We are really trying to design our service to enhance the artist. The better we are, the better the artist looks, and the better the label does.

WHAT ADVICE WOULD YOU GIVE TO YOUNG PEOPLE WHO WANT TO WORK FOR THE NASHVILLE NETWORK?

Artists have an entry-level program called "You Can Be a Star." This was designed to present new talent on television. So if you are someone who hasn't had a shot at it, "You Can Be a Star" tapes twice a year. Between 7,000 and 9,000 tapes per series are narrowed down to about 200. Then those folks are invited to come in.

For the other positions, including the technical positions, we are generally looking for people who have had a good deal of experience. We don't have the time to do the training. Currently, experience is the best prerequisite for being hired. We do hire out of the local Nashville television market and other places around the country, depending on the need.

ANY OTHER COMMENTS?

Our television service will not lead the way for new trends; that has to come from the people creating the music. So we will react to a new trend, or to whatever the public seems to be responding to, with our different formats. We will wait to see what the next steps are.

CHAPTER FOURTEEN

TRADE MAGAZINES AND MUSIC CRITIQUE

The purpose of trade magazines is to serve as a news source for the industry. Probably the most important features of a trade are the charts—Country 100, Hot 100, Adult Contemporary charts. Trade magazines also have record reviews that are written for radio programmers to look at as they select their ads each week for the radio-station play lists. They have news of late-breaking stories, pricing returns, radio company policies, quarterly reports for labels, new signings, and marketing blitzes behind certain artist products.

Interestingly enough, the advertisements are very important in trades because they show the commitment of a label to spend money on an artist. They also serve to alert the industry and, in particular, radio, that an artist is out on the marketplace and has a new product to watch for. That's why you'll find record companies paying $3,000 to $6,500 for a full-page ad.

Trade magazines are to the music industry what the newspaper is to regular people. They carry news that's basically hard line. You'll find soft features, like a talent interview, or an in-depth, close-up review of an album; but basically their function is to diffuse the news for people in the industry. The most popular trade magazines today are *Billboard, Cash Box, Radio & Records,* and *The Gavin Report.*

KIP KIRBY

Nashville bureau chief/country music editor for *Billboard* magazine. Freelance writer: articles appear in such magazines as *Country Music*, *Playboy*, *Songwriters Digest*, *Tune-In, and Off Duty*.

HOW DOES BILLBOARD *SERVE THE ENTERTAINMENT INDUSTRY?*

Billboard is a trade magazine. As such, it's geared toward those who work in the entertainment industry: record companies, producers, songwriters, publishers, retailers, radio stations, video companies, syndicated programmers, booking agencies, concert promoters and so on. A trade magazine's function is to provide news and information to its readers, keying on trends, headline news, and in-depth profiles. We also publish a significant number of charts each week that cover everything: the Hot 100 pop singles and albums as well as individual Hot 100 charts for country, black, and adult contemporary music. We also have European charts, video software rental and sales charts, and even computer software.

We also reflect what's going on in the industry and how current events will have an impact on that industry.

For instance, one story, which illustrates the kinds of articles we look for, involved an in-depth survey on upcoming country

Compact Disc titles to be released by the major labels, along with information about sales volume they expected to do in country CDs by the end of the year. And we also do "softer" features, such as talent reviews, artists' profiles and album and singles reviews.

IS THERE ANYTHING DIFFERENT ABOUT WRITING FOR A MUSIC TRADE MAGAZINE?

Yes, definitely. We're writing for the industry, not for the average reader. Our audience is actively engaged, in some way or another, in the entertainment industry. We're dealing with facts, figures, analysis, compilations, and trends. *Billboard*'s readers generally know a great deal about their industry; our job is to keep them up-to-date with new or pertinent information.

Writing for a trade can be technical. It's not "fanzine" feature writing. We have to conduct the surveys, get the information, find the right people to talk with, figure out what's important and relevant, and then

205

write the story clearly and concisely. You don't have a lot of space in a trade magazine to get your point across. You've got to keep things succinct.

For instance, I might interview Emmylou Harris for *Country Music* magazine and chat about her children, her thoughts about life on the road, where she thinks her career is going and what a normal day for her might be. For *Billboard*, none of that would apply. For *Billboard*, I would focus on her latest album, how it was recorded, why she chose those songs, any changes or new directions in her production or touring schedule, and how the album is being marketed.

HOW DO ARTICLES IN BILLBOARD EN-COURAGE CREATIVE TRENDS WITHIN THE INDUSTRY?

We don't create trends; we write about them. We talk about them and analyze them. Sometimes, if we're lucky, we see them coming and predict them in advance! That makes us valuable to our readers and is why *Billboard* has been around so long and will continue to be around. This is how, in my opinion, our editorial expertise is so worthwhile and important. We use quotes from industry sources, experts in their fields, so we can accurately reflect what's really going on.

WHO ARE YOUR NEWS SOURCES?

Of course, we work closely with publicists and public relations firms who pitch us stories and ideas. It's in their interest to see "ink" about their clients or artists in *Billboard*. It's our responsibility to make sure there really is a good news angle, though; something that warrants space in the magazine. We aren't writing for fans, remember.

HOW DO YOU HANDLE NEGATIVE PERSONAL STORIES ABOUT ARTISTS AND DRUGS, OR LAWSUITS?

Lawsuits, which are relevant to the industry or the act's career, are covered as news items. We always go to the court and obtain a copy of the legal documents, however,

and use that wording for accuracy. We usually will try to talk to the lawyers involved as well to see if a response filing is planned. As far as stories about drugs, rehabilitation, and so forth are concerned, well, I might mention something in my weekly column if an artist is working on a come-back or something; but again, since we're not writing for fans, gossip items aren't a priority. I've done artist profiles on acts who have quit drugs and alcohol—artists like Larry Gatlin and Johnny Rodriguez, for example—and then I'll ask them what changes this has made in their recording, their touring, their performing.

WHAT ARE YOUR FEELINGS ABOUT THE ARTISTS YOU'VE INTERVIEWED?

Oh, for the most part, I've found them very nice, very friendly, easy to talk with—especially country artists! I think it's important for writers to realize that artists may sit down and be 100 percent yours for the duration of an interview, but that doesn't mean you'll end up friends, or even that the artist will cross the floor to say hello to you at a party. You may knock yourself out writing a story that conveys their creativity, and their talent and their artistry—and never hear a word from them when the article is printed. You have to get used to the unalterable reality of journalism: you probably won't end up pals with the people you interview—and it's probably better that way. It's awfully hard to be objective in print about someone you're friends with. Journalists have to maintain their integrity and independence in print, and it isn't easy if you have a personal relationship with a particular performer.

Understand that the writer isn't the star. It's not our job to insert ourselves into stories; it's our job to get quotes correct, write a strong story, and showcase the subject of the piece. My own personal self-satisfaction comes from writing a story that I think is really good. It's great when an artist or executive takes the time to write a note or call up and say, "Gee, that was a wonderful article you wrote . . . Thank you." But get used to the fact that it doesn't happen often!

DO ARTISTS REALLY OPEN UP TO YOU?

When you spend time with them, sometimes they do, especially if you've interviewed them before and they know your work. Writers hear a lot. Artists will complain about record companies or their producers, why their last single didn't go to Number One, problems with radio stations, any number of things. But I certainly don't print everything I hear, even when I'm writing a story for a feature publication rather than *Billboard*. You try to get the whole picture—and sometimes it's not the same picture the artist himself sees.

Writing for a news magazine like *Billboard* is like sitting at the hub of a wheel, with spokes going out all around you. The spokes lead to every aspect of the industry, and you get this amazing view of how everything fits together.

WHAT'S YOUR FAVORITE PART OF WRITING FOR BILLBOARD?

Helping to expose new acts. Helping to "break" artists through my influence. Convincing radio to take a chance on unknown talent—or helping labels get word about new artists out in the industry. When I look back over the years and think about some of the superstars I was able to help when they were still unknown, I feel pretty good.

A record company executive once said that we shouldn't take our business too seriously. "After all," he pointed out, "it all boils down to the fact that we're trying to sell little pieces of vinyl with holes in the middle." Of course, that's a simplistic summary; but yet there's some truth to it. We're selling a commodity that can't be measured. Is it a necessity or is it a luxury?

The important thing, to me, is that talent is the lifeblood of this industry. We're selling creativity; and I don't think you can take that lightly. These days, artists are called "product," their records are "product." We package them, develop them, market them, expose them, exploit them, all in the name of commerciality. A record company executive hears an exciting new album and what does he say? "Hey, great album—how many singles are there? How can we promote it?" There are formulas today which didn't exist in the past.

WHAT ADVICE WOULD YOU GIVE PEOPLE WHO WANT TO WRITE FOR A MUSIC TRADE MAGAZINE LIKE BILLBOARD?

First of all, listen to music. Study the albums. Read other publications that talk about music whether it's *Downbeat* or *Mix* or *Rolling Stone*. Figure out what part of the industry does what. Go visit a recording studio. Intern at a radio station, or work in a record store for a summer. Get some on-the-job training.

Read everything you can. Go to the library. Get familiar with certain industry terms, how things interact, who does what. Freelance. Interview artists at local clubs for local publications. If you're college-bound, enroll in a school with a music program. Write for the student newspaper, review concerts, and review albums.

Don't get an attitude and think just because you can go backstage after a concert and shake hands with the act, you're a star. It's not your job as a writer to compete with celebrities. Worry about shining in what you write.

You don't have to be a great writer to write for a trade. In fact, if you're a very creative writer, working for a trade may stifle you. It's not the most feature-oriented kind of writing. Trade writers are journalists, reporters, always digging. We get our creative kicks in, usually, when we freelance on the side.

WHAT ARE SOME OF THE PROBLEMS PEOPLE HAVE GOING INTO THE INDUSTRY AS TRADE WRITERS?

Lack of experience and lack of talent are two. The first can be overcome; I'm not so sure about the second. There are people who are great writers but haven't got the initiative or determination to follow through. You have to be persistent, but it pays off.

You have to be able to meet deadlines, get facts straight, take notes fast, spell, transcribe tapes—and understand how the industry works so you can come up with good news stories.

DID YOU HAVE FORMAL TRAINING?
No, I actually was doing publicity for a Nashville showcase club, Exit/In, when I was hired as a reporter for *Billboard*. I had done some freelance writing for local publications; but nothing in my portfolio qualified me on the surface for the position. However, I had gathered a wealth of information by working at the club. I had a good association with name acts who played there, and I'd worked with the record companies on special showcases and projects, so they were familiar with me. I learn fast; and when I don't know something, I'm not afraid to ask. I think these are two traits of a good writer!

WHAT ARE THE PITFALLS OF ENTERTAIN-MENT JOURNALISM?
You have to maintain a level attitude, not burn out. You have to learn how to separate truth from fiction and not get egotistical. Don't expect "perks" just because your byline appears in print.

HOW ABOUT INTEGRITY?
To me, integrity is vital. So is being objective and not taking out personal problems or "vendettas" in print. Just because you've had a bad experience with an artist doesn't mean you have any right to give his new album a bad review. If it's a good album, it deserves a good review. You have to separate yourself—and personalities—from your job. Fairness is important.

HOW MANY JOB OPPORTUNITIES ARE THERE TODAY FOR WRITERS IN THE MUSIC INDUSTRY?
There are still a lot. I've seen interns who've worked for me in the past go on to great positions in the industry—or manage to support themselves on freelance assignments from what they've learned at *Billboard*. Interns often get promoted from within and end up on record company payrolls, or in some other facet of the industry. Believing in yourself, and being persistent, really pays off. It's competitive, sure; but sometimes the only difference in getting a job and not getting a job is how many times you've knocked on the door.

Contacts are valuable. Try to meet everyone you can. You may have to write twenty pitch letters to get one assignment; but each assignment leads to new contacts and perhaps more assignments.

WHAT PERSONAL TRAITS HELP?
Positive, cheerful attitude, and the ability to get along with others are invaluable. Make your job fun. Don't be afraid to ask questions. How else are you going to learn? Stay abreast of all new developments within your industry. Learn about new technology, new products, new companies.

HOW HAS THE INDUSTRY CHANGED SINCE YOU STARTED AT BILLBOARD?
As we do this interview, I've been at *Billboard* almost eight years, from reporter to editor to bureau chief. At the same time, the industry has gone through tremendous changes which have made it more professional, more competitive, more technological. It's much more expensive to do business today in every area. When an act goes to a record company A & R department today, he isn't walking in with a guitar-and-voice demo tape. Albums these days aren't just vinyl—they're digital and Compact Disc! We're in the midst of a video revolution, not to mention a computer software evolution.

The future isn't very bright for independent labels and small businesses without capital. Jerry Moss and Herb Alpert admitted not long ago that if they were to attempt to launch A & M Records now, chances are it wouldn't succeed. There's no chance of success without a lot of money or major label distribution.

Like everything else, entertainment is big business now. Movies cost millions of dollars to make; albums cost hundreds of thousands. Still, there are plenty of opportunities. Five years ago, there was no MTV; today, MTV has dramatically changed the way albums and rock artists are marketed.

There's still a need for management, booking, marketing, promotion, merchandising and publicity. Artists still get signed; records are still hits; concerts still sell out. New artists still become superstars; people still enter the industry in some strength every year.

BILL
BURK

Independent entertainment writer.

WHAT ADVICE WOULD YOU GIVE TO PEOPLE WHO WANT TO CRITIQUE RECORDS, CONCERTS, ETC.?

First, they must have an overbearing love of music. They should become as knowledgeable as possible about the artists, getting to know them away from the stage or dressing room, if at all possible. That's what I've always tried to do. I feel that my strong point is my personal friendships with the artist.

HOW DO YOU RELATE TO THE ARTISTS THAT YOU INTERVIEW?

My basic approach is to treat them as people. In doing so, with rare exceptions, I find that they appreciate it and will respond as people. Over the years I've had a lot of them visit my home. The approach is if they want to get away from everything and just unwind, they'll be treated like normal people. It has been a real drawing card; a lot of them do come out. My neighbors have finally gotten to the point that they are not awestruck anymore. If they see somebody out there playing softball in the backyard,

they know it's just people having a good time.

HOW ABOUT ELVIS PRESLEY? DID YOU EVER GET TO INTERVIEW HIM, MEET HIM?

Elvis and I were very close friends, because when I first started with the paper, he had just signed with RCA. He was a night person and I worked the night shift (I was the lone night-shift reporter). We got thrown together by necessity on the paper's part and became friends. It got to the point that I was sometimes his confidant. If something was troubling him, he'd call me at three or four o'clock in the morning, which was noon for him. We'd always lived within a mile of each other, so it was easy to get together. He had gotten away from that, I always thought at the Colonel's insistence; but three months before he died, he called me. We met at a doughnut shop on Elvis Presley Boulevard. We talked for a couple of hours about where he had been and where he was then. He felt that I had knocked his last concert in Las Vegas. It was the first time I had ever knocked him; it may have been the first time I had ever reviewed one of his concerts. He thought I was knocking him personally. But I told him it was nothing personal.

DID HE FEEL EMBARRASSED ABOUT TRYING TO UPHOLD THIS IMAGE THAT EVERYBODY HAD OF HIM?

Frankly, he was on drugs so much that he didn't know where he was. He was unable to feel embarrassed.

WHY DID HE GET SO HEAVILY INTO DRUGS?

My source was of the opinion—and he was with Elvis quite a bit throughout the drug situation—that it was psychological, that Elvis was coming up on the "fat and forty" syndrome. The closer he got to forty, the more it worried him. He was worried that his fans would desert him.

SINCE YOU KNEW HIM FOR SUCH A LONG TIME, DO YOU THINK HE ENJOYED DOING WHAT HE WAS DOING?

Being from north Memphis, it was sort of like a toy with him. He enjoyed it. The enjoyment came from being able to say, "Hey, look at this. I'm a little kid who came from Lauderdale Courts and all these people are making a big to-do over me."

LAUDERDALE COURTS IS A HOUSING DEVELOPMENT, ISN'T IT?

It's a public housing project. We had come from different ends of town, but I was only about a step out of the project. In our last conversation, he was accusing me of being jealous of his having "made it." I told him, "Wait a minute. We have to define what 'made it' is. I've always been proud of you because you came out of the north end of town, and you made it on your own. Nobody ever gave it to you. You didn't inherit it. What you did, you did on your own."

WHAT HAPPENED BETWEEN ELVIS AND PRISCILLA?

She got fed up with the guys being around all the time. I can't say that I blame her. I'd say that she had very good reasons for leaving. How can you ever be intimate with your husband or just be yourself when there are always a bunch of guys around?

WAS THIS AN IMAGE THAT ELVIS WAS TRYING TO BUILD?

No, it just seems that he was comfortable with the guys hanging around. He was always the little kid, and they horsed around a lot. They did a lot of things that 30- and 40-year-old people shouldn't be doing anymore.

OBVIOUSLY THINGS WENT ON WITH ELVIS THAT THE GENERAL PUBLIC DOESN'T KNOW OR DOESN'T NEED TO KNOW.

It's his private life on the one hand. I've said many times that "20/20" with Geraldo Rivera thinks that they really got into it, but they didn't even scratch the surface. I think all of us have skeletons in our closet. I'm very image conscious about myself as well as artists. Kids look up to sports figures and artists, and the artists owe it to the kids to at least set a public example and make every effort to keep their private lives private.

DO YOU THINK THE LIFESTYLE—THE PRESSURES OF BEING ON THE ROAD, OF BEING AN IMAGE OR IDOL—CAUSE PEOPLE TO ABUSE ALCOHOL AND DRUGS?

The drugs are there, people are on them, and I think the pressures of the road contribute. But I've always looked at pressure as something that you put on yourself. There are a lot of people who are on the road who are not on drugs. It depends on how you handle it.

One time Charlie Rich and I bumped into each other at a Liberty Bowl function. He told me that he wished he could hang out with me like we used to—when we would go to clubs and he would jump on-stage and perform. But after "Behind Closed Doors," he felt his fans wouldn't let him. He said they would mob him. Elvis had told me the same thing once, sitting in front of Graceland. I told Elvis to just get out there because the novelty will wear off in a week or two, and you can be a person again. Then you won't have to lock yourself behind these gates. Charlie had bought a big place that had a fence around it, too. I told Charlie, "Let me take you out in public some night, you and Margaret Ann, and we'll go out and test it." We picked the Bill Cosby concert at the Hilton. There were 800 people there. We sat through the whole show; nobody bothered us before the show. Afterwards, a little grandmother-in-tennis-shoes type came up and said, "Aren't you Charlie Rich?" He said, "Yes, Ma'am." She said, "I thought so," and then walked off. We later went to a couple of places, but to my knowledge he still stays behind those gates.

BECAUSE YOU ARE A NEWSPAPER WRITER AND YOU SEE THE ENTERTAINERS AFTER THEY HAVE MADE IT, WHAT KIND OF ADVICE WOULD YOU GIVE TO YOUNG PEOPLE WHO WANT TO BECOME ENTERTAINERS?

I see so many young people today who don't want to pay their dues. They want to be famous right off the bat. The thing is to get out there and get the experience. Always be around where it is happening. If you keep hanging around without making a pest of yourself, there may come a day when someone doesn't show up, and you'll get a break. It's like the old story of the understudy on Broadway when the star doesn't show.

WHAT ARE THE PITFALLS OF TRYING TO BE A LOCAL MUSIC CRITIC?

The hardest thing I have to deal with is the people who surround the artist. Getting through that outer layer to get to the person can be difficult. I can get through the record companies, since they want the publicity. I can get through the manager, wherever his office is. But the road manager or whoever is with the artist is the guy you have trouble with. They get that real power ego; they can control who sees the artist and who doesn't.

HOWARD LANDER AND TOM POWELL

Lander is publisher and Powell, editor, of *Amusement Business* magazine.

TELL ME A LITTLE ABOUT YOUR MAGAZINE.

Amusement Business is the founding property of Billboard Publications. Since there wasn't a record business in 1894 (the year *Billboard* magazine was founded) our roots go back to the carnival industry. *Amusement Business* was launched out of *Billboard* magazine in 1961. It was started because the recording industry and the live entertainment industry were growing rapidly and could best be served by having two publications.

Billboard went with the record business and we had to come up with the name *Amusement Business* for our publication. We feel very strongly that there is a need for coverage of the talent marketplace. We really believe the industries we cover are very closely linked. They all have the same task of getting as many people through the gate as possible, to make sure they're happy and entertained, and to have them come back again.

WHAT IS YOUR MARKET?

We identify our market as managers and department managers at arenas, stadiums, amusement parks, carnivals, and fairs across the country.

Tom Powell: You reach all the potential buyers with *Amusement Business*. You're going to the promoters and building managers, including the building managers that co-promote, and to the fairs and the fair managers who buy talent. You're reaching the people who would buy your act.

Howard Lander: To give you an example, the International Association of Auditorium Managers had a survey that asked their members what publication they received and read regularly. *Amusement Business* was cited by 78 percent compared to *Variety*'s 20 percent and *Performance*'s 47 percent.

Every week we have a talent section with hard news, and our "Boxscore" column. We also list the Top 25 singles from the pop and country music charts, because many of our readers don't get *Billboard*. We have found that the activity in the singles market is very important to the talent buyers.

Tom Powell: We do this also for the park and fair managers who aren't in tune with the industry as much as your typical promoter. Your average fair manager probably isn't reading *Billboard*. Some of the smaller fairs managers may even be the county agent.

WHAT'S THE PUBLICATION ALL ABOUT?

Tom Powell: It's a news vehicle. It's as up-to-date as we can provide. If we get some hot news on deadline or even after, we'll get it in there.

Howard Lander: Tom had fifteen years of newspaper experience before joining us. We pride ourselves in getting the news out.

AMUSEMENT BUSINESS *IS ALSO IN-VOLVED IN SEMINARS?*

Howard Lander: We realized last year that in every section of the paper, the big news was corporate sponsorship. At every convention we went to, they talked about it. So we created a corporate sponsorship seminar. We had so many people at the first one, that we had to turn people away. We repeated the seminar in Chicago.

WHY IS CORPORATE SPONSORSHIP SUCH A BIG THING?

Tom Powell: Many of the acts going out on the road are not getting record-company tour support. They have to find another source of money. Fairs have a free stage. As an example, the Texas State Fair will have seven free stages. They may have Lee Greenwood on one and someone else on another. Instead of having to pay for the talent, the fair gets a sponsor, like Pepsi, to present someone on-stage. It works to the benefit and exposure of both the artist and the advertiser. In addition, the sponsor can put a picture of the artist on the product's can or wrapper or in a newspaper ad. It's something that corporations, talent, and venues have found to be very beneficial.

THERE ARE A LOT OF ARTICLES ABOUT FACILITIES AND THEIR MANAGERS IN AMUSEMENT BUSINESS.

Tom Powell: We are considered the "Bible" for the markets we reach, that includes the carnivals, circuses, arenas, fairs, and parks. We also publish seven annual source directories. One is the *Auditorium, Arena, Stadium Guide*, which has about 250 pages of advertisements. That book is sent to talent promoters, booking agencies, and to the acts themselves. The guide can help put a show together.

Tom Powell: A good example is the Foreigner tour. It went all over the world, but the show started in Albany, Georgia, because the act heard about the facilities there through an ad in the guide. Some people may think Albany, Georgia, is the end of the world, but it's got a 10,000-seat auditorium. They had a nice gross for their performance there, and they worked out some of the bugs for worldwide tour.

HOW DO YOUR STORIES HELP IMPROVE THE ENTERTAINMENT BUSINESS?

Howard Lander: It's not unusual for people to read the entire paper. What's happening is arena managers, talent managers, and park managers are reading the entire paper because they are discovering that they all have a common link. What works at one end of the industry can work at the other.

Howard Lander: You'd also be surprised at how many carnival managers get involved in the booking of acts at fairs. In fact, Mike Williams, who is the manager of a carnival, recently signed a fair where he is in charge of both putting on the carnival and booking the grandstand acts.

This is really a live industry. After salaries and the mechanical cost of putting out the paper, we spent the most money on travel. At any time of the year, we've got somebody on the road. We have datelines from all over the world. We feel it's important, since we're looking for the backstage happenings, that we're involved in the business end. We're not very concerned, at a sold-out concert, about the quality of the artist's voice or the group's performance. We are interested in who did the sound and lighting. Were there any security problems? What were the receipts and potential? What were the tickets prices?

Tom Powell: We ask them the questions nobody else asks them.

CHAPTER FIFTEEN

BOOKING AGENTS

There are approximately 1,300 booking agents (1,000 in the U.S., 300 in Canada) sanctioned by the American Federation of Musicians. The booking agents represent the musicians that they work for. They acquire employment for musicians by hustling for jobs—contacting nightclubs, hotels, and any other establishments that need live entertainers. In some instances, the establishments seeking musicians to entertain their guests will contact the booking agent. It's not as easy as it sounds. It's a lot of hard work on the telephone and a great deal of shoe leather, walking on the streets, looking for establishments to book talent.

The booking agent may form an agency and hire sub-agents to work with him in getting establishments to hire entertainers. The agent's job is to acquire employment for the people he represents and to make sure they are paid properly. In return, he is paid 15 percent of the entertainer's salary for that booking.

Agents must be self-motivating individuals, with a true love of music and people. They are the middlemen who help the musicians secure work and the entertainment establishments find the proper performers. An agent puts the two together. He also may contact concert promoters in an effort to "sell" recording artists. "Sell" means that the agent wants the promoter to give the talent he represents a chance. The more famous the talent the booking agent represents, the easier it is to secure work for that talent. Everyone knows the artist and what to expect. Breaking a new act can be super hard because the concert promoters or entertainment establishments are afraid of losing their money. If the act doesn't draw a crowd, the booking agent and musicians still get paid. But the concert promoter or entertainment establishment loses its shirt.

JACK
SUBLETTE

President of Top Billing International, an artist booking
agency. Artists represented include Tom T. Hall
and Jerry Clower.

**WHAT IS YOUR JOB AS A BOOKING
AGENT? WHAT DO YOU REALLY DO?**
First of all, the whole idea is to negotiate
contracts on behalf of your clients, and our
clients are recording artists. We solicit dates
from buyers. We set up concert appearances, radio shows, television shows,
nightclub engagements—that type of thing.
We negotiate the contracts. We're responsible for their personal appearances.

**RIGHT NOW YOU ARE ONE OF THE TOP,
IF NOT THE TOP, AGENT IN NASHVILLE.**
I don't know how you determine that. If
dollar amount or number of days booked
have anything to do with it, probably so. I've
heard that I'm right up there, but I don't
know how you rank people in the industry.
Billboard doesn't have a Top 10 agent list.

**I THINK SUCCESS HAS SOMETHING TO
DO WITH IT, AND YOU'RE VERY
SUCCESSFUL.**
I'm also with a successful company, which
makes it a little easier. I might not have been
so successful with other firms, who knows? I

do know it feels right to me, and I'm happy
with what I've done so far.

DO YOU ENJOY THIS?
I love it, yes. It's fun. It's quick. You see
immediate results. We're sales people. Our
job is to sell entertainment. We've got
people calling here who are looking to put
on a show, so it's up to us to recommend
what we think would go in their market. It's
our job to figure out, first of all, who would fit
into that particular situation.

**YOU HAVE TO KNOW ABOUT THE MARKET
AND THE PEOPLE THAT ARE THERE.**
We try to, yes. And if we don't know, we ask.
We'll sit there and gather enough information
to make recommendations.

Of course, to be honest with you, our main
concern is the welfare and the best interests
of the artists that we represent. Therefore, if
a guy calls in from a particular location and I
have an act that's within 200 to 300 miles of
that location the day before, I'm gonna zero
in on selling that act.

The artists are what we've got to be

concerned with and that's what we've got to keep in mind. We are building their careers. By playing key markets and key venues and performing in front of the right people, that's what we are doing—building careers. It's in the act's best interest to pick up that third or fourth day. It may not be in the buyer's best interest, but the buyer should know his market. It's his job to know what will go over and how to promote it. It's my job to sell what I've got.

YOU'RE SOMEWHAT LOCKED INTO LIMITATIONS WITH THE TOUR SITUATION. YOU ALMOST WANT TO DO A TOUR, BECAUSE OF THE COST OF TRAVEL AND EVERYTHING. IS THAT CORRECT?
The tour is everything to an agent. I can't send an act to the state of Washington or the state of Oregon to work one show. That's ridiculous. The expenses would be so exorbitant that there's no profit in it. I've got to put together six, eight, or ten days in a row. So, if I can work the act out there and back, I have my tour. It's not nearly as simple as it sounds, though. You don't just snap your fingers and set a tour.

We spend a lot of the time calling out. We develop a list of potential buyers or a list of buyers we've dealt with in the past. Depending on where you want to put the act, in a club or something, you can offer the buyer a deal. It's like having a sale on tour tie-in days. We pick a route based on where we are going, a group of dates that pay well, and we work on prospective buyers who are 300 to 500 miles from those key markets and then we work our way closer to home. When all the days are booked, we can start in another direction. It never ends.

WHAT IS THE AVERAGE COST TO HIRE AN ARTIST? DOES THE PRICE USUALLY GO UP WITH THE NEXT HIT RECORD?
In our roster, the acts run from $2,000 to $12,500. Your really top-notch promoters know the business, know the acts, and know their markets. Even if an act has a big, big hit record, you can't jump the price out of reason. There's only so much an act can draw in any market, and the promoter should know that. You can't hype them too much. Artists should be priced according to their drawing power. Naturally, hit records influence drawing power.

HOW ABOUT CASH UP FRONT, ADVANCED PAYMENT OF THE ARTIST'S SALARY? AGENTS USUALLY STIPULATE THAT THE ESTABLISHMENT PAY HALF OF THE SALARY ON SIGNING THE CONTRACT AND THE OTHER HALF AFTER THE ENGAGEMENT HAS BEEN COMPLETED.
We normally get half of it up front, depending on how far in advance the engagement is booked. If it's six months or so, we won't demand 50 percent with a contract. That's tying up too much promotion money for too long a period of time. But we might ask for 10 percent just as good faith deposit. Normally, thirty days before the date, we pretty much have half of the payment in our office.

DO THE ARTISTS HAVE ANY OPPORTUNITY TO TURN DOWN CERTAIN JOBS?
Sure they do. The artists hire us. If a guy's going to sign with us and give us a certain percentage of his income, hopefully, we've got enough good judgment within this company to put them in the right places. That is not to say we are never second-guessed. We can be overruled by the act. The entertainers are in ultimate control.

We have to work within guidelines. Some acts will say, "Here's my price spread. Here's my lowest dollar. I won't work for any less than that, and this is what I want to average." If there's a borderline case, we may be real flexible. We think that it's better for an act to work a date that just pays expenses than to be off on the road and pay expenses. Often we go to the act for approval. It all depends on the situation, the supply, and the demand.

IT SOUNDS AS IF A PROMOTER CLOSE TO A BIG MARKET COULD EASILY MAKE SOME GOOD MONEY, COULD GET BARGAINS.

Your club owners get the best deals, and they should. The club owner has the least to make. He's usually got a very confining facility; he can only seat 500 to 1,000 people. Some clubs are bigger, but not many. A promoter can go into a 15,000-capacity coliseum. He is not limited the way a club is. He also does not have an ongoing overhead. The club that can use a date that is convenient for the act and tour is in a better position to get a bargain.

ARE PROMOTERS HURT BY ECONOMIC BAD TIMES?

I don't think they hurt as bad as their screams would indicate. My reasoning behind that is that any time inflation is high and the economy is down, you have a lot of unemployment. Usually the breadwinner has an enormous burden on his shoulders, just to make ends meet. And let's face it, the mass audience of the country music fans are blue-collar workers. You depend on those factory workers to buy records and concert tickets.

Their income is down and their expenses are up. They are having a hard time making it, if they do at all. Their problems are big ones, and—with those problems hanging over them all the time—they need some release. Something to make their emotions react, to make them laugh or cry about something besides money. I would bet they would go out, get drunk, listen to country music, have a good time, and forget about not being able to pay the rent. They need low-cost entertainment to which they can relate. If they can get a ticket to a concert for $7 or $8 but they've got to pay $4 to a movie that might later be on television anyway, they'll go to the concert.

When times are hard, the entertainment business should boom. It is cheap release. I've heard it recommended that when bad times are upon us, one should buy beer

stock. People can't buy whiskey, so they'll go to a bar and drink beer. They'll listen to sad country songs on the jukebox and relate to them.

DO THE CHARTS ON RECORD SALES AFFECT YOUR MARKETING OF TALENT?

The charts are a good indication of potential markets. We get a read-out sheet from the label, about once a week, that pretty much charts the sales of albums and the radio action of singles. In other words, a record may be No. 25 in Los Angeles and No. 1 in Minneapolis. Naturally, we're going to pitch the Minneapolis market while it's hot. Sure, it gives us an edge when approaching a market.

THIS IS REALLY A BUSINESS, ISN'T IT?

Hell, yeah. It's definitely a business, a big business. It's serious to a lot of people, myself included.

Some acts—I don't think we represent any—but some acts treat it as a plaything. It's a toy for them. But most of the artists obtain 80 percent or more of their income from personal appearances. It breaks my heart to see some talent screw up by not taking it seriously. It's a big waste.

Acts that travel have huge overheads. They've got six to twelve people on the payroll; they've got a $120,000 Eagle Bus that they've got to maintain. They have a large business, and a lot of the fun is replaced with responsibility and pressure.

WHAT DO YOU DO DURING AN AVERAGE DAY? WHAT TIME DO YOU COME IN? WHAT TIME DO YOU LEAVE?

I get here about 8:20 A.M. I usually start by writing letters, researching markets, and doing things that don't require me to be on the phone, because the switchboard doesn't open until 9:00 A.M. At 9:00, we usually start taking and making calls. If we're not getting a whole bunch of calls, then we start looking for dates we need. We start calling out and selling our wares. Trying to get somebody excited about bringing that act to a market can be rewarding or very frustrating.

We'll have a meeting once a day, usually a sales meeting. We talk about dates we need on acts, the priority for the day, that kind of thing. Most of the day is spent on the phone. I probably talk to thirty people a day by phone, and it's either selling or servicing a date. Once you sell a date and issue a contract, your responsibility is not over until the date is played, the act is paid, and we get our commission. So you've got to stay with it, follow up on it. You have tons of details to worry about.

AT TIMES, THERE SEEMS TO BE A PICTURE OF THE OLD BOOKING AGENT WHO IS SOMEWHAT OF A CRAFTY, SNEAKY PERSON.

When I first came into this business, my vision of a typical agent was a New York theatrical agent—little thin mustache; slick, greased hair; loud clothes; obnoxious as hell, sitting behind a desk full of papers with a line of people waiting outside to audition. A real crafty individual to be watched. I didn't want to have any part of it. That may be the picture of some theatrical agents, but that is not what we do. Of course, the company that I work for is a very reputable company, a very up-front company. I don't know if I'd be happy working for other agencies. I have never given it very much thought. Thank God, I've never had to.

Our business is based on repeats. If a guy is successful, we'll do business with him year after year, and that's what we're after. Let's face it. We don't want to book a good act with a sorry promoter who's going to get out there, do one show, and lose his shirt. We don't want to have 200 people in a 5,000 seat auditorium and make the act or us look foolish. That's not our goal. Our goal is to make the promoter successful and to turn around and do business with that guy again. That's what we want. To do that, you've got to be as fair as possible.

You can hype some people and sell them a bill of goods. There are a lot of suckers out there, and if you're just out to make a quick buck, you can do it in this business. But if you're out to establish a working relationship, you had better play it straight.

We dress in business suits. We're probably the only agency in Nashville that dresses this way, but the boss feels it gives us a psychological edge. You're talking to a guy on the phone. You're dressed up; you feel confident; you feel good (except for this tight feeling around my neck). You've got a psychological edge on selling and negotiating. I try to picture the man on the other end wearing overalls. So it's our policy.

On the agency level, a company can make a great deal of money if it has a great roster, if it has big acts. An agent can make a fair living. An agent who works for somebody is not going to get rich by any means, but in most instances it depends on your individual performance. It's like most salesmen; you get a commission. So, depending on your figures and ability you can make a good living. Every company's different; every deal is different.

AGENCIES HAVE TO BE SANCTIONED BY THE AMERICAN FEDERATION OF MUSICIANS. IN OTHER WORDS, YOU HAVE TO HAVE A LICENSE.

The primary agent and the agency do. I'm a sub-agent of Tandy Rice and he has the license. But I'm still sanctioned; I'm on the good list.

DO YOU HAVE ANY ADVICE FOR YOUNG PEOPLE WHO WOULD LIKE TO GET INTO THE MUSIC BUSINESS?

My advice would be to make damn sure that's what you want more than anything else in the whole wide world, because there's no easy way to do it. You've got to have the desire eating away at you almost constantly. There's no prerequisite, no education that's required, no proving ground. It's all chance, politics, hard work, long hours, and who you know that gets you in a place where you can be successful. And a lot of times, it is very hard to do.

There is a personal sacrifice and you have to neglect your family. If you're not willing to starve, you can forget it. Don't come to Nashville if you're $20,000 in debt, and you've got to make $2,000 a month immediately to pay off that debt. Don't do it. You'll never make it; you'll go bankrupt. Come to Nashville not owing anybody, with as few possessions as possible. Be able to come in and say, "Hey, I'm gonna stick it out, and try to make something happen." Then be willing to give it about two years before you give it up and go home.

DO YOU SEE A LOT OF PEOPLE WHO WANT TO GET INTO THIS BUSINESS?

I do. I never advise anybody to get into this business. I'll talk to a guitar player in Beaumont, Texas, or a fiddle player, or an agent who has a small agency booking nightclub acts around a little area, and they'll say, "I want to come to Nashville. I want to really break into it." I say, "Don't do it, man, stay at home. If you're doing okay there, just don't do it. Stay where you are."

WHY IS THIS A ROUGH BUSINESS?

There are no prerequisites. You can walk out of the University of Tennessee with a degree in accounting and know where your job market is. Your grade point and college record impress potential employers. It is next to impossible to impress people in our business. They have seen it all, or think they have. It's a hard business. There's not a placement service to help find you a job. You've just got to come around and knock on a bunch of doors. It's very difficult.

I'd like to add that the agency business is not the business that it's made out to be. A lot of people have the idea that an agent sits around all day in a big, fancy office, comes in at 11:00, takes two hours for lunch, and knocks off early to go to the spa. He takes a bunch of calls and turns down offers all day. He picks and chooses where his acts work. That's not the case. It is full of pressure, and it never lets up. It's one of those businesses where you've got to be on top of it from the minute you walk in until the minute you leave; you've got to keep your nose to the grindstone, if that's not too old a cliché. You've got to stay on top of it. It's not an easy job.

It's very hard work. The agents have a massive responsibility. It's a high-stress business. There is an enormous amount of pressure on the agents in this industry to keep the income level of the artists up to that certain point, to keep them out of trouble. You've got hundreds, literally millions, of dollars' worth of paperwork on a product that is intangible. You can't repossess it.

When I sell entertainment, I'm selling a human commodity. Now that human commodity may die tomorrow, and so does my income. He may have a wreck. His bus may break down on the way to the show. There are just so many "ifs" and "buts" in this business that there's an enormous amount of pressure on everyone in it to produce. We've got to keep acts happy; we've got to keep promoters happy. We've got to keep record labels happy; we've got to keep managers happy. We've got to keep everybody in this industry moving because we generate the income. And yet, the agents get more blame than credit. If an act does well, it's because the act is hot. If the act does poorly, it goes looking for another agent.

It's not unusual for an act to get the big head and say, "What the hell are these people doing? Sitting back here and turning down dates. I have to pay my fat-cat agent 15 percent of my income. I'll just hire me a guy and book myself." They don't know the marketplace. They don't know what they are worth. Entertainers can't handle rejection. When a promoter says "that act won't draw," I can handle it better than an act can.

ARTISTS ARE VERY CREATIVE PEOPLE. ARE THEY HARD TO WORK WITH?

They're hard to work with because of their egos. They have a view of themselves that is often over-inflated, but that's fine because it takes an enormous ego to get in front of thousands of people and come off looking good. You can't be shy and bashful and do it. You've got to have an ego. I want an act with a big ego.

And it's hard sometimes to tell an act, "Look, you're not drawing people right now. You're asking $5,000 and your average attendance figure at a concert is $3,000. Something's wrong. People are losing money on you." It's hard to tell an act that. It's hard for them to believe you, too.

YOU MUST GET A LOT OF ENJOYMENT, THOUGH, OUT OF THE SUCCESS YOU DO HAVE.

It's financially rewarding. If I can book 1.5 million dollars' worth of entertainment, I'm going to be financially rewarded. I'm going to be overrun with dates, too.

I've got 20 acts that are working 200 dates a year each. On any given day, I may have 6 to 10 acts working 6 to 10 different places. And it's my responsibility to know every detail. Ultimate responsibility for everything that happens at those dates is on the agent. I've got to, or I am supposed to, know every detail—contracts, the money, everything. But it's fun, too. Every day is a different challenge and a different thing going on. We just always stay energetic and excited, and it's a trip. It's life in the fast lane.

ANDREA SMITH

President of International Celebrity Service (ICS) booking agency. Artists represented include Jim Ed Brown, Donna Fargo, and John Hartford.

YOUR SPECIALTY IS IN THE OVERSEAS MARKET. HOW DO YOU FEEL THAT DIFFERS FROM THE AMERICAN MARKET?

I personally think the overseas markets are very much like this country was for country music fifty or sixty years ago. It's much easier to break an act over there. You can break artists sometimes by touring and by playing big concerts. Records are not quite as important. They're much more open about accepting new acts.

In many ways they're behind. They like old-time country music. Slim Whitman's still a big star over there, and they like the basics. They like nice, simple arrangements and nice, simple music. They know all about it, and they're interested in the history and the roots of the artists. They're very much into the music. Over there, an artist is popular for a long time.

IN REGARD TO DIFFERENT PARTS OF EUROPE, DOES NATIONALITY AFFECT THE WAY PEOPLE LISTEN TO MUSIC OR WHAT TYPES OF MUSIC THEY LIKE?

I can't figure if it affects the types of music they like. It certainly affects the reception. I think British audiences are terribly warm, and German audiences are less warm. They have to really like an act. They're more the type who, instead of stomping for an encore, will clap politely in unison. They're less receptive, and I'd say that has to do with their personality.

I have never played acts in a major way in southern Europe; I don't think country music has much following. I did go to Paris and was amazed at that reception. They played country rock acts that received a passionate reception.

DOES THE PROMOTION OF CONCERTS IN EUROPE HAPPEN THE SAME WAY AS IN THE UNITED STATES? DO INDIVIDUAL PEOPLE PRODUCE THEM OR ARE THEY GOVERNMENT SPONSORED?

Both. When you go behind the Iron Curtain, the acts are almost always an exchange between governments. Artists are not paid; it's more a publicity outing. But the dates that we do in Western Europe are sponsored by individuals.

THERE SEEMS TO BE A LARGE ENTHUSIASM FOR WESTERN MUSIC IN THE IRON CURTAIN COUNTRIES.

Well, I agree. When Elton John went over, he was greeted so wildly it was beyond anybody's imagination. I do not have much information about country music firsthand. I've never seen anybody behind the Iron Curtain. I've not pursued it because there's not much money in it. If somebody came and asked me to put together a tour I'd be glad to, but my job mainly is to make money for my artists.

I think you have to have the right act, too. For country music, it's my understanding you have to have an artist who's very dynamic or whose music is just so acceptable. I think it takes a Roy Clark, who's been fairly successful, or Tennessee Ernie Ford, or somebody who would have real broad appeal in a lot of ways.

HOW ABOUT FROM THE ARTISTS' POINT OF VIEW? DO THEY LIKE TO TOUR EUROPE?

I think they're more and more accepting of it. When I first started taking artists to Europe, they complained about the food. They couldn't understand television, and they thought anybody who didn't speak English must be crazy. But it's becoming such an important record market that artists who are seriously interested in pursuing a career are just very foolish to ignore the international market.

An artist who is interested in his career—who is progressive, who understands what is going on, and who is committed to his career—is willing to make some sacrifices. It takes some commitment to make those tours. But I think they like to.

LET'S COME BACK TO OUR CONTINENT AND TALK ABOUT THE CANADIAN MARKET. WHAT IS IT LIKE?

The Canadian market is enormous for country music. I would say we probably do 5 percent of our business in Canada, which is a lot.

HOW ABOUT ADVICE?

As somebody who has hired many booking agents and tried to solve the problem of what it takes to be a good agent, I'm not sure how to answer. I think a good place to start would probably be to spend some time on the road, plus any kind of music experience. I love to hire musicians. I think they just somehow have an innate understanding, sympathy, and communication with performers, and I like that.

I think you need to have a great sense of discipline. It's very detailed work. If you're not a detail person, you're going to have the wrong person show up at the wrong time and the wrong place. Until you've had an artist do that, you don't know what furor is.

I would also say you need patience. I personally never take an agent who's less than 25-years-old. I know it seems unfair to young people, but you have to remember that an agent is responsible for many artists and often for 100 percent of the artist's income. In the country music field, you almost act as manager a lot of times. You make decisions that really affect their careers, and I think it takes experience in life and good judgment. If you're willing to put in your time on the road and come in as assistants in different areas, it's well worth doing.

CHAPTER SIXTEEN

CONCERT PROMOTION

Probably the biggest gamble in the music business is concert promotion. The financial rewards are enormous but so are the losses. Why is it a gamble? Concert promoters must pay a lot of money up front for the auditorium rent, insurance, police protection, ushers, union workers, advertising, and talent. Concert halls require a base fee, plus a percentage of the gate receipts. Base fee depends upon the size of the arena. A one-night rental can cost anywhere from a few hundred dollars to several thousand. Insurance depends upon the size of the hall, the number of people expected, the type of entertainment being booked, and the location. Insurance costs the promoter anywhere from $100 a night to a few thousand. The stage hands—union employees—build the set and operate the sound and lights. These employees are paid from $10 to $13 an hour and receive additional benefits, including tips from the performers. In addition, a certain number of stagehand employees are required for each concert, depending on the room.

The promoter must also pay for the police protection and the ushers. Usually the number of policemen and ushers depends on the expected number of people attending the concert. For every 200 people at the concert, one usher or policeman is required. Advertisements in the local newspapers, on television, and radio stations must be paid in advance. The cost of radio advertising differs with the size of market. A 30-second spot on a radio station in New York City costs more than $300; and in smaller markets (say, of around 200,000 people) radio advertisements cost from $20 to $50. Concert promoters like to co-sponsor concerts with the local radio stations to save the financial burden of radio advertising. Newspaper ads again depend upon the market size, and the cost can be a few dollars to several hundred. Television advertisements, depending on the market size, can be a few hundred dollars to several thousand dollars.

A promoter also pays the performer, with from 30 to 50 percent of the base salary being paid in advance. In addition to the base salary, some well-known acts receive a percentage of the gate. And, of course, the promoter must pay BMI, ASCAP, or SESAC for the use of their music. A performance license costs about $20 to several hundred dollars.

The selection of the artist or group that will draw a large audience is vital to success. The promoter has to be in touch with what type of entertainers will draw in his own market. Sometimes the biggest stars won't have a sell-out. Booking the wrong act into your marketplace will cost the promoter a lot of money.

Not only can you lose money in concert promotion, but you will find it almost impossible to break in. A good suggestion is to start in an area where current concert promoters are not operating. This is usually in small cities or towns that aren't unionized, and where you can learn the business. The existing promoters have established themselves. They have the contacts in the local market and know the booking agents of major entertainment acts.

The competition for the public's money is fierce, and a hot act can make the promoter thousands of dollars in one night. But to remain in business, the concert promoter must be honest and sincere and must provide good-quality entertainment to the audience through well-prepared shows. Anything less will give the promoter a bad reputation in the local market and in the music business.

Concert performances help build the image of the artist and notify the public of new record releases. A good performance will help boost record sales. It's all tied together. Concert promotion and entertaining make money and sell records. But what is more important is that concerts allow for personal contact between the entertainer and the audience. When an audience leaves a concert feeling good, the entertainer usually feels the same way.

JOE
SULLIVAN

President of Sound Seventy Concert Promotions. Artist manager for the Charlie Daniels Band, Dobie Gray, and Jimmy Hall.

A LOT OF PEOPLE IN THIS INDUSTRY GOT HERE BY GAMBLING. WOULD YOU AGREE WITH THAT?

Yes, and concert promotion is probably the biggest gamble of all. The first six months I was in business, I lost $50,000. That was all the money I'd saved up all my life.

I read a couple of self-help books, *Think and Grow Rich* and *Power of Positive Thinking*. I went out and bought myself a new car and a couple of new suits, and I started looking more successful and feeling more successful; and it turned around. I think it has a lot to do with mental attitude.

If you start sliding and you get down about it, you're going to keep going down. If you can manage to bring yourself back up mentally, your chances of succeeding are a whole lot better.

SO YOU FEEL THAT PEOPLE IN THE INDUSTRY NEED TO HAVE A REALLY POSITIVE OUTLOOK. DOES THAT APPLY TO SINGERS, TOO?

Yes. Charlie Daniels and I got together about 9½ years ago. At first, it was looking so bleak for both of us that everybody was suggesting that we should just split up and Charlie should just go back to studios. (He was a studio musician.) He refused to give up, and he kept a real positive attitude all along and, of course, the rest is history.

Personal appearances are very important. A lot of artists really build a following on personal appearances, just by grinding it out, staying on the road. They already may be headlining before they ever have a big record.

WHAT ADVICE WOULD YOU GIVE TO YOUNG PEOPLE WHO WANT TO GET INTO THE INDUSTRY?

That's a difficult question. We have this guy here who's our concert production manager. He applied for the job a couple of years before he ever got it. He ended up working backstage at concerts for ten or fifteen dollars a show, until he just wouldn't go away. He worked his way in the back door basically. He had just come out of college. He had taken some music courses and was just interested in being in the music business. He stayed here and hung out, made himself available, until finally the job came open for him.

SO YOU ARE SAYING PEOPLE SHOULD HAVE A LOT OF DESIRE TO SUCCEED AND GET IN?

If the door is closed the first time, don't let it discourage you. If you really want that job, keep going back, be visible, be around. Eventually it just might happen for you.

WHAT QUALITIES DO YOU LOOK FOR IN PEOPLE YOU HIRE?

Desire and positive attitude. The people who love the music industry don't look on it as just a job; they really want a career. Of course, I look for honest people. I think that's very important.

I want people who don't mind doing whatever it takes to get the job done. If the stage needs to be mopped but it's not your job to do it, grab the mop and mop away. That type of attitude.

WORKING MORE THAN FORTY HOURS A WEEK?

I don't know anybody in this business who has made it working forty hours a week. Double that and you've about got it, I think; eighty hours a week is a pretty short week sometimes.

YOU ALSO HAVE TO TRAVEL A LOT, DON'T YOU?

You've got to be able to do that. I keep an apartment in New York because I'm up there so much. Artists we manage expect to see me at a certain number of their shows, or they start feeling like I'm not interested.

WHAT DOES A CONCERT PROMOTER HAVE TO DO? WHAT DOES YOUR JOB CONSIST OF?

It starts with who's where, what tours are going out, and who's available for the market. Then a certain amount of research and a certain amount of gut feeling are needed to determine if that artist is going to draw. You might have one that will draw in

Spokane, Washington, but wouldn't draw fifteen people in Nashville, and vice versa. You have to really know the market.

Then you have to be willing to put a whole bunch of money on the line. The profit margin is in about the last 15 percent or 20 percent of receipts. You can go to the auditorium, and it looks full lots of times, and we're still only breaking even or losing a few dollars because we didn't sell that last 20 percent.

You have to really know how to get people there—know how to advertise properly and get people excited about the concert. You can sell-out an act and that act can walk out with $40,000 to $50,000 and still leave unhappy if you haven't looked after the details properly. There are more promoters available than there are artists to go around, so it's a competitive business.

HOW DO YOU SELECT THE ARTIST YOU WANT TO PUT INTO A CERTAIN CITY? IS IT JUST A CERTAIN FEELING? IS IT A MARKET SURVEY?

It's a little bit of both. In many cases we've put the artist in that city before, so we have past track records to go by. We watch the gross figures in *Billboard* and *Amusement Business* to see who's doing business where. We get a feeling about cities similar to Nashville, say, so that the artist might do well here, too. And, of course, if the artist is getting a lot of air play, that makes a big difference. If he is not getting air play, the chances are the people aren't going to know who he is.

ONCE YOU'VE DECIDED THAT YOU'RE GOING TO PUT A CERTAIN ARTIST ON A WEST COAST TOUR, HOW ARE YOU GOING TO DO THE PUBLICITY? ARE YOU GOING TO TAKE OUT NEWSPAPER ADS, TELEVISION ADS, RADIO ADS, OR IS WORD OF MOUTH VERY IMPORTANT?

Word of mouth is very important in the business. We have a public relations firm that works closely with the concert pro-moter; they contact television stations and newspapers, set up interviews, and so forth.

The record company is very instrumental in doing that. Newspaper, music magazine interviews, that sort of thing, is very important. But word of mouth you can't beat.

We have a young lady here who handles the public relations in-house. That's her full-time job. She goes to the newspaper, makes sure that they have plenty of up-dated, fresh publicity material, and looks for a little hook or an angle to get a story in the newspaper. We make the disc jockeys at all the radio stations aware the artist is coming, try to get them excited about it, and get a little chatter going on the air about this particular artist. All that is in addition to just regular time-buys on the air and regular newspaper ads.

I have a theory about promotion. If you can get a lot of tickets sold the day tickets go on sale, if you can create enough interest to get lines around the corner, then you've got the word of mouth going for you. It can't be beat. So we would gear a schedule for the radio and newspaper ads to be very heavy the week before tickets go on sale, promoting the day they go on sale. Then we would advertise pretty heavily for a couple of days afterwards, and then we would slack off a bit until maybe the last week before the show.

WHEN A RADIO STATION SAYS, "SOUND SEVENTY AND [THE NAME OF THE RADIO STATION] PRESENTS [SO-AND-SO]"—IS THAT CO-OPERATIVE ADVERTISING?

It is, to some extent. There are certain limitations on what you can do. The Federal Communications Commission has ruled that radio stations can't say they're presenting the show unless they really are, that is, unless they have a financial interest in it. So, if you've noticed, they say, "Sound Seventy Presents for KDF [or Rock 106]," or something like that. Radio programmers have a theory that the affiliation with that show is prestigious for them. Listeners feel that the station is interested in bringing in talent for them to see.

There was a very low volume of concerts in Nashville and promoters here weren't really interested in bringing rock music. I had approached a couple of them about bringing in more shows because listeners would call the radio station all the time and ask, "Why is it we have to drive to Memphis or Birmingham or someplace to see a show? Why doesn't WMAK bring in concerts?"

The station wasn't interested in doing it, but I dabbled with it a little bit. I had a partner who was doing the same thing. We decided to give it a try and got about ten or twelve shows that first year. They all did well. We only had two losers out of twelve concerts.

IS IT CASH UP FRONT ALL THE TIME?

A new promoter getting into the business would probably have to pay 100 percent up front until he was well established. Then the normal rule is 50 percent deposit, and it varies with the agency-promoter relationships as to when you have to send that deposit in. When I first started, I managed to get in without having to pay all the money up front, but they wanted that deposit 30 to 45 days in advance. Once you're well-established, the deposit can get in within a week before the concert, and you're not going to hear too much screaming from the agents.

The artist always gets a percentage. Ten or fifteen years ago, artists began to realize that they only were getting $10,000 and the promoter was making $20,000. It's now gotten down to a science as to how the deals are structured. A pretty standard deal is a certain guarantee, maybe a $25,000 guarantee against 85-15 on the net, the amount after the building rent, all the security costs, all the staging costs, and similar expenses have been paid.

THE CONCERT PROMOTER HAS TO PAY FOR ALL OF THOSE THINGS.

The concert promoter guarantees all of those things. So practically any show now, you're looking at a $60,000 to $70,000 break even point on the show. And then you get only 15 percent of the net after that.

CHAPTER SEVENTEEN

RECORD DISTRIBUTION AND RETAIL STORES

Now I know it's hard to believe, but the records are placed in the stores. All of the work, people, time, creativity, and money means zero unless you buy it. Record stores, drugstores, specialty shops, mail order, and TV commercials are just a few of the places and ways to purchase a record.

Stores are set up for one purpose—to sell records. The size and shape of the building, eye-level displays, posters, and even the background music induces you to buy a record. Two-for-one, price discounts, and other sales tactics are also used.

Store owners hope that radio-station air play, concerts, word of mouth, music television, and magazine or newspaper articles will bring the customer into the store with a record in mind to purchase. In addition, store owners try to sell more albums of the same artist or same type of music.

Per-inquiry advertising is used to sell records with television commercials. The advertisements are run free on late night TV in exchange for a percentage of the money generated by mail-in orders. People who buy records by mail rarely visit record shops or purchase records in stores.

HUTCH CARLOCK

President of Music City Record Distributors, Nashville.

ONCE YOU RECEIVE THE RECORDS FROM THE PRESSING PLANT, WHAT HAPPENS?

The industry has changed quite a bit in the past few years. We were the prime distributor of all products for certain record labels. As the years have passed, we now are not the prime distributor, but more of a one-stop for all the labels. Some of the labels are distributing their own products through various branches of their own.

WHY DO THEY DO THAT?

I don't know if it is more profitable, but through certain areas of the country there are some distribution problems. As an example, in New York City, some of the companies felt if they controlled their own destiny they would be better off. It's just worked out that way for them. It's a better means of distribution for them; they control everything that way.

We are still the prime distributor for many of the local labels here in Nashville. We buy from the manufacturers or from their branch warehouses just like a one-stop. That way we offer all products to everybody.

LET'S LOOK AT THE STRUCTURE OF DISTRIBUTION. ONCE IT LEAVES YOUR COMPANY, WHERE ARE YOU GOING TO SEND IT—TO AN INDEPENDENT DISTRIBUTOR, TO A RACK JOBBER?

We would send it directly to a retailer or to our own shops. We have some small shops ourselves. They go there for the final sale to the customer.

WHAT IS THE PROFIT MARGIN FOR THE RETAILER?

Years ago it would run about thirty-eight percent. Today they can squeeze twenty-eight to thirty percent out of it, and if they get that much they have a good operation going. The cost of doing business is tremendous; those costs have gone up while the gross for the people has not increased that much.

HOW ABOUT IN YOUR BUSINESS? WHAT KIND OF A PROFIT MARGIN CAN YOU GET?

In the wholesale business we run fifteen to sixteen percent. If we get seventeen percent we're very lucky.

231

WHAT IS A RACK JOBBER?

A rack jobber is a person or company who takes the records and physically puts them in a truck and hauls them to a K-Mart store, for example. This guy would probably own the racks in the store and the fixtures. His employees put the records out and put the price tags on them. It is quite an additional service. The rack jobber's prices should be higher to his customers than ours would be to our retail customers who do those jobs themselves.

LET'S TALK ABOUT ONE-STOPS. YOU CONSIDER YOURSELF A ONE-STOP, RIGHT?

In today's sense, yes. In the old days, a one-stop was started on the premise of supplying 45 rpm records to jukebox operators with title strips. Some of those one-stops haven't evolved into the kind of service we offer. We distributed to the one-stops. Today they're in the same business that we're in.

HOW ABOUT THE MOM-AND-POP STORES? WHAT DOES THAT MEAN? DO THEY STILL EXIST?

A lot of them still exist, although competition has really eroded them. The original mom-and-pop store was a small store that was operated by one or two people. They did a nice job. Record chain stores and retail chain stores in the shopping malls came along and forced most of them out. High interest rates forced out some of them. Traditionally, most of the small shops would borrow a little money in the spring to last through the summer. Business is a little softer then, and they'd plan on making it back in the fall and winter when the record business was much stronger.

IT APPEARS THAT, BECAUSE OF COMPETITION, SOME OF YOUR RESPONSIBILITIES HAVE CHANGED IN THE PAST FEW YEARS.

Our functions have changed to the extent that, in the old days, we were responsible for promotion. We were responsible for whatever displays were out, along with a little better gross margin. As competition came along, the big companies are now doing their own distribution and have their own promotion and poster people. Our functions along those lines ceased. We are now just a supplier of product to our customers.

It's a big change, but I think the industry may be a little healthier as a result. It's now all coordinated where before it was a hit-or-miss proposition. In Nashville, we might have had our own ideas about how to do something and people in Atlanta would do it entirely different.

I KNOW THE DISTRIBUTOR USED TO SUPPLY TO THE STORES, BUT THEY ALSO HAD ADVERTISING BUDGETS, PROMOTION PEOPLE, AND ALL KINDS OF THINGS.

We still have promotion persons, and we do our own in-house advertising for the stores. We do a lot of functions, but we are now doing them for ourselves.

DO YOU GET CO-OP MONEY FOR THAT?

Most of the companies operate on a budget for X amount of dollars per record. If they feel the record has potential, they'll elect to spend so much money in various areas of the country. They'll allocate those funds to us or to other wholesalers as they become available. We, in turn, share it with our people—our customers.

THERE USED TO BE A POLICY OF 100 PERCENT RETURN ON RECORDS, AND I UNDERSTAND THAT A LOT OF RECORDS WERE SHIPPED GOLD AND RETURNED PLATINUM.

They had some funny policies years ago. A manufacturer could do $50 million a year and wind up losing money, which is perfectly ridiculous because their profit margin was much greater than ours. But by the time they pay the artist, the studio expenses, and everything else, it comes down. If XYZ artist had a big name, he might tell the company to ship out so many pieces of his new album, whether it had any merit or sales value. Shipping them out cost us a lot of money as the wholesaler, and they would later be returned. It was a very expensive thing. The companies have cut those types of things out now. If they do ship, it's because the record is selling. They want it out there when it does come through. They justify it before it's done.

THEY DON'T GAMBLE AS MUCH AS THEY USED TO. IF IT'S GOING TO BE RELEASED NATIONALLY, WILL THEY PRESS THE RECORDS IN DIFFERENT AREAS OF THE COUNTRY?
Right. Shipping costs are soaring now.

DO DISTRIBUTORS HAVE A HARD TIME COLLECTING MONEY?
It's always a problem. It happens in many industries. Two or three years ago, the people that we buy from tightened their credit policy, so we in turn had to tighten ours. We no longer had the luxury of carrying an account for 90 days like we used to do. We had to be more business-like, collect the money, and turn it over to the people we owed. We are probably operating more efficiently as a result.

IS THERE ANY ADVICE YOU WOULD GIVE TO PEOPLE WHO WANT TO GET INTO THE MUSIC INDUSTRY? SPECIFICALLY IN THE DISTRIBUTION AREA.
There are a limited amount of openings at all times with any wholesaler because we don't use that many people. If a person will come into the warehouse, learn to sweep floors, and doesn't mind getting his hands dirty, he can certainly make it in the music business. You need to be flexible. Things are changing so fast that ten years hence we might be looking at an entirely new industry. We are on the brink of many things with VHS and Beta systems—new things that are coming technologically.

JAN
RHEES

President of Dancing Water Music, Inc., and
Flying Cloud Music, Inc.
Jan Rhees Marketing. Record promotion to retail outlets,
jukebox operators, and stores.

HOW DO YOU GET A RETAILER EXCITED? WHAT DO YOU SAY TO HIM?

I care about what the retailer thinks. What I say is, "I want you to get involved. I want you to personally give me your input." When you involve people, you get a great reaction. People love to be a part of an artist, the entertainment business, and that's what I do—involve them totally in what I've got.

EXPLAIN WHAT HAPPENS TO A RECORD FROM THE TIME THAT IT IS SHIPPED AND YOU GET A CALL FOR HELP. WHAT IS THE FIRST THING YOU DO?

Let's do singles. Jukebox operators are 80 percent of your singles sales. Consequently, I would concentrate on jukebox operators. They usually do not purchase a single until it's in the 20's on the chart, unless they believe in the record and know that it's going to come home.

I'll go to the jukebox operators and say, "Look, order the record. The record is out" I'll make them aware of the product. Jukebox operators, interestingly enough, buy off the *Cash Box* charts. I asked them why, and they said because the print is bigger.

ARE YOU KIDDING ME?

No. I've gone to *Billboard* and all the other trades with that information, and they don't necessarily think anything about it. Consequently, I watch *Cash Box* very carefully. So we're into the second week of the record, we're at 65 with a star, bullet, or whatever. The jukebox operator has ordered the record, and it's going to take a week or two weeks to get it in. In the meantime, I'm instigating sales, jukebox sales, early on the record. And in the meantime, the salesmen come in and the retailer or the jukebox operator says, "I hear you've got a new Mac Davis single," and he orders it.

Now, if I've got a rapport established with that jukebox operator, you may have forty box operators come in to buy a single that day, or his singles. He's buying for fifteen accounts. Now, it makes sense, "Do me a favor this week. (I'm telling this to the head of the operator, the guy behind the counter.)

234

Play the Mac Davis single for everybody; tell them how serious we are about him. Tell them there's an album coming out. They can feel safe; they can go out there on a limb and put this record on the jukeboxes." That's what it's all about.

DO YOU EVER CONTACT RADIO STATIONS?

Radio stations have a lot of problems with stock in that they add a record one week; they give it two weeks. They have a Research Department. They not only have a request line, but they have a guy calling out to retailers exclusively and finding out how the record's selling. They want to know that when ratings come that they're selling records; that's very important. Mac Davis has been on station KDA here in Nashville for three weeks. KDA calls Discount Records. Discount Records has no stock, is not aware of the record. We're into the second, third week now, and nobody's contacted them. KDA calls the Polygram salesman and says, "I'm dropping your Mac Davis record." The salesman asks why, and KDA says, "There's no product in the market. Why am I playing this record?" The consumer's getting jerked around. He's listening to something and it's not available.

I make sure those holes are covered because we're in this business to sell records. An album is what it's all about. Album sales are what the record company is going to look at when it's renewing a contract for the artist. A single is a tool for the album; that's why the company releases a single and then follows up with an album with a sticker on it saying it contains the hit single.

SO YOU USE A SINGLE TO . . .

To educate the consumer with the artist. When I work an album, I instigate in-store play. I instigate involvement in the entire album with the artist in that I'll have the artist autograph the album. I'll have the artist do in-store promotions on the album. I get to the record company and get involved with their display material, their point-of-purchase material, where it's placed, in what bin. Also I want to know about the visibility of the album, the visibility of the artist, is the artist on tour?

THOSE THINGS ARE ALL IMPORTANT INSIDE A STORE, AREN'T THEY? WHERE THE RECORD IS AND IF IT'S VISIBLE TO THE CONSUMER.

Another thing that's important is where the point-of-purchase material is placed. Eye-level and above is the prime target area for the consumer's focal point, visual point.

In-store play, you don't even realize how much it affects sales. If you walk in and think you hear an artist that you dearly love and find out that it's an unknown artist, you'll buy the album anyway. So it's a very important aspect of breaking records and breaking artists.

Having artists appear in-store is very dangerous, in that it can kill an artist. You set up an in-store promotion in Dallas, Texas, and nobody shows up. At this point—and you may sell a ton of records—what you're doing is you're not only killing the artist's enthusiasm but your timing is so completely off that you're affecting the retail operation also.

YOU MENTIONED SOMETHING THAT I WOULD LIKE TO TALK ABOUT, THE TIMING. HOW MUCH TIME DO YOU HAVE TO BREAK A RECORD, ONCE IT HITS YOUR DESK?

As much time as the team requires. When I say the team, I'm taking into consideration all efforts from management, manufacturer, promotion, marketing. It's a whole team involvement, and once one part of the team quits, the rest of the team falls.

WHO HAS THE FINAL SAY IF THE RECORD IS GOING TO BE A HIT OR NOT?

The consumer. The street. That's why it's vitally important in this business that you stick to the street, that you're in the retail. When I go on the road as a marketing company, I go in and I listen. What's selling. I ask, "How do you feel about the return policies that WEA's coming up with? How is $5.98 as opposed to $7.98, with only a 5 percent return on the initial order, how is that going to affect you? How's it going to affect your customers? What do your customers want to hear more of? What are jukebox operators tired of? Do we need ballads? Do we need women? Do we need duets? What's missing?" And as long as you stay there, hopefully you'll never stray off too far.

CHAPTER EIGHTEEN

BREAKING IN

Nashville has over seven million visitors a year, and many of those visitors would like to be in the music business. Face it, if you want a career in the music business, it's competitive. If you want in, you should move to a place where it's happening, usually Los Angeles, Nashville, Memphis, New York, or Toronto.

It's hard to get into the clique as a singer, musician, artist, artist manager, booking agent, or any other area of the business. But there is room for qualified people. The good people—and there are a lot of them—will help you. They take the time to answer the questions because they were once where you are and they probably asked the same questions. They want to be helpful because someone helped them when they were starting out. Hopefully, you will listen to what they say.

Be a good, honest person. It's important to be honest with yourself and with other people—those you work with and those who help you. Professional people in the music business don't want to work with people who

are on ego trips or who have drug, alcoholic, or emotional problems. They would rather work with people who accept this industry as a business and approach it as a business.

It's hard to break in; it takes at least a year to even get the people interested in you. They want to know that you're for real and that you're here to stay. It takes years to develop a career. You can begin by meeting the right people. Join a professional music organization. If you want to be a songwriter, join the Nashville, Los Angeles, or New York songwriting associations. By joining the professional organizations, such as the National Academy of Recording Arts and Sciences (N.A.R.A.S.) or the Nashville Entertainment Association or whatever association that's in your city, you will meet some of the top people in the industry. A lot of the top producers, recording artists, and artist managers in the business belong to these organizations. Become an associate member, go to the meetings, and meet the right people.

Record companies and publishing companies are always looking for talented people. They look for that exceptionally talented person. So, be yourself, which makes you unique. If you have a special talent and want to be in the music business, go for it. Join the organizations that give you the opportunities to meet the right people. They will be there.

WHAT IT TAKES TO MAKE IT

People who become stars were born to be stars. It seems to be their destiny. In addition to feeling that way, they center their daily lives around being a personality. If it's not your dream to become a successful recording artist, then don't try. Stay out of it. Usually it takes years to develop the qualities of a recording artist. You've got to dream it; you've got to live it.

Kris Kristofferson and Larry Gatlin—and almost every other songwriter or artist—have creative talents that astonish the average person. Everyone involved in the music business industry is an expert at his skill. If he's not, he won't last long in the industry. People who have been in the industry for years have developed a knowledge and ability to accomplish their jobs. Successful songwriters know how to write songs. Producers have tremendous talent that allows them to communicate with people, to produce music in any style, and to motivate musicians and recording artists to create a piece of magic that is imprinted on a piece of plastic. Audio engineers have the talent to operate equipment that would make an astronaut shake his head. It's space-age technology run by men and women who happen to be creative and technical at the same time. That takes talent.

Singers are a dime a dozen, but a singer who has a unique style can be a marketable item. A recording artist's own unique, personal style and qualities make him stand out. People want to be entertained by somebody special. They pay good money to see and hear somebody do something that they can't do. A lot of us can sing, but very few of us can perform.

Some people's vocal characteristics make them unique for example, Bing Crosby, Elvis, Janis Joplin, and Rod Stewart. Bing Crosby preferred being recorded early in the morning, around 8:00 AM, because he wanted a certain type of characteristic that his voice had at that time of the morning.

Some have unique lifestyles, like the hippie and drug lifestyle. Others have a lifestyle that people can identify with, such as the classy Frank Sinatra. Waylon Jennings is considered to be the musical "outlaw."

There isn't any reason to copy an established recording artist's style. The public already has an original. Why would they want to spend money on a copycat? If you want to make it as a recording artist, be yourself. Therefore, you'll be unique. There is only one you.

If you don't believe in yourself and your talents, who will? You'll get a lot of rejection in your life, because you just can't please everyone. Your life is very public and, therefore, open to public discussion and criticism. You've got to be able to live with it and handle it.

The public has a way of knowing your true feelings. You can't hide them; you simply can't hide a lack of confidence on-stage or in a recording. If you're a performer, you'll probably be scared to death before every performance, but when the spotlight hits you, you'll turn on.

You've got to believe in yourself and what you do. You've got to trust yourself and believe you can and will accomplish whatever you want. If you're good enough, you will succeed. If not, at least you gave it your very best shot.

Many artists have achieved their success because of their talent, persistence, and determination for success. Anne Murray was a schoolteacher. Donna Summer had to move to Germany to become famous before she was accepted in the U.S. as a recording artist.

They had to work hard to make it to the top. They were determined to do it, and they have accomplished it. It's a lot easier to give up than to keep struggling for success in such a competitive career. Their determination and persistence are the crucial factors in their continued success.

Sometimes we actually believe everything people tell us. When you're an artist, it's easy to lose touch with reality because you're living in a plastic world. It's hard to know who you are when you're living in the finest hotels, eating the best foods, and receiving constant admiration.

It's easy to get a huge ego. It's easy to forget what is really important. Unfortunately, big egos have a way of messing up your head and will mess up your social life and professional career.

Keep in touch with reality. Remember that your fame and income last only as long as the public wants you. A recording artist is a servant of the public. It can be perceived the other way around, but, in the long run, it's the entertainer's career that exists because of the public's favor. Having an ego can end a career faster than losing your voice.

It takes a lot of guts to leave your hometown and move to a town where the music business is. But you can only accomplish so much, you can only go to a certain level of success in your hometown, so you've got to move on. You'll leave your friends and family and move to a city where there are opportunities. That can be scary and fun. Act like it's a gamble (because it is), and it will be an adventure. Have fun along the road of success or failure. It sometimes takes many years (seven is the average) before you get a real shot or break. You'll usually have to earn that break by preparing yourself, knowing the right people, and being in the right place at the right time.

Some people sweep floors, do many kinds of odd jobs, or even get married, waiting for that break to happen. Most of us never know when or if we'll be famous. Don't just wait and waste time until it happens, because it may never happen. Have a good time, meet new people, make new friends,

and have the time of your life. It may just take all of your life before you accomplish all of your goals.

DRUGS

Let's look at it realistically. Some of the top stars in the music industry are dead—Janis Joplin, Jimi Hendrix, Elvis Presley, and hundreds of others. Agents, managers, musicians, hangers-on, groupies, fans, you name it, and you'll find that people in almost every area of the music industry have died from drug overdoses. Some of the biggest stars of the past are still alive today, but they have either become part-time vegetables or they're strung out on cocaine or whatever drug happens to be in. If you haven't heard from one of your favorite stars of the past, there is a possibility that he may have blown it with drugs. It's hard to perform stoned and really inspire someone else.

So, why do people do it? The music business creates a lot of pressures. The bigger the star, the more pressure they have. Part is caused by their fans; part is the pressure applied by the artist himself when he tries to perform better each time for the fans. Then there is the obvious problem caused by separation from home and loved ones, and being on the road day after day, month after month. In addition, somewhere while all of this is going on, you still have to be creative; you still have to be happy and spontaneous.

For many entertainers, marijuana or booze is the answer. They are not the only ones. Unfortunately, a small hit leads to a bigger one. It's not uncommon for a rock star to have a $150,000 drug habit. Once you're hooked on drugs, it becomes an endless cycle of working to pay the habit and having the drugs to escape the problems of the work.

How bad is the drug problem in the music business? One person said that on almost every bus or in every recording session, you could find somebody on drugs. That tends to be changing today because many of the people who have survived have lost friends who were on drugs. It comes down to either getting straight or getting out of the business. The survivors are looking around and deciding that booze and drugs must be avoided.

The music industry is a business. As soon as a record company realizes that you're a liability to them, you'll be off the label at the end of your contract. Being realistic about your worth and place on this earth will at least keep you in touch with reality.

CHAPTER NINETEEN

A WORD OF ADVICE

So you've decided to give it a shot. It's inside of you, and you can't stand it until you give it a try. Well, good for you. Go for it. By all means, try to become what you want to be! The personal satisfaction of self-accomplishment is what it's all about. Be realistic and understand what it is all about. If you want to be in the music business and you've got the talent it takes, you still must understand how the business operates.

Don't discount your education. No matter what part of the industry you want to join, an education is an important asset. Whether you take business or accounting courses or get your degree in music composition, the time you spend in the classroom can help to give you a solid background before you start paying your dues.

Record company entry-level jobs are usually very low paying. The secret is getting that first job! After you get in the business and gain the contacts and commitments, a lot of doors will open. It's very hard and sometimes stressful work. It's also a lot of fun because you'll work with people you've read about all your life. It's not a dream or a fantasy, and in many cases the jobs will be the hardest you've ever had. But if it's what you want with all your heart and you're willing to make sacrifices, then go for it and good luck!

JAY
COLLINS PH.D.

President, Nashville Musicians Union, Professor of Music Business, Belmont College, Nashville. Past President, Music Industry Educators Association. Member, National Academy of Recording Arts and Sciences, Country Music Association, Nashville Entertainment Association.

WHAT ADVICE WOULD YOU GIVE TO PEOPLE WHO WANT TO GET INTO THE MUSIC INDUSTRY?

The first piece of advice I would give is for them to get themselves to the point of being as realistic as possible and to do an intro-spective survey of their own attitudes about the industry. In other words, why do they have this interest?

If their answer approximates someone who is star-struck, they're not ready for a business that is hard, demanding, requires lots of hours, and has its frustrations as well as its moments of happiness. If they're the kind of people who like to go to bed early at night, forget it. This is the wrong industry. If they like going to a 9-to-5 job that they can shelve at 5:00 PM in order to go home, go bowling, or something, forget it.

If a person finds out that he truly wants a career in music, then I would not worry about how many opportunities there are. I'd simply go after it in the most direct way possible. Many of the people who get into this industry get in through their technical skills while they temporarily put aside their

creative ambitions. By that I mean they manage to get a foot in the door as an engineer and then go on to become booking agents or managers.

We have a commercial music program that is devoted to people who are interested in getting into the commercial performance arena. In our music business program here, we require a four-year degree with an emphasis on learning all of the managerial skills along with their specialized technical skills. We know that when our students graduate and become engineers or players in sessions, they're not going to be doing that all their lives. You don't see a lot of 60-year-old people in the studios recording or behind the console. They have either be-come disenchanted with it, or they have been promoted up to administrative posi-tions. They've made their money.

IS THE INDUSTRY STARTING TO NEED TRAINED PEOPLE?

I'd say that there is a special need in the area of administration. Administrators need to have studied the music industry and to have also acquired, by study or experience, all sorts of administrative skills that apply to professional positions.

The industry does not have time to train administrators. They have to come in prepared and ready to keep that industry working so that the bottom line is in the black and the quarterly report is not book juggling.

WHAT IS MIEA?

MIEA is Music Industry Educators' Association. MIEA consists of educators who specialize in music-industry curricula at various colleges and institutes throughout the United States and Canada. The association's activities include setting educational standards, assisting in the development of educational programs, promoting research, and recognizing outstanding achievements. MIEA publishes a newsletter, and it holds an annual meeting for people who are in the business of music-industry education. It's a matter of interchanging ideas and being helpful to one another.

WOULD YOU SAY THAT THE COLLEGES AND THE EDUCATORS WHO BELONG TO MIEA ARE HELPFUL?

As an organization, we get letters from people inquiring about programs and advice. If you get into the industry and don't have the qualifications to back you up, you're not necessarily going to be ready when you have that opportunity to be appointed to a certain position. If you're fortified by getting all that you can in the process of getting a degree in music business (or whatever it's called in each school), then you have self-confidence, and you generate it to others. You're not afraid to act and stand on your own two feet. In essence, you

become a good top administrator, and that is what the industry is looking for.

YOU WOULD ENCOURAGE PEOPLE TO GO TO SCHOOL AND TRY TO DEVELOP THESE TALENTS.

Absolutely. I'd be scared to death to try to be in the music business today without going to school and studying it. Twenty years ago, it was a different ball game. Today, it's changed.

I think of so many people in the Nashville music community who are really the go-getters and at the top of their organizations. Either they grew up with the industry and consequently got a good education as a part of the industry, or they came to their positions well-prepared and well-educated. The problem with the former is that you can't get your foot in the door and grow up with the industry anymore; it's already grown up.

The way to get in this industry now is to come in prepared, with education and experience. You get that experience not necessarily in the industry, but through studying the industry and interacting with it while getting your education. That's why you see so many programs in the colleges throughout the country. It's because there is a demand for it.

People who want to get into the industry find that the people who are holding jobs *have* abilities. They begin to say, "How do *I* get those abilities?" They know they cannot be hired without experience. The only way to get that experience, unless you've got an Uncle Joe or somebody who will hire you, is to get some good strong background, such as a four-year degree from a program like the one at Belmont College or several other colleges and institutes around the U.S. and Canada.

APPENDIX

RECORD COMPANIES

Some of Nashville's major country music record companies and independent labels include:

CBS RECORDS
34 Music Square East
Nashville, TN 37203

CAPITOL/EMI AMERICA RECORDS
1111 16th Avenue South
Nashville, TN 37212

**COMPLEAT ENTERTAINMENT
(DISTRIBUTED BY POLYGRAM)**
21 Music Circle East
Nashville, TN 37203

GUSTO RECORDS
1900 Elm Hill Pike
Nashville, TN

MCA RECORDS
1701 West End Avenue
Nashville, TN 37203

MTM MUSIC GROUP
P.O. Box 121347
Nashville, TN 37212

MERIT RECORDS
20 Music Square West
Nashville, TN 37203

NATIONWIDE SOUND DISTRIBUTORS
1204 Elmwood
Nashville, TN 37203

POLYGRAM RECORDS
10 Music Circle South
Nashville, TN 37203

RCA RECORDS
30 Music Square West
Nashville, TN 37203

WARNER BROS.
1815 Division Street
Nashville, TN 37203

RECORDING STUDIOS

Some of Nashville's studios include:

AL JOLSON ENTERPRISES
31 Music Square West
Nashville, TN

THE BENNETT HOUSE
134 4th Avenue
Franklin, TN

BULLET RECORDING STUDIOS
49 Music Square West
Nashville, TN

CREATIVE WORKSHOP INC.
2806 Azalea Place
Nashville, TN

DOC'S PLACE RECORDING STUDIO
394 West Main
Hendersonville, TN

FANTA PROFESSIONAL SERVICES
1213 16th Avenue South
Nashville, TN

FIRESIDE RECORDING STUDIOS, INC.
813 18th Avenue South
Nashville, TN

HILLTOP RECORDING STUDIOS
902 New Due West Avenue
Nashville, TN

HUMMINGBIRD STUDIO
50 Music Square West
Nashville, TN

JACK'S TRACKS RECORDING STUDIO
1308 16th Avenue South
Nashville, TN

THE MUSIC MILL
1710 Roy Acuff Place
Nashville, TN

POLLYFOX
920 19th Avenue South
Nashville, TN

SOUND EMPORIUM RECORDING STUDIOS
3102 Belmont Blvd.
Nashville, TN

SOUND STAGE STUDIO
10 Music Circle South
Nashville, TN

SOUNDSHOP RECORDING STUDIOS, INC.
1307 Division
Nashville, TN

TREASURE ISLE RECORDERS
2808 Azalea Place
Nashville, TN

WILD TRACKS RECORDING STUDIO
805 18th Avenue South
Nashville, TN

WOODLAND SOUND STUDIOS
1011 Woodland
Nashville, TN

MUSIC BUSINESS ORGANIZATIONS

Some of Nashville's trade associations and organizations include those on this list, provided by The Nashville Entertainment Association.

THE NASHVILLE ENTERTAINMENT ASSOCIATION (NMA)
P.O. Box 25309
Nashville, TN 37202

THE COUNTRY MUSIC ASSOCIATION (CMA)
P.O. Box 22299
Nashville, TN 37202

THE GOSPEL MUSIC ASSOCIATION (GMA)
P.O. Box 23201
Nashville, TN 37202

THE NASHVILLE SONGWRITERS ASSOCIATION INTERNATIONAL (NSAI)
803 18th Avenue South
Nashville, TN 37203

THE SONGWRITERS GUILD
50 Music Square West
Suite 207
Nashville, TN 37203

**THE AMERICAN FEDERATION
OF MUSICIANS (AF OF M)**
(Musicians Union)
P.O. Box 1203999
Nashville, TN 37212

**THE NATIONAL ACADEMY
OF RECORDING ARTS AND
SCIENCES
(NARAS)**
(Grammy Awards)
7 Music Circle North
Nashville, TN 37203

**THE NATIONAL ACADEMY
OF TELEVISION ARTS AND SCIENCES
(NATAS)**
(Emmy Awards)
1717 West End Avenue
Penthouse
Nashville, TN 37203

SMPTE
37 Music Square East
Nashville, TN 37203

**THE AMERICAN FEDERATION OF
TELEVISION AND RADIO ARTISTS
(AFTRA)/
THE SCREEN ACTORS GUILD (SAG)**
1101 17th Avenue South
Nashville, TN 37212

**AUDIO ENGINEERING SOCIETY
(AES)**
2200 Hillsboro Road
Executive Center
Nashville, TN 37212

**NATIONAL ENTERTAINMENT
JOURNALISTS ASSOCIATION
(NEJA)**
P.O. Box 24021
Nashville, TN 37202

**AMERICAN SOCIETY OF
COMPOSERS, AUTHORS &
PUBLISHERS (ASCAP)**
Southern Regional Executive Director:
Connie Bradley
2 Music Square West
Nashville, TN 37203

BROADCAST MUSIC INC. (BMI)
Senior Vice President:
Frances J. Preston
10 Music Square East
Nashville, TN 37203

**SOCIETY OF EUROPEAN STAGE
AUTHORS AND COMPOSERS (SESAC)**
Country Director: Dianne Petty
11 Music Circle South
Nashville, TN 37203

INDEX

LARRY E. WACHOLTZ is an independent television producer and is Assistant Professor of Music Business at Belmont College in Nashville, Tennessee.

Wacholtz served as the Director of the Television Production Center and Director of Audio Engineering at Eastern Washington State University, and was instrumental in the coordination of the music business curriculum at Memphis State University.

His professional associations include the National Academy of Television Arts and Sciences, the Nashville Entertainment Journalists Association, the Country Music Association, the National Academy of Recording Arts and Sciences, the Audio Engineering Society, and the Nashville Music Association.
A Vietnam veteran, Wacholtz is the recipient of the Air Force Commendation Medal.

Book design by **Damien Alexander**
Cover illustration by **Jim Cherry**
Graphic production by **Hector Campbell**